All Things New

COLUMBIA SERIES IN REFORMED THEOLOGY

The Columbia Series in Reformed Theology represents a joint commitment of Columbia Theological Seminary and Westminster John Knox Press to provide theological resources for the church today.

The Reformed tradition has always sought to discern what the living God revealed in scripture is saying and doing in every new time and situation. Volumes in this series examine significant individuals, events, and issues in the development of this tradition and explore their implications for contemporary Christian faith and life.

This series is addressed to scholars, pastors, and laypersons. The Editorial Board hopes that these volumes will contribute to the continuing reformation of the church.

Editorial Board

Shirley Guthrie, Columbia Theological Seminary

George Stroup, Columbia Theological Seminary

B. A. Gerrish, University of Chicago and Union Theological Seminary and Presbyterian School of Christian Education

Amy Plantinga Pauw, Louisville Presbyterian Theological Seminary

Donald K. McKim, Westminster John Knox Press

Columbia Theological Seminary wishes to express its appreciation to the following churches for supporting this joint publishing venture:

First Presbyterian Church, Tupelo, Mississippi

First Presbyterian Church, Nashville, Tennessee

Trinity Presbyterian Church, Atlanta, Georgia

Spring Hill Presbyterian Church, Mobile, Alabama

St. Stephen Presbyterian Church, Fort Worth, Texas

COLUMBIA SERIES IN REFORMED THEOLOGY

All Things New

Reform of Church and Society in Schleiermacher's *Christian Ethics*

JAMES M. BRANDT

© 2001 James M. Brandt

Originally published in hardback in the United States by Westminster John Knox Press in 2001.

2011 paperback edition
Published by Westminster John Knox Press
Louisville, Kentucky

All rights reserved. No part of this book may be reproduced or transmitted in any form or by any means, electronic or mechanical, including photocopying, recording, or by any information storage or retrieval system, without permission in writing from the publisher. For information, address Westminster John Knox Press, 100 Witherspoon Street, Louisville, Kentucky 40202-1396.

Scripture quotations from the New Revised Standard Version of the Bible are copyright © 1989 by the Division of Christian Education of the National Council of the Churches of Christ in the U.S.A. and are used by permission.

Book & Cover design by Drew Stevens

This book is printed on acid-free paper that meets the American National Standards Institute Z39.48 standard. ∞

PRINTED IN THE UNITED STATES OF AMERICA

11 12 13 14 15 16 17 18 19 20 — 10 9 8 7 6 5 4 3 2 1

Library of Congress Cataloging-in-Publication Data

Brandt, James M., 1952–
   All things new : reform of church and society in Schleiermacher's Christian ethics / James M. Brandt.
      p. cm. — (Columbia series in Reformed theology)
   Revision of the author's thesis (Ph. D.)—University of Chicago, 1991, originally presented under the title: Die christliche Sittenlehre.
   Includes bibliographical references (p.) and index.
   ISBN 0-664-22448-2 (alk. paper)
   1. Schleiermacher, Friedrich, 1768–1834. Christliche Sittenlehre.
2. Christian ethics. I. Title. II. Series.

BJ1251 .B73 2001
241—dc21   2001026548

ISBN: 978-0-664-23730-1 (paper edition)

To Heidi,
And our boys:
Matthias, Jesse, and Micah

CONTENTS

Acknowledgments	xi
Foreword	xiii
Introduction: Schleiermacher's Life and Its Reflection in the *Christian Ethics*	1
Schleiermacher's Life in Outline	1
The *Christian Ethics*	4
Schleiermacher's Life and *Christian Ethics*: Correspondences	8
1: Schleiermacher's Life and Thought to 1802	**13**
What's in a Name?	13
Years of Preparation: 1787–96	15
The First Berlin Period: 1796–1802	17
A New Era in Theology: The *Speeches on Religion*	20
2: Life and Thought, 1802–1834	**24**
Halle: *Christmas Eve Dialogue* and New Political Consciousness	26
Return to Berlin	28
Public Figure in Berlin	29
Brief Outline on the Study of Theology	34
The Christian Faith	36
3: Schleiermacher among the Moravians and the *Christian Ethics* as an Ethics of Piety	**41**
Pietism in the Schleiermacher Family	41

Schleiermacher at Niesky and Barby	43
Piety in the *Christian Ethics*	46
Piety in *The Christian Faith*	48
Descriptive Method in the *Christian Ethics*	51
Piety and the Structure of the *Christian Ethics*	52

4: Philosophy and Theology in Schleiermacher's *Ethics*: The Contrast with Hegel — 58

Ideational, Professional, and Personal Divergence	59
Hegel on Philosophy and Theology	61
The *Christian Ethics* on Philosophy and Theology	62
Form, Method, and Structure in Philosophical Ethics and Christian Ethics	65
Schleiermacher's Architectonic of Knowledge	67
The *Philosophical Ethics*: Speculative Philosophy of Culture	70
Christian Ethics on Its Own Terms	74

5: Pastor Schleiermacher and His Ecclesial Ethics of Piety — 82

The Nature of the Church in Schleiermacher's Theology	86
The Status of the Church in *The Christian Faith*	86
The Character of the Church in *The Christian Faith*	88
The Life and Activity of the Church in the *Christian Ethics*	90
Restoring Action in the Church: Discipline and Reform	92
Broadening Action: Christian Education and Missions	96
Representational Action: Public and Household Worship and Christian Virtue in Daily Life	100

6: Schleiermacher as Reformer and Transformation in the *Christian Ethics* — 109

Schleiermacher as Social-Political Actor	109
Transformation of Culture in the *Christian Ethics*	116
Restoring Action and Transformation as Prophetic Critique	118

Prophetic Critique in Relation to Broadening
    and Representational Actions   122

Broadening Action and Transformation
    as the Transvaluation of Cultural Goods   124

Representational Action and Transformation
    as Christian Permeation of Culture   127

7: A Calvinist of a Higher Order:
The *Christian Ethics* in Schleiermacher's
Revisionist Reformed Theology   **135**

Bibliography   149

Index of Subjects   155

Index of Names   158

ACKNOWLEDGMENTS

This book has been a long time in the making. Those who have helped and encouraged me in the process are legion. I want publicly to thank them all. Because of the contributions of many colleagues and friends, this book is much better than it otherwise would have been. Where it stands in need of improvement or radical revision, the responsibility is mine.

Brian Gerrish was there from the beginning. In 1983 at the University of Chicago, when I was casting about for a dissertation topic, he suggested I look at Schleiermacher's *Christian Ethics*. It took but little reading in the text to know I wanted to engage it. Gerrish was a helpful adviser as I navigated my way through the dissertation process. Even more, he provided and still provides a model of scholarship I seek to emulate, though I fall short of its lofty standards.

I first read portions of the *Christian Ethics* in an independent study with James M. Gustafson in the spring of 1984. As members of my dissertation committee, David Tracy and Don Browning made helpful suggestions about my work.

The work that is now published has been significantly expanded and revised from the earlier dissertation. When I told Saint Paul colleague Tex Sample stories from Schleiermacher's life, he encouraged me to use biographical material as a way into the *Ethics*. He also read several chapters of the manuscript and gave me valuable suggestions.

Others who read one or more chapters and gave me feedback were Saint Paul colleagues Young Ho Chun and Richard Randolph, as well as Walter Wyman, Jonathan Strom, and my spouse, Heidi Peterson. Each gave insight and encouragement that improved the work.

Institutional support included a sabbatical leave from Saint Paul School of Theology for the spring semester, 2000. I am grateful for the opportunity to labor in Saint Paul's corner of the Lord's vineyard and for the support the institution has provided for my scholarship.

I thank the Wabash Center for Teaching and Learning in Religion and Theology for the summer 1999 grant that enabled me to travel to Berlin for two weeks of research. Even more, the grant allowed me to concentrate on research and writing during the remainder of the summer and to build momentum on the project.

The staff of the Saint Paul library was of tremendous assistance. During the sabbatical, I was given a study carrel for use, a fruitful place for thinking and writing. Library Director Logan Wright was always gracious in his hospitality and had good suggestions about tracking down research leads. Bobbie Bean and Sandy Chen were helpful in securing texts from other sources, and Melissa Casper led me out of many a computer dead end into which I'd wandered. Student assistant Kevin Fox helped in a variety of ways, with a diligence for which I am extremely grateful.

This book has found its best possible home in the Columbia Series in Reformed Theology, and I am thankful for my editor at Westminster John Knox Press, Donald McKim. His faith in the project and his judicious editorial suggestions have made this a better book. Project editor Linda Watkins kept me on task and caught innumerable mistakes before it was too late. My coach, Caroline Otis, has been a valued partner in my research and writing. She sees the best in me and helps me call it forth.

My family has supported me through the long years of research, writing, and revision. My parents-in-law, Top and Jane Peterson, were always interested in my work and have been pleased that their Lutheran son-in-law was so committed to the study of a Reformed theologian. My brother John; sister Debbie and her partner Matt; sister Ruth, her husband Mike, and daughters Rachel and Claire are all dear to me: their love and support have helped me keep the faith.

My parents, Victor and Irene Brandt, inspire me still with the steadiness of their love and their continuing commitment to serve through the ministry of the church. I learned faith from them and was encouraged by them to think theologically, even when it took me down unusual paths.

And finally, the people with whom I live and whom I love the most: my spouse, Heidi, and our three Peterson-Brandt boys, Matthias, Jesse, and Micah. Without them my life and work would be empty. With them I know love and fullness of life and am encouraged to pursue insight and justice, confident of my contribution to the wider world. With affection and gratitude I dedicate this book to them.

James M. Brandt
Saint Paul School of Theology
Kansas City, Missouri
March 2001

FOREWORD

Friedrich Schleiermacher's reputation as one of the greatest theologians in the history of the church rests mainly on his dogmatic masterwork, *The Christian Faith*. But in his own mind, *The Christian Faith*, as a work of Christian *doctrine*, presented only half of his dogmatic theology; the other half was Christian *ethics*, which he dealt with separately. The need to treat Christian ethics by itself, he believed, is that the practical side of Christian faith might otherwise be overshadowed by the theoretical. Nevertheless, he did not consider the separation essential. The propositions of Christian ethics too, like those of dogmatics in the narrower sense (Christian doctrine), are propositions of faith. They are about the selfsame Christian consciousness, but in its particular manifestation as motive for action. For this reason, he thought it would be appropriate if the two parts of dogmatic theology were occasionally treated together.

Schleiermacher never succeeded in preparing his lectures on Christian ethics for publication. Shortly after the first edition of *The Christian Faith* appeared (1821–22), he wrote to a friend of his wish, if he could find the time, to present his Christian ethics as a companion work. But when the second edition of *The Christian Faith* came out (1830–31), the ethics was still not ready for the printer, and by the time of his death in 1834 he had delegated the unfinished task to a former student, Ludwig Jonas. From an assortment of Schleiermacher's own handwritten manuscripts and notes taken down by his students, Jonas was able to put together and publish posthumously Schleiermacher's *Christian Ethics Presented Systematically According to the Principles of the Evangelical Church* (1843). The title was exactly parallel to the full title of *The Christian Faith* (which was shortened by the English translators). A hefty book of more than nine hundred pages, like *The Christian Faith* it was structured by a precise systematic framework, but it still lacked the polish and tightness of the companion work. The relationship between the two works is grounded in Schleiermacher's belief that the abstract essence of religiousness, though in itself a matter of feeling or immediate self-consciousness (the "feeling of absolute dependence"), is both an impulse to thought and an impulse to action. Hence religiousness gives rise to two disciplines, logically independent of each other but springing from a common source. Further, he established a particular link between thought and action, doctrine and ethics, in Christianity by describing the distinctively Christian modification of religiousness as a religion of the "teleological" type. By a "teleological" religion, he meant a religion directed to moral ends—marked, that is, by "a predominating reference to the moral task," represented in Christianity as activity in the kingdom of God.

The Christian faith, however, is distinguished from all other religions of the teleological type by the fact that everything in it is connected with the redemption accomplished by Jesus of Nazareth. This is the defining characteristic of Christianity that determines Schleiermacher's understanding of the way Christian ethics is to be done: its aim is to indicate the patterns of behavior that result from fellowship with the Redeemer. He found the Kantian ethic of duty distasteful, and he advocated instead a descriptive ethic that would drop the imperative mood altogether. With Christ something new entered history, and it continues to work in the church as an active power. Christian ethics must describe this power and its effects. Of course, Schleiermacher did not deny that a Christian ethic could be presented in the imperative mood, and he admitted that his descriptive ethic hardly offered a purely empirical account of the way things presently are in the Evangelical Church. But the crucial point for him was that every genuinely Christian activity flows from the transforming influence of the Redeemer, mediated through the "common Spirit" of the Christian community. In 1 Corinthians 13, the Apostle Paul gave a description of love, and in Galatians, renouncing law, he described love, joy, peace, and all the other characteristics of Christian behavior as the fruit of the Spirit (Gal. 5:16–24). Here, in Paul, Schleiermacher found two models for the purely descriptive form of Christian ethics that he advocated.

Except for the introduction, which has been translated by John C. Shelley, the *Christian Ethics* has never been translated into English. Students and teachers will be grateful for Professor Brandt's sure-footed guidance through a long and complex German text, which has been undeservedly—if understandably—neglected in the English-speaking world. Two features of this study should prove especially appealing.

First, although he provides an admirable introduction to the principles of Schleiermacher's Christian ethics, including the vexed question of its relation to philosophical ethics, Brandt also reviews many of the issues to which the principles are applied. I can well imagine that for some readers this may be the most engaging feature of the book, whether or not they find Schleiermacher's moral judgments persuasive. He believed that the distinctive spirit of Christianity is a principle of action that should encompass the whole of life, and he brought this principle to bear on an astonishing number of activities, sorted out by means of a somewhat artificial scheme of two *spheres* of action (church and culture) and three *kinds* of action (purifying or restoring, broadening or disseminating, and expressive or representational). Readers will find here his thoughts on the implications of faith in Christ not only for such inner-churchly concerns as ecclesiastical discipline, reform, religious instruction, missions, worship, and the Christian family, but also for such outward-looking cultural concerns as the state, labor, capital punishment, revolution, war, colonization, the arts, games—and more. As Professor Brandt puts it, "The *Christian Ethics* is not only an ecclesial ethics of piety, but also a theology of culture. . . . The *Ethics* promotes its vision of culture transformed by Christ."

Second, and equally engaging, Brandt does not simply give a chapter-by-chapter exposition of the *Christian Ethics,* but sets its main themes in the context of the author's sometimes frantic life and labors. The result is a portrait of an amazingly resourceful man who, along with his official duties as pastor, university professor, and civil servant, was an energetic political activist. He aligned himself with the advocates of social and economic reform, and he openly resisted the design of King Friedrich Wilhelm III to bring the church more completely under the control of the crown. There were times in his life when prophetic protest led him into political agitation. His activities were then closely monitored by the Prussian authorities, and he was in danger of losing his appointments. Brandt concludes with good reason: "The transformative impulse of the *Ethics* can be seen as a theoretical reflection of Schleiermacher's reformist activities."

But why a book on Schleiermacher's ethics in a series devoted to Reformed theology? In *The Christian Faith* and in his *Christian Ethics,* he spoke as a Protestant. The full title of both works made explicit his intention to do theology "according to the principles of the Evangelical Church," by which he meant in particular the Prussian church formed in 1817 by union of the Lutherans and the Reformed. Limitation of the theological task to the faith and life of a particular Christian community required, as he said expressly, that he renounce any wish to produce a universal Christian ethics for all time. There could be no certainty that what was once taken to be right and good would be so regarded in the future, and he thought it inevitable that in his own day theology would be pursued either as Catholic or as Protestant theology. In the *Christian Ethics,* he invoked the Reformation doctrines of justification by faith and the priesthood of all believers as formative ethical principles, and he repeatedly drew attention to the differences between Catholic and Protestant teaching (although he believed they would eventually be overcome). One constant refrain in the *Christian Ethics,* for example, was that Catholic ethics demanded obedience to the church, whereas a Protestant ethic appealed directly to the conscience informed by scripture.

Schleiermacher spoke as a Protestant, accepting the division between Catholics and Protestants as a *fait accompli*. But he played down the old antagonism within Protestantism itself between the Lutherans and the Reformed. The Marburg Colloquy notwithstanding, he believed that there was no difference of "spirit" between them. The theological disagreements did not reflect a dissimilarity in the religious affections, but rather in the way they were represented; and the disagreements had no bearing, he said, on Christian ethics. It is true that he could occasionally profess his continuing allegiance to the Reformed *school*, as he called it, even after union with the Lutherans had brought into existence a single *communion*. But it by no means followed that he considered himself bound to come out on the Reformed side of every dogmatic issue. In his *Christian Ethics*, as elsewhere, he located the disagreement in two doctrines: election and the Lord's Supper. On the first, he did come to Calvin's defense, though he modified what he defended; on the second, because neither the Lutheran view nor the Reformed was free of difficulties, he was content to await further help from New Testament exegesis. He denied that either difference affected the questions with which his *Christian Ethics* was concerned.

But these two, of course, are not in fact the only issues on which Lutherans and Calvinists have spoken with their own distinctive accents. On some, Schleiermacher did seem to betray his Calvinist origins. Lutherans who are uneasy with his talk of "religiousness" (*die Frömmigkeit*), for instance, have sometimes traced the troublesome concept back to "piety" (*pietas*) in the theology of Calvin. But on other issues, Schleiermacher departed unambiguously from his Reformed heritage. Fundamental to his ethics was his suspicion of law, and he explicitly rejected the "third use" that Calvin had described as the principal use of the law. Again, there was a difference between Luther and Calvin on the way they understood the priesthood of all believers, and on this theme, too, Schleiermacher echoed Luther rather than "our Calvin" (as he sometimes called him).

It is a further contribution of this important book that Professor Brandt, himself a generous observer of the Reformed tradition rather than an insider or an advocate, takes up the mooted question of Schleiermacher and his Reformed heritage. In the concluding chapter, he cites Wilhelm Dilthey's judgment that in the *Christian Ethics* is the clearest indication of Schleiermacher's Reformed identity, because the work manifests the "aggressive spirit" of Reformed religion. This seems to me entirely right. It touches on a difference between historic Lutheranism and historic Calvinism that has often been discussed but is commonly overlooked when Schleiermacher's relation to his Reformed heritage is debated. His *Christian Ethics* plainly exhibits the so-called christocratic tendency of Reformed theology, which is sometimes held to confuse the distinction, so fundamental to Lutheran social ethics, between the "two kingdoms." The negative side of the christocratic tendency has been the refusal to permit the state to control the church, which accordingly must have its own independent "government." Schleiermacher shows his Reformed roots here, too, when he advocates a presbyterian form of government for the Prussian church. Readers will be grateful to Professor Brandt for opening up this side also of a many-sided churchman who is still insufficiently known and appreciated.

Union Theological Seminary and
Presbyterian School of Christian Education

B. A. Gerrish

INTRODUCTION: SCHLEIERMACHER'S LIFE AND ITS REFLECTION IN THE *CHRISTIAN ETHICS*

February 14, 1834, was a day of mourning in the city of Berlin, the likes of which the capital of Prussia had rarely seen. A funeral procession made its way through the city toward a cemetery outside its boundaries. Leading the way was a coffin borne aloft by twelve hearty students from Berlin's Humboldt University; three groups of twelve students alternated in carrying the casket. Behind the casket came a line of mourners on foot, stretching over a mile in length. Behind these mourners came some one hundred horse-drawn coaches; in the first of these rode Friedrich Wilhelm III, King of Prussia, along with his son, the crown prince, six years later to be Friedrich Wilhelm IV.[1] Lining the streets were additional throngs, conservatively estimated at 20,000 to 30,000 people. Contemporary observers said that the whole event, a spontaneous expression on the part of the people of Berlin, was meant to honor the one who had died.[2]

The one mourned and honored was Friedrich Daniel Ernst Schleiermacher. He had been a pastor in the Reformed and then the Union church, a professor of theology and philosophy, and a leader in the cause of social-political reform. He was loved by the people of Berlin. The capital city of Prussia stopped on that day in February 1834, and there can hardly have been a person unaffected by the salute to this person, small only in his physical stature.

SCHLEIERMACHER'S LIFE IN OUTLINE

The young Schleiermacher rebelled against the narrow constraints of churchly formation, theological rigidity, and social convention. He was asked to leave the Moravian Brethren seminary in Barby in 1787 because he insisted, with a small circle of friends, on independent thinking. Nor did he shy away from the skeptical conclusions to which this independent thinking led him. He would not submit to the seminary's authoritarianism, nor would he desist from reading "worldly" humanistic writers like Goethe.

In the period 1796–1803 as a young minister at the Charité hospital in Berlin, he broke with social convention by his participation in "salon society" and in the Romantic circle of poets and scholars. Salon society pushed the envelope with its mixing of social groups in defiance of the norms of the day: men and women, Jews and Gentiles, commoners and nobles all came together for intellectual and social intercourse. The Romantic circle took aim at the dominant Enlightenment orthodoxy of the day and developed an alternative worldview, stressing intuition, poetry, and sympathy over reason, science, and order. The Romantics also protested the tradition of arranged marriage where love was absent; living out this credo led to divorces and alignments of love. Schleiermacher fell in love with Eleonore Grunow, a young woman unhappily married to an older Lutheran minister. For a time they planned for her to leave her husband that they might marry. In this context Schleiermacher burst on the public intellectual scene in Berlin with the 1799 publication of his controversial *On Religion: Speeches to Its Cultured Despisers*.[3] The *Speeches* was a countercultural work, subverting rationalist, pietist, and orthodox views of religion; its revisionist understanding of religion and theology led to charges of Spinozistic pantheism and caused concern on the part of the young minister's ecclesiastical superiors.

Schleiermacher's early rebelliousness becomes in subsequent years a commitment to reform of society and church and revision in theology pursued from within the system. He becomes a professor and pastor within the established and state-sponsored university and church, playing a crucial role in the founding of the new University of Berlin in 1810. His accomplishments as an intellectual stagger the imagination. As a professor and scholar in theology and philosophy, he lectured and published in a wide array of areas, from hermeneutics to ethics, from dialectics to pedagogy, from biblical studies, church history, and dogmatics to disciplines in practical theology. In all this he contributed to the creation of a new intellectual world opened up by Romanticism and Speculative Idealism.

At his death, Schleiermacher had served for more than twenty years in Berlin as professor of theology at Humboldt University and as preacher at Trinity Church. In the latter role he was a charismatic leader, drawing reform-minded persons to the congregation and leading resistance to state efforts to impose its will on the Prussian Church. Schleiermacher was also a contributor in the cause of social and political reform. He played a leading role in rallying the populace to the cause of the liberation of Prussia when the French under Napoleon had conquered it. He also gave energy and vision to the "Prussian springtime"[4] of 1806–13, a significant period of democratic reform. When the Reform Movement was definitively halted in 1819, the repressive measures of the reactionary government were trained on all reformers, and Schleiermacher's work was carefully monitored, his person suspect. Spies reported to the government on his academic lectures and sermons. During this same period, he was the leader in the newly formed Prussian Union (of Lutheran and Reformed) Church, particularly in resisting the king's imposition of a new liturgy for all churches in Berlin. The battle raged for seven years, from 1822–29; the king won and made few concessions. Toward the end of his life there may have been some rapprochement, for in July of 1830 Schleiermacher was given the order of Red Eagle by the king. Be this as it may, for most of his life Schleiermacher was a leader of social and political reform and a thorn in the king's side.

Beyond his role as a public figure, Schleiermacher was also deeply engaged in his life as a husband and father, and a veritable "virtuoso of friendship."[5] In 1809 Schleiermacher married the young widow Henriette von Willich and became stepfather to her children. Together they had four more children. By all accounts, Schleiermacher was a devoted husband and father. In his masterful study of the early Schleiermacher, Albert Blackwell demonstrates how sympathy for others was "the pulse of Schleiermacher's life and ethics." He writes:

> To judge from his correspondence and the testimony of his friends, Schleiermacher had a virtually inexhaustible reservoir of sympathy for others and a correspondingly insatiable need for love and sympathy in return.[6]

Schleiermacher was a true *mensch*; he was admired for his humanity, the person he was, especially in his relationships with others. Friedrich Schlegel says that "what Goethe is to poetry, and Fichte is to philosophy, Schleiermacher is to humanity," and Bettina Brentano von Arnim says that he "was not the greatest man (*Mann*) of his time, he was the greatest human being (*Mensch*)."[7]

Physically, Schleiermacher was a small person, and he had a stoop to his back that prevented him from standing erect. But he was a great human being, and the people of Berlin knew it. So it is that on February 14, 1834, they turned out *en masse* to express their respect for a man small in stature, but great in so many ways. To his contemporaries he was "one of those representative [individuals] in whom are concentrated as it were, in a focus, the moral and intellectual life of the nation and the period to which they belong."[8]

Today Schleiermacher is little known outside academic circles. Theologians know him as the "founder of modern Protestant theology." Philosophers recognize him similarly for founding modern hermeneutics and for having set the measure against which all subsequent German translations of Plato are measured.

THE *CHRISTIAN ETHICS*

This book concerns itself with a lesser-known work in Schleiermacher's theological corpus, the *Christian Ethics* (*Die christliche Sitte* or *Sittenlehre*). Theological students who know of Schleiermacher are perhaps able to identify the trilogy of works rightfully seen as central to his theological corpus: the *Speeches*, the *Brief Outline*, and *The Christian Faith* (or *Glaubenslehre*). Few know of his work in ethics.

In fact, a great number of otherwise careful scholars have concluded that Schleiermacher's theology is ethically deficient. In the history of Schleiermacher interpretation, there has existed a general consensus that his ethical position is woefully inadequate. Even those who are otherwise friendly to Schleiermacher have voiced dissatisfaction with his theological ethics. Albrecht Ritschl, a theologian decisively influenced by his Reformed predecessor, complains that Schleiermacher fails to work out the implications of his ethical vision: the importance of the ethical moment is seen, but not incorporated into his theology.[9] H. Richard Niebuhr, a theologian who is quite similar to Schleiermacher in important respects,[10] classifies Schleiermacher's theological ethics as belonging to the "Christ of culture" type; that is to say, an ethics that surrenders a distinctive Christian identity in order to accommodate itself to its cultural context.[11] As one would expect, Karl Barth and Emil Brunner, leaders of twentieth-century "Dialectical Theology" and harsh critics of Schleiermacher and the trajectory of the New Protestantism, register important criticisms against the ethical aspect of Schleiermacher's theology.[12] In the latter half of the twentieth century, the rejection of his theological-ethical legacy became more vehement, building on the Neo-Orthodox critique but fueled also by a Marxist analysis of social and economic reality.[13]

Schleiermacher is read as ethically deficient, at least in part because the *Speeches* are the lens through which his work is considered. The *Speeches* identify intuitive awareness as central to religion, and relegate action and thought to secondary roles. Although Schleiermacher never repudiates the *Speeches* perspective, the importance of the ethical moment in religion comes to a new prominence for him, especially after the political upheavals of 1806.

The *Speeches* of 1799 are responding to the rationalistic threat to reduce religion to morality. Of the significant religious and theological currents that flowed from the 1700s into the next century, there is one that shapes the *Speeches* in a profound way. This is the pronounced tendency in the eighteenth century toward an exclusive identification of religion with morality. Enlightenment rationalism, the eighteenth century's most significant intellectual movement, "was characterized by a deep and pervasive moralism."[14] This included the conviction that "morality is the better part, the final meaning and content of religion" and that "religion is the acknowledgment of moral duties as divine commands."[15]

Kant represents the culmination of this moralistic rationalism. Not only does he agree that the essence of religion is to be identified with morality; for Kant "the rationally permissible belief structure now explicitly rests on the self-certifying moral experience."[16] Kant's second critique, *The Critique of Practical Reason*,[17] moves from the sense of moral obligation as a given in human life, to the postulation of human freedom as the necessary ground for the possibility of moral experience, and the postulation of the existence of God and the immortality of the soul as necessary to the fulfillment of the moral sense in the unity of virtue and happiness, duty and desire. In the second critique, morality is not only the real meaning of religion; it is also the ground for those religious "postulations" that can be made. Kant's program represents an almost complete moralization of religion and theology.

Schleiermacher's *Speeches* must be seen as a countercultural work deliberately swimming against the tide of rational religion and its moralism. Schleiermacher insists that religion in its essence be identified as intuition rather than as either morality or knowledge. The *Speeches* preference is to speak of the "infinite," or the "world spirit," rather than God. Religion is understood as "intuition of the infinite,"[18] a "holy soul stirred by the universe,"[19] or "love of the world spirit."[20] By defining religion in this way, Schleiermacher identifies religion in its essence as intuition or pious feeling, immediately given in experience. Against Kant, Schleiermacher insists that one does not move from moral sense as the given to the postulation of religious claims, nor is morality to be identified as the real meaning of religion. This commitment to the centrality of intuition or religious consciousness as the basis from which theological analysis can proceed is one to which Schleiermacher remains loyal throughout his intellectual career, from the first edition of the *Speeches* to the second edition of the *Christian Faith*. By means of this focus on piety Schleiermacher is able to offer a clear alternative to a rationalistic reduction of religion.[21]

Clearly then, a sharp distinction between the "religious" and "ethical" moments is an important feature of Schleiermacher's theological program. Because Schleiermacher is concerned with preserving the integrity and irreducibility of religion, he insists on religious feeling or piety as the center of his theological (i.e., dogmatic and ethical) program. This being so, it is not surprising that interpreters of Schleiermacher, especially as they fail to give clear attention to his historical context, judge the ethical aspect of his theology to be deficient.

Although Schleiermacher insists throughout his theological work on a careful distinction between piety or religious feeling, on the one hand, and ethical action and reflective thinking, on the other, he in no way wants to separate these elements. The conclusion that his theology is ethically deficient misses the fact that for Schleiermacher Christian piety as feeling gives rise to both action and reflection. Christian piety is by its very nature active and morally responsible. It is crucial to consider the place of ethical action in Christian piety and, correspondingly, the relation of Schleiermacher's less well-known *Christian Ethics*[22] to his famous *Christian Faith*[23] if we are to attain an accurate assessment of his position.

Another problem presents itself. It could be argued that the *Christian Ethics* is not deserving of careful attention. It is not, after all, a work written and prepared for publication by Schleiermacher himself. Rather, the *Ethics* was published posthumously by Ludwig Jonas in 1843 from lecture notes (both those from students and some from Schleiermacher's own hand). The work we have is not a finished product. On the other hand, Schleiermacher offered semester-long lecture courses on Christian ethics no fewer than twelve times,[24] and we have the testimony of Jonas that "No course of lectures by Schleiermacher ever made a greater impression on me than those in the summer of 1817 on Christian ethics."[25]

So, what is the status of the ethical action in Schleiermacher's theological scheme? And what importance is to be assigned to the *Christian Ethics*? A preliminary way of addressing these issues is to consider how Schleiermacher views the relationship of the dogmatic and ethical elements in his theological scheme, attending to the explicit theological self-understanding he articulates. Of what does theology consist? What are its component parts? Consistently, Schleiermacher affirms that only as dogmatics and ethics are considered together is the whole of Christian teaching constituted. Christian doctrine consists of the science of Christian dogmatics and the science of Christian morals. Schleiermacher addresses this issue in paragraph 26 of his *Christian Faith,* asserting, "It is clear that only the two taken together represent the whole reality of the Christian life."[26] Because the modes of action described by ethics are "expressions of the religious affections of the Christian,"[27] they qualify as propositions or doctrines of faith. In the *Ethics* itself, Schleiermacher affirms, "[T]his discipline must be seen as an organic part of the whole theological study."[28]

Schleiermacher views dogmatics and ethics as two sides of the same coin; together they form a unity—the science of doctrine. He argues for the unity, even the interchangeability, of the two disciplines:

> Evidently, we must say that Christian ethics is also dogmatics. Because that in the Christian church to which Christian ethics always returns is completely a matter of faith [*Glaubenssache*], and the presentation of Christian rules of life is nothing other than a further development of that which is contained in the original faith of the Christian. And is Christian

dogmatics not also ethics? Of course! Because how could the Christian faith be fully presented without presenting the idea of the kingdom of God on earth?[29]

The presentation of the idea of the kingdom of God on earth is, in fact, a presentation of the Christian manner of living and acting, which is nothing other than Christian ethics. Christian ethics is grounded in Christian piety, and any complete exposition of piety must include ethics. Schleiermacher envisions these two disciplines as complementary, as comprising an organic unity. This note is sounded also in *The Christian Faith* and the *Brief Outline*. In the former work, Schleiermacher affirms that it is easy to understand how these two disciplines could be treated together, as they were throughout most of Christian history. In the latter work, we read that the separation of the two disciplines "cannot be regarded as something essential."[30] In fact, the discussion of the separation in the *Brief Outline* concludes with the affirmation: "It will always remain desirable that the undivided treatment should regain currency from time to time."[31]

The obvious question given this affirmation of unity is why dogmatics and ethics should be separated at all. The answer consistently given—cited in all three of the aforementioned works—is that Christian ethics requires independent treatment so it can come out from the shadow of dogmatics. By being presented separately, each discipline can be seen in its own interconnectedness. "It has brought to Christian ethics the further advantage of undergoing a more elaborate treatment."[32] Thus the *Brief Outline*. In both *The Christian Faith* and the *Christian Ethics*, Schleiermacher discusses the union of the two disciplines, noting that usually this has meant that the concerns of ethics are "as a whole or in pieces referred to one locus (or several loci) of dogmatics."[33] Then ethics is divided up, subsumed under the doctrine of God as commands, and under "revelation," "church," and "kingdom of God." Divided in this manner, ethics appears as "no rightly regulated, well-shaped organism;"[34] therefore, "it was inevitable that the ethical interest should lead sooner or later to the two disciplines being separated from each other."[35] In spite of their fundamental unity, Schleiermacher justifies the separation of these two disciplines in the interest of ethics.

The above analysis shows that based on *The Christian Faith*'s own self-presentation, dogmatics and ethics are complementary *in principle*. One might wonder whether this is also the case *in fact*. Evidence of complementarity can be seen in *The Christian Faith* itself. At key points in that work, a border is reached, analysis halted. This can be a source of frustration to the careful reader of *The Christian Faith*: a certain ideational momentum builds as a particular notion is discursively developed, consequences drawn out. Then one arrives at the ethics border, and the development of ideas stops. For example, the Christian consciousness of grace, analyzed in terms of the divine attributes that correspond to it, climaxes with a discussion of the divine wisdom. Here Schleiermacher is a Moses who does not cross over into the ethical promised land:

> The divine wisdom, as the unfolding of the divine love, conducts us here to the realm of Christian Ethics; for we are now confronted with the task of more and more securing recognition for the world as a good world, as also of forming all things into an organ of the divine Spirit in harmony with the divine idea originally underlying the world-order, thus bringing all into unity with the system of redemption.... Hence the world can be viewed as a perfect revelation of divine wisdom only in proportion as the Holy Spirit makes itself felt through the Christian Church as the ultimate world-shaping power.[36]

Rhetorically, this is *The Christian Faith* rising to a rare instance of kerygmatic oratory. And in doing so, it points beyond itself to the *Ethics*, where the task of analyzing the church as the instrument of revelation will be done. Here, as elsewhere,[37] in concrete ways, Schleiermacher's dogmatics points beyond itself to its completion in ethics.

Schleiermacher chooses to treat dogmatics and ethics separately, even while insisting upon their complementarity. And he does so for the sake of ethics. It is undeniable that his decision resulted in his *Christian Faith* being universally known and his *Christian Ethics* almost as universally ignored. Schleiermacher's announced intention in making this division is noteworthy—to present Christian ethics in a more complete and integrated manner. Schleiermacher claims to have the interest of ethics at heart in offering separate dogmatic and ethical treatments. Ethics has a standing equal to that of dogmatics within Schleiermacher's theological system; the two are complementary, and only when both are considered together can Schleiermacher's whole system be comprehended. The *Christian Ethics* completes *The Christian Faith*. Without knowing the former we really don't comprehend Schleiermacher's theology in its entirety. So we need a careful examination of *Christian Ethics*. That is the task of this book.

SCHLEIERMACHER'S LIFE AND *CHRISTIAN ETHICS*: CORRESPONDENCES

To this point, the argument of this chapter has developed two seemingly unrelated themes. On the one hand, we have examined the breadth and depth of Schleiermacher's accomplishments in his life and the high regard in which his person was held by his contemporaries. On the other hand, we have seen the *Christian Ethics* as the overlooked completion of his theological system. These two themes come together in the approach this book will take: Schleiermacher's life is used to illumine his *Christian Ethics*.

In no other work that Schleiermacher authored is there such a correspondence with his life. Schleiermacher lived as a Christian pastor, theology and philosophy professor, husband and father, leader in movements of social and political reform, and genius of friendship and relationship. We will show that his *Christian Ethics* is best characterized as an ecclesial ethics of piety and a transformative theology of culture that is comprehensive in scope. The *Christian Ethics* analyzes all areas of life in the church and in the wider culture and attends to the material issues of life (e.g., questions ranging from Christian worship, education, service and caring, to war and peace, criminal justice, social relations, and the arts), as well as the more formal issues of ethics. Similarly, Schleiermacher's life included deep participation in a wide range of ecclesial and cultural life. Schleiermacher was not a reclusive scholar, but a true *mensch* who lived a rich and full life.

The agenda for this book will be to lift up experiences from Schleiermacher's life as an entry into aspects of his *Christian Ethics*. After Chapters 1 and 2 provide an overview of Schleiermacher's life in its historical context, Chapter 3 considers Schleiermacher's early educational experiences among the pietistic community of the Moravian Brethren and then examines piety as the ground and goal of the *Christian Ethics*. Chapter 4 considers Schleiermacher's relationship with his contemporary, the philosopher G. F. W. Hegel, and examines the relation between Christian and philosophical ethics as seen in the *Christian Ethics*. Chapter 5 looks at Schleiermacher's pastoral experience, particularly his years at Trinity Church in Berlin and the *Ethics'* view of the "inward" mission of the church in terms of church discipline and reform, education and missions, and worship. Chapter 6 analyzes Schleiermacher's involvement in the social and political arena and demonstrates the *Ethics* vision of cultural transformation. Finally, Chapter 7 draws together the lines of the argument and considers the question of the Reformed character of the *Ethics*.

So, the task of this book is to investigate Schleiermacher's life and use it as a lens to view his *Ethics*. Who was this Prussian preacher and university professor, why did he have such impact on his contemporaries, and what correspondence is there between his own life and his vision of the Christian life as laid out in the *Ethics*? Before turning to the heart of the book, where vignettes from Schleiermacher's life are brought into correspondence with his *Christian Ethics*, the outline of his life and his achievement in theology need attention. That is the task of the first two chapters.

NOTES

1. Translator's introduction to *The Life of Schleiermacher, as Unfolded in His Autobiography and Letters*, trans. Frederica Rowan, vol. 1 (London: Smith, Elder, and Co., 1859), ix–x.

2. Martin Redeker, *Schleiermacher: Life and Thought*, trans. John Wallhausser (Philadelphia: Fortress Press, 1973), 213.

3. Friedrich Schleiermacher, *On Religion: Speeches to Its Cultured Despisers*, trans. Richard Crouter (Cambridge: Cambridge University Press, 1988). The German version, which is a critical synopsis of all three German editions, is *Friedrich Schleiermachers Reden über die Religion*, ed. G. Ch. Gernhard Pünjer. Kritische Ausgabe (Brunswick: C. A. Schwetschke and Son [M. Bruhn], 1879). Crouter's translation makes the original edition available to English readers once again. Referred to as *Speeches*. Terrence N. Tice's translation of the first edition (Richmond: John Knox Press, 1969) has been out of print for some time. John Oman's translation (New York: Harper & Row, reprint edition 1958) has been the most readily available English-language version since its original publication in 1894. It is of much less value than Crouter's translation for scholarly purposes however, as it is a compilation of the three editions published in Schleiermacher's lifetime and includes many changes from the first German edition of 1799.

4. This is a name I give to the Reform Movement of 1806–13 to suggest the parallels with the Guatemalan springtime of 1944–54. Both were hopeful times of democratic reform followed by returns to oppressive, autocratic rule. On the Guatemalan springtime, see Jim Handy, *Gift of the Devil: A History of Guatemala* (n.p.: South End Press, 1984), esp. 103–23.

5. Albert L. Blackwell, *Schleiermacher's Early Philosophy of Life: Determinism, Freedom, and Phantasy* (Chico, Calif.: Scholars Press, 1982), cites this comment by Eleonor Grunow, 274.

6. Ibid.

7. Ibid., 174–75. Schlegel quotation from a letter of 1798, Br. III, 81. Von Armin's letter is reported in Ehrenfried von Willich, *Aus Schleiermachers Hause: Jugenderinnerungen seines Stiefsohnes* (Berlin: G. Reimer, 1909), 127. The testimony of stepson Ehrenfried von Willich concurs: "I have never seen anyone in whom knowledge and life were so in unison as they were in him, anyone who so lived what he thought and knew" (26); cited in Blackwell, 2.

8. Rowan, ix.

9. Albrecht Ritschl, *A Critical History of the Christian Doctrine of Justification and Reconciliation*, trans. John S. Black (Edinburgh: Edmonston and Douglas, 1872), 440–511. Cf. also Albrecht Ritschl, *The Christian Doctrine of Justification and Reconciliation: The Positive Development of the Doctrine*, trans. H. R. Mackintosh and A. B. Macaulay (Clifton, N.J.: Reference Book Publishers, 1966), 8–14.

10. Richard Crouter, "Schleiermacher and the Theology of Bourgeois Society: A Critique of the Critics," *Journal of Religion* 66, no. 2 (July 1986): 306. Crouter cites the following positions, shared by Schleiermacher and Niebuhr: "stress on divine oneness and radical monotheism, the need for an ethics that is broadly rooted in human sociality and a sense of history, as well as in the openness of theology to the pluralism of academic disciplines."

11. H. Richard Niebuhr, *Christ and Culture* (New York: Harper and Row, 1951), 93–94.

12. See Karl Barth, *Church Dogmatics*, vol. 2, pt. 2, *The Doctrine of God*, ed. G. W. Bromiley and T. F. Torrance (Edinburgh: T. & T. Clark, 1957), 509–781; see also Emil Brunner, *Das Gebot und die Ordnungen* (Tübingen: Verlag von J. C. B. Mohr [Paul Siebeck], 1933).

13. Yorick Spiegel, *Theologie der bürgerlichen Gesellschaft: Sozialphilosophie und Glaubenslehre bei Friedrich Schleiermacher* (Munich: Kaiser Verlag, 1968); Dieter Schellong, *Bürgertum und christliche Religion: Anpassungsprobleme der Theologie seit Schleiermacher* (Munich: Kaiser Verlag, 1975); and Frederick Herzog, *Justice Church: The New Function of the Church in North American Christianity* (Maryknoll, N.Y.: Orbis Books, 1980).

14. Claude Welch, *Protestant Thought in the Nineteenth Century* (New Haven and London: Yale University Press: vol. 1, 1972; vol. 2, 1985), 1:34.

15. Ibid.

16. Ibid., 47.

17. Immanuel Kant, *The Critique of Practical Reason*, trans. Lewis White Beck (Indianapolis: Bobbs-Merrill Educational Publishing, 1956).

18. *Speeches*, trans. Crouter, 90.

19. Ibid., 92.

20. Ibid., 115.

21. Schleiermacher's appeal to piety also enables him to offer an alternative to Orthodoxy and its apparent identification of assent to dogma as the essence of religion. The focus on piety is also critical in his later work *Kurze Darstellung des theologischen Studiums zum Behuf einleitender Vorlesungen*, ed. Heinrich Scholz (Darmstadt: Wissenschaftliche Buchgesellschaft, 1961). The English translation is *Brief Outline on the Study of Theology*, trans. Terrence N. Tice (Richmond: John Knox Press, 1970). In this work Schleiermacher recognizes and appropriates the radically historical character of all theology. The clear distinction between piety and theology enables Schleiermacher to admit both change and development at the level of theological expression—as historical it is ever in flux, ever subject to change—and the more basic continuity at the level of piety—piety in its immediacy remains constant throughout history. The focus on piety is crucial to the two most significant issues that Schleiermacher's theological program addresses: the nature of religion and the historical character of theology.

22. Friedrich Schleiermacher, *Die christliche Sitte nach den Grundsätzen der evangelischen Kirche im Zusammenhange dargestellt*, ed. Ludwig Jonas, in *Sämmtliche Werke*, div. 1, vol. 12 (Berlin: G. Reimer, 1843). The *Sämmtliche Werke* consists of thirty-one volumes, divided into three divisions: theological works, sermons, and philosophical works. References to the *Sämmtliche Werke* are to division, volume, and page. The new reprint edition of the *Die christliche Sitte* is from Waltrop: Verlag Hartmut Spenner, 1999. All translations from this work are my own; hereafter referred to as the *Christian Ethics*.

23. Friedrich Schleiermacher, *Der christliche Glaube nach den Grundsätzen der evangelischen Kirche im Zusammenhange dargestellt*, 7th ed., ed. Martin Redeker, 2 vols. (Berlin: Walter de Gruyter, 1960). Referred to below as *The Christian Faith*. The standard English translation is *The Christian Faith*, trans. H. R. Mackintosh and J. S. Stewart (Edinburgh: T. & T. Clark, 1928).

24. The lecture course from the winter semester 1826–27 at the University of Berlin may be taken as typical. It began on October 23 and ran for an hour each weekday until March 30. It totaled about ninety-five hours of lecture. Friedrich Schleiermacher, *Christliche Sittenlehre: Einleitung,* ed. Hermann Peiter (Stuttgart: Verlag W. Kohlhammer, 1983), xxvii–xxviii. The body of this work, without the editor's introduction and the textual apparatus of the text itself, has been translated in *Friedrich Schleiermacher: Introduction to Christian Ethics,* trans. John Shelley (Nashville: Abingdon Press, 1989).

25. *Ethics,* vii.

26. *The Christian Faith,* 111. The complementary character of Schleiermacher's works in dogmatics and ethics is signaled by the parallelism of their German titles. Translated, the titles are "Christian Ethics" or "Christian Faith" "set forth according to the principles of the Protestant church in their interconnections." The shorthand titles also reflect this parallelism: *Sittenlehre* (doctrine of morals) and *Glaubenslehre* (doctrine of faith).

27. Ibid., 111.

28. *Ethics,* 2.

29. Ibid., 12–13.

30. *Brief Outline,* 82.

31. Ibid.

32. Ibid., 80.

33. *Ethics,* 15.

34. Ibid., 10.

35. *The Christian Faith,* 112.

36. Ibid., 736–37.

37. Cf. *The Christian Faith,* 560 and 613.

1
SCHLEIERMACHER'S LIFE AND THOUGHT TO 1802

The relation between Schleiermacher, the Reformed theologian and pastor, and the city of Berlin developed over the course of his lifetime. Its roots go back even further; Schleiermacher had family connections in the city. His mother, Katherine-Maria née Stubenrauch, was born there in 1736. Both her father and her paternal grandfather had served as Reformed chaplains at the royal court in Berlin. Schleiermacher's father, Gottlieb, was also the child of a Reformed parsonage. Gottlieb served as a Reformed chaplain in the Prussian army. Friedrich's lineage was solidly Reformed clergy and Prussian on both sides of his family.

The Christian identity of Prussia, and of Brandenburg and Brandenburg-Prussia before it, was unusual. In 1613 John Sigismund, the Elector of Brandenburg, had announced his adherence to Reformed Christianity, but had not required that his subjects follow him into the Reformed fold. Lutheranism remained the dominant confession of the people of Prussia, and the unusual result was a Reformed ruler with a majority of Lutheran subjects. This situation remained until the church of the Prussian Union joined the Reformed and Lutheran confessions into one church in 1817. As Reformed pastors, the Schleiermachers and Stubenrauchs were part of a "royal minority" in Prussia.

WHAT'S IN A NAME?

Friedrich Daniel Ernst was born in 1768. The three men after whom he was named were all Prussian and Reformed, and each played a powerful role in his life, directly or indirectly.[1] "Friedrich" was after the Prussian king, Friedrich II (the "Great"), in whose army Gottlieb served and whose great nephew, Friedrich Wilhelm III, ruled for much of Schleiermacher's life. Under Friedrich II (ruled 1740–86) and his father before him, Friedrich Wilhelm I (ruled 1713–40), Prussia became a military and political power and an absolutist state.

Friedrich's shadow is cast on all subsequent German, and even European, history. Prussia's rise to power altered the political landscape of Europe permanently. Prussia's ascendancy made it the western rival to Austria in the German east. The balance of power had Prussia and Austria on ends of the teeter-totter with the hundreds of small states in between.

Friedrich Wilhelm I and Friedrich II succeeded in making Prussia a military and economic power by building up the army, encouraging manufacturing and trade, and modernizing and rationalizing the state bureaucracy. Previously, positions in the state had been awarded to members of the nobility on the basis of their noble status; this changed so that intellectual acumen and administration ability became the new criteria for government positions. This change functioned to support concentration of power in the hands of the king; both Friedrich Wilhelm I and Friedrich II were autocratic rulers who demanded strict obedience and employed fear to undergird their sovereignty. The nobles of the Prussian countryside, the Junkers, were made the officer corps of the army—positions of prestige and stature, given the army's prominence—and thus their loyalty was ensured and military leadership provided. Both kings were shrewd politicians who knew significant success in achieving their goals of military and economic strength.

Friedrich Wilhelm I was a disciplined, hard-working ascetic and soldier-king who transformed the flower garden in front of his modest palace into an army drill ground. He dressed daily in his military uniform. He doubled the size of the army during the course of his reign, from 40,000 to 80,000 soldiers. In terms of religion, he inclined toward pietistic Lutheranism, as evidenced by his termination of the rationalist philosopher Christian Wolff from the faculty of the University of Halle.

Although Friedrich II shared with his father the goal of economic and military development of Prussia, he was in other ways very different. Friedrich was deeply immersed in the Enlightenment and a lover of all things French. He admired and befriended Voltaire; for three years the French *philosophe* lived with Friedrich in Potsdam and Berlin. Friedrich rejected confessional Christianity and allowed religious toleration in his kingdom. Believing that humanity could elevate itself through reason, Friedrich eased censorship and eliminated torture in his regime; immediately on his accession to the throne, he reinstated Wolff at Halle, and he later built an opera house in Berlin for the production of French opera. Friedrich accepted Rousseau's "social contract" theory of the state and believed that the ruler was to serve the people by promoting their security and happiness. On the other hand, Friedrich believed that, in a ruthless world of struggle and strife, to fulfill his mandate to the people he needed to exercise power unchecked by anything save his own reason. This he did. Friedrich was an autocratic ruler; he gave his ministers and generals no real responsibility. He ruled by fear. On the basis of his brilliance and daring, Friedrich became a great military strategist; Napoleon looked back in awe at his prowess. Friedrich won great military victories against superior forces. He greatly expanded Prussian territorial claims, adding Silesia through the Seven Years War of 1756–63 and West Prussia by means of the partition of Poland he brokered among Prussia, Austria, and Russia in

1772. Friedrich was a person of genius and contradiction—at once a rationalist committed to toleration, openness, and the pursuit of happiness and a ruthless militaristic power broker who prospered at the expense of others. When his son was born in 1768, Gottlieb Schleiermacher named him after the Prussian king he then admired.

"Daniel" was for Gottlieb's father, Daniel Schleiermacher, who was also a Reformed pastor. When the seven-day-old Friedrich was baptized in November 1768, his grandfather Daniel was an absentee godfather. Daniel had fled into exile in the Netherlands in 1749 after being charged with sorcery and witchcraft. This father-son separation repeated itself with Gottlieb and Friedrich. In 1783, Friedrich was sent to boarding school; he was never to see either of his parents again. His mother died later that same year, and although his father lived until 1794 and there was a regular and often passionate correspondence between father and son, they never saw each other again.[2]

Father Gottlieb adopted a rationalist theology at least in part as a reaction against his father's disgrace resulting from the charges of witchcraft and sorcery. But this changed in 1778 when Gottlieb experienced a pietistic reawakening. His life was infused with a new and deep sense of devotion to Christ that led to a transformation of his ministry, his theology, and his family. The result for Friedrich was that he was placed in a Moravian (pietist) boarding school in Niesky where he, too, had a pietist conversion experience. The Moravians schooled him for four formative years, 1783–85 at Niesky and 1785–87 at their seminary at Barby. Schleiermacher's identity as a rebel emerged for the first time at the seminary. He fell in with a group of fellow students who developed their own educational program, reading Kant and Goethe. Eventually, Schleiermacher was forced to leave the seminary. The events leading up to his withdrawal from the seminary occasioned a distressing rift between Friedrich and Gottlieb, which was healed only by the passage of time and much correspondence.

Having left the seminary, Friedrich had no place to go—for education or even for shelter. In the end, his father granted Friedrich's request that he might go to Halle, live with his uncle Samuel, and study theology there. He promised to underwrite his son's expenses there for a year and a half. Friedrich left the Moravians behind physically and moved to Halle, as he had left them behind intellectually and spiritually and moved into doubt, uncertain about where he stood.

YEARS OF PREPARATION: 1787–96

In Halle, Friedrich lived with his uncle, Samuel Ernst Timotheus Stubenrauch, a professor of theology at the university. This uncle was the source for Friedrich's third given name, "Ernst." The uncle's befriending of the young rebel inaugurated a period of personal and intellectual self-formation that paved the way for the later accomplishments as pastor, theologian, and reformer. The years 1787–96 were a "decade of analytic philosophical preparation . . . years of almost ascetic philosophical concentration."[3]

Schleiermacher lived in Halle with his uncle Stubenrauch from 1787–89. The record of these years suggests that he attended few lectures in theology; instead, he busied himself with Kant's first and second *Critiques* and the *Groundwork of the Metaphysic of Morals*, listening to the lectures of the philosopher Eberhard, a critic of Kant. His developing theology at this time moved in a rationalistic orbit with an emphasis on moral living. In 1789 he went with his uncle to the town of Drossen, where Stubenrauch had accepted an appointment as pastor. The year in Drossen was a low point in Schleiermacher's life: his health was poor and his spirit depressed. However, in 1790 he passed his first set of theology exams and accepted a position as tutor for the children of Count Friedrich Dohna, at the beautiful manor in East Prussia.

Schleiermacher's three years with the Dohna family were as rich and positive as the year at Drossen had been difficult and depressing. He loved being part of the family's domestic circle, and he was happy in his tutor role, cultivating the minds and sensibilities of the Dohna children. He also fell secretly in love with one of the daughters, Frederika. He experienced a religious revitalization and enjoyed the opportunities he was given to preach. The sermons of this period have a "deeper tone which suggests that the author was inwardly at the point of going beyond the Enlightenment" and a recognition that "piety is the deeper source and spring of morality."[4] During his time with the Dohnas and in the following two years when Schleiermacher worked as associate pastor in Landsberg, he continued to engage Kant, fastening on the notion of transcendental freedom and the unbridgeable gap between noumena and phenomena. Schleiermacher develops an alternative ethical vision. This vision stresses the practical application of the moral law, the partiality of all human knowledge, and the cultivation of character as the moral task facing humans.[5]

Schleiermacher spent the next two years, 1794–96, working as assistant pastor of the Reformed church in Landsberg. In order to take this position, he stood for and passed the second set of theology exams in March 1794. He did well in all the exams except dogmatics, where he received a "satisfactory." The key addition to his own intellectual development in this time was his engagement with Spinoza, mediated to him through the philosopher Jacobi. In retrospect, it is evident that the decade of intense academic work and personal formation prepared Schleiermacher; he was ready to make his public debut in Berlin.

THE FIRST BERLIN PERIOD: 1796–1802

The Berlin of Schleiermacher's first stay there had slipped some from the heights under Friedrich II. When he came to the Prussian capital, the king was Friedrich Wilhelm II (ruled 1786–97); when he left Berlin, the ruler was Friedrich Wilhelm III, who ruled for the remainder of Schleiermacher's life.

The rule of Friedrich Wilhelm II was undistinguished. Fearing the political consequences, he turned away from Friedrich II's Enlightenment orientation and love of French culture. Instead he cultivated native German culture, for example, befriending and supporting Mozart. Friedrich Wilhelm was a sexual libertine; he had many mistresses and persuaded church officials to bless two of his bigamies. He had no gift for politics and was governed by the flatterers who surrounded the throne. In contrast to the indulgence of his personal life and in synch with his rejection of ways French and Enlightened, in his governance of the church he attempted to exclude rationalism and reinstate Orthodoxy: ministers were to hold strictly to orthodox Lutheranism. This order was unenforceable and led to much hypocrisy, but it was a portent of things to come in the Prussian church. Friedrich Wilhelm's moral and political deficiencies symbolize the weakening of the Prussian state, and his reign paved the way for Napoleon's conquest.

Friedrich Wilhelm III ruled Prussia for the final thirty-seven of Schleiermacher's sixty-six years. In contrast to his father's sexual libertinism, he was happily married to Queen Louise; this set a different moral tone in the land. But like his father, he was an inept, nervous politician. Friedrich Wilhelm relied heavily on his personal secretaries for political counsel, excluding his ministers of state from influence. This isolated the king politically, and, without a good working relationship with his ministers, he lost the insight and support they could have garnered him.

German intellectuals of Schleiermacher's day, like generations before them, focused on religious and philosophical issues. In contrast to their French and English counterparts for whom political action and reflection were central, the thinkers of the German Enlightenment maintained their distinctive focus. This may be due in part to the fertility of German soil for religion. The strong tradition of German Mysticism, the Reformation, and Pietism are noteworthy examples of this. Even more was it due to the tight control that German princes exercised over intellectuals. Having little opportunity to wield influence in the political arena, they continued to plow in the fields of religion and philosophy.[6]

Enlightenment Rationalism was the eighteenth century's most significant intellectual movement. The German *Aufklärung* begins with Gottfried Wilhelm Leibniz (1646–1716), a broad-ranging genius. His faith in reason, his cosmic optimism, and his religious vision based on the goodness of creation and the universal love of God come to be characteristic of the *Aufklärung,* the German version of the Enlightenment. After Leibniz, German Rationalism was dominated by a view that identified religion and morality. As was noted above, Kant represents an almost complete moralization of religion and the end of the rationalistic program. Kant recognized the extreme limits inherent in human reason. In Kant's epistemology, knowledge of empirical reality is secured, but knowledge of transcendent realities (*noumena*) is deemed to be inaccessible. Romanticism and Critical Idealism seek an alternative to the limits placed on knowledge by Kant and his identification of religion with morality. These thinkers reorient the German intellectual program, and Schleiermacher is a key player in this reorientation.

Orthodoxy and Pietism carried the banner of traditional Christianity in the eighteenth century. Although different in emphasis, both affirmed historic claims to Christian truth on the basis of divine revelation. Orthodoxy stressed right doctrine and insisted on assent to the revealed truths of Christianity; here the emphasis is clearly on knowledge. Pietism's emphasis is the renewal of faith and life; in its own way, it shares Rationalism's concern for morality. In response to God's goodness in sending Christ to deliver sinful humanity from sin, Christians are to live in service to neighbor and avoid the vices of the world. Although doctrine was not their central concern, pietists remained conservative theologically, affirming traditional claims about God, Christ, humanity, and the world. In Berlin in 1799, Schleiermacher makes his mark as a theologian, providing a new and distinctive alternative to the Kantian Rationalism, Protestant Orthodoxy, and Pietism of his day.

On Religion: Speeches to Its Cultured Despisers caused a tremendous stir with its biting critique of contemporary theology and church practice, and the surprising and unconventional way it spoke about religion. It was a work of rebellion against the dominant religious and intellectual culture of the time, but it was also a work of reconstruction that appropriated insights from the as yet unnamed Romantic movement and forged a path ahead for religion and theology. Although the book was published anonymously, soon everyone knew the author to be Schleiermacher, the 31-year-old minister serving as a chaplain at the Charité hospital. The reformulation of religion in the *Speeches* leads historians of Christian theology to mark 1799 as the dawn of a new epoch, known variously as "Modern Protestant Theology," or "the New Protestantism." The *Speeches* set theology on a new footing, but the new era in Protestant theology blooms only with Schleiermacher's later works, the *Brief Outline* and *The Christian Faith*. In them the vision of the *Speeches* is brought to fruition.

The *Speeches* were the offspring of the relationship between Schleiermacher and Berlin. Without Berlin and the sense of belonging, affirmation, and challenge that Schleiermacher found there, the *Speeches* would not have been conceived. More specifically, it was in the "new Berlin society" that Schleiermacher found soul mates whose lives and intellects inspired his own development and production. Two interconnected communities provided the young minister with social space: the salon hosted by Markus and Henrietta Herz and the Romantic circle of artists and poets. It was at Herz's salon that Schleiermacher first met Friedrich Schlegel, who in turn brought him into the Romantic circle that also included A. W. Schlegel and the poets Novalis, Ludwig Tieck, Friedrich Hölderlin, and Jean Paul.

The salon society was an important expression of the "new Berlin," which was deeply influenced by Goethe and in opposition to the enlightened (and French) Berlin of Friedrich "the Great." The salons were social gatherings usually hosted at the homes of wealthy, non-noble, often Jewish (such as Henrietta and Markus Herz) members of the small but growing bourgeoisie. Invited to the salons were cultured folk including young intellectuals—both commoners and nobles, and the women of the newly wealthy bourgeoisie class. This mixing of folk made for a richly diverse community; it was particularly the mixing of women and men that gave the salons a countercultural flavor and was scandalous in the eyes of many. What brought this diverse group together was interest in the cultivated and social life revolving around the arts and intellectual questions. Social and economic conditions made possible the new culture of the salons. In the second half of the eighteenth century, the Prussian government sought to stimulate the economy and keep the clamps on social change. Government policies led the fortunes of many nobles to sink and those of some commoners to rise. At the same time, positions for young intellectuals were hard to come by, and their time could be devoted to the salons. So Jewish women, like Henrietta Herz, became the hosts who brought together diverse folk who shared common intellectual interests.[7]

Schleiermacher quickly became Henrietta Herz's confidant and close friend. Her husband Markus was a well-known physician who had been Kant's favorite student. Henrietta was seventeen years younger than her husband, but their marriage appears to have been grounded in mutual respect and commitment. Henrietta was, by all contemporary accounts, beautiful and brilliant. She knew ten different languages. A tall and full-figured woman, she towered over Schleiermacher, who was short and slightly humpbacked. They were an odd-looking couple, but their friendship was deep and enduring, as evidenced by the rich and affectionate correspondence they exchanged for many years.

A NEW ERA IN THEOLOGY:
THE *SPEECHES ON RELIGION*

Friedrich Schlegel and the Romantic circle were particularly crucial in the creation of the *Speeches*. Schleiermacher and Schlegel became fast friends; for the year of 1898 they were inseparable, living together and viewed by themselves and their friends as "married." On Schleiermacher's twenty-ninth birthday, Schlegel elicited from his friend a promise that he would write "something original"[8] in the coming year. After initial grumbling and hesitation, Schleiermacher fulfilled the promise; the result was the *Speeches*.

Because of Schlegel's role in the creation of Schleiermacher's youth work and the way the *Speeches* are imbued with the language and conceptuality of Romanticism,[9] the influence of Romanticism on the *Speeches* is sometimes overemphasized. Schleiermacher was a member of the Romantic circle—the odd member. Where the other members were poets and aesthetes for whom art was the pinnacle of human creativity, Schleiermacher was a minister, his focus religion. And as Blackwell notes, Schleiermacher consulted Henrietta Herz, Schlegel, and Dorothea Veit concerning the *Speeches*, "but typically ignored their advice."[10] In fact, the Romantics were among the "cultured despisers" Schleiermacher sought to engage and convert in the *Speeches*.

The Romantics celebrated nature in its wild diversity and burgeoning life, not its mechanical order as had the Enlighteners. They affirmed historical particularity and the individual uniqueness of persons, nations, and families in opposition to Enlightenment universality and uniformity. They stressed the imagination and embraced myth, fairy tale, and dream,[11] seeing in these forms of expression (which were not taken seriously by the Enlightenment) a celebration of the wonder, delight, and mystery of the world. For the Romantics, the world is imbued with grandeur, the finite is pregnant with the infinite, and to discover and celebrate the unfolding of the infinite in nature, history, and individuals is the highest calling of persons. With much of this Schleiermacher agrees, but he would lead the Romantics beyond art to religion, and finally Christianity, as the place where communion with the infinite is most accessible.

How did the *Speeches* attempt to engage the Romantics and other cultured despisers on their own terms, and how did they open a new view of theology? The genius of the *Speeches* resides in their compelling reconstruction of the character of religion. Religion is understood as "sensibility and taste for the infinite,"[12] an "intuition of the infinite,"[13] a "holy soul stirred by the universe,"[14] or "love [of the] world spirit."[15] In this way, the *Speeches* identify the essence of religion with its inward, experiential side.

Against Kant, the *Speeches* insist that one does not move from moral sense as the given to the postulation of religious claims, nor is morality to be identified as the real meaning of religion. Similarly, against Deism's claim that religion is a matter of knowledge and Orthodoxy's emphasis on "right doctrine" (again, a matter of knowledge), the *Speeches* assert that religion consists, in the first place, neither in knowing or doing, but in intuition. Because he is concerned to preserve the integrity and irreducibility of religion, Schleiermacher insists on "intuition" or "piety" as its heart and center.

This commitment to the centrality of intuition or piety is one to which Schleiermacher remains loyal throughout his career, from the first edition of the *Speeches* to the second edition of *The Christian Faith*. In fact, it is arguable that this commitment is the touchstone of Schleiermacher's whole theological system. In this youth work we have, then, at once a countercultural attack on the dominant religious practices and understandings, and a reconstruction of religion that sets the parameters for Schleiermacher's ongoing project.

The *Speeches* inaugurate a new era in Christian theology because of its reconstructed concept of religion, its commendation of Christianity as the place where true religion is to be cultivated, and the beginning it makes toward the reconstruction of theology in light of this new concept of religion. The *Speeches* affirm the superiority of "positive religion" (e.g., Judaism, Christianity) over the "natural religion" of the Deists. Where natural religion is cold and abstract, stressing autonomy and reason (a true product of the eighteenth century), positive religion is warm and definite, stressing instead piety and corporateness. In the end, natural religion is indeterminate and brings forth no definite religious feeling. Natural religion

> is therefore no determinate form, no truly individual presentation of religion; and those who confess only it have no specific dwelling in its realm, but are strangers whose home, if they have one (which I doubt), must lie elsewhere.[16]

In contrast to this, Christianity is specific and focused, providing a definite place where religious cultivation can occur. Christianity's "original intuition" is

> the intuition of the universal straining of everything finite against the unity of the whole and of the way in which the deity handles this striving, how it reconciles the enmity directed against it and sets bounds to the ever-greater distance by scattering over the whole individual points that are at once finite, and infinite, at once, human and divine.[17]

Even while giving Christian faith an elevated position, the *Speeches* depart from traditional understandings. Christianity is elevated, in part, because its awareness of the finite world's universal resistance to the unity of the whole issues in searching criticism, including self-criticism. Paul Tillich was later to name this the "Protestant Principle." In the *Speeches* it means that Christianity "must everywhere disclose all corruption, be it in morals or in the manner of thinking."[18] When the *Speeches* apply this critical moment to Christianity, they conclude that Jesus himself "never claimed to be . . . the sole mediator."[19] Christianity is essentially free and open, and it imposes no restrictions, allows no narrowness; it is always expansive, anticipating further disclosures of the Christian principle manifest in Jesus. The *Speeches* point to the established church and say it has departed from Jesus precisely by departing from his openness and elevating him, unself-critically, above all others.

By placing religion on a new footing, Schleiermacher founds a new epoch in Christian theology. Religion is not based on knowledge or action; it is *sui generis* and claims its own domain—a domain that is irreducibly intuitive and historical. The *Speeches* are distinctively Christian in a way that Deism was not. They affirm positive, historical, revealed religion in place of Deism's natural and universal religion of reason. The *Speeches* connect with Pietism in its focus on the inwardness that is characteristic of religion, and they bring self-criticism into the theological tradition in a new way. The theological proposals in the *Speeches* are at once Christian confessions and a critical reappropriation of the faith that claim the freedom to reexamine traditional understandings. The *Speeches* open up a space where theology can be done in a new way, with attention to the lived experience of religion, with an affirmation of tradition and a critical approach that allows for, even demands, revision of theological understanding. After the *Speeches*, theology was never to be the same.

The *Speeches* were the first flowering of the deep relationship between Schleiermacher and Berlin. He became a recognized public figure in the Prussian capital. This relationship continued to develop during Schleiermacher's second period as a resident. He lived in Berlin for the final twenty-eight years of his life, and, as we have seen, the city celebrated his life and mourned his death in grand style. The story of his life from the end of his first residence in Berlin until his death, and the development of his theological and ethical program in that period are the subjects of the next chapter.

NOTES

1. See Martin Redeker, *Schleiermacher: Life and Thought,* trans. John Wallhausser (Philadelphia: Fortress Press, 1973), 7, for the source of Schleiermacher's names.

2. Albert L. Blackwell, *Schleiermacher's Early Philosophy of Life: Determinism, Freedom, and Phantasy* (Chico, Calif.: Scholars Press, 1982), 8.

3. Ibid., 19.
4. Redeker, 20–21.
5. Blackwell, 50–51, 53, 68.
6. Hajo Holborn, *A History of Modern Germany*, 3 vols. (New York: Alfred Knopf, 1959–69), vol. 2 (1648–1840), 308.
7. Deborah Hertz, *Jewish High Society in Old Regime Berlin* (New Haven: Yale University Press, 1988), 20–21.
8. *Briefwechsel 1775–96*, vol. 2, edited by Andreas Arndt and Wolfgang Virmond (Berlin and New York: Walter de Gruyter, 1988), 214, as quoted in Julie Ellison, *Delicate Subjects: Romanticism, Gender and the Ethics of Understanding* (Ithaca: Cornell University Press, 1990), 33.
9. The very notion of "Romanticism" is problematic and slippery, for it refers to such a wide diversity of individuals and groups, times and places. Because the term needs to be retained for purposes of scholarship, it is perhaps preferable to speak of "romanticisms." See Ellison, ix–x.
10. Blackwell, 139.
11. The Grimm brothers, Jakob (1785–1863) and Wilhelm (1786–1859), stand in the Romantic tradition; their work collecting folk tales was inspired by the Romantic interest in ancient culture and literature.
12. Friedrich Schleiermacher, *On Religion: Speeches to Its Cultured Despisers*, trans. Richard Crouter (Cambridge: Cambridge University Press, 1988), 103.
13. Ibid., 90.
14. Ibid., 92.
15. Ibid., 115.
16. Ibid., 206.
17. Ibid., 213.
18. Ibid., 215.
19. Ibid., 219.

2
LIFE AND THOUGHT, 1802–1834

In 1802 Schleiermacher left Berlin under pressure from his ecclesiastical superiors. The pressure had been building since before the publication of the *Speeches* and had to do with Schleiermacher's writing and his friendships and associations. By 1800 Berlin was no longer a small city; it had grown to be the second largest city (to Vienna) in central Europe with a population of about 172,000. Still, it was not a place where a public person could hide, and Schleiermacher's relation with members of the Romantic circle, particularly Friedrich Schlegel, was well known. In fact, Schleiermacher had written and published a defense of Schlegel's controversial novel, *Lucinde*. Then there was his involvement with Eleonore Grunow. Schleiermacher was deeply in love with Eleonore. The two had made a secret betrothal, and Schleiermacher hoped Eleonore would divorce her husband and be free to marry him.

Relations between men and women, particularly in the context of marriage, were an important aspect of the issues swirling around Schleiermacher. Part of the Romantics' credo was an affirmation of individual self-cultivation and a rejection of formality and structure. Marriage where love was lacking was seen as an empty pretense. At this time, Schlegel was deeply involved with Dorothea Veit, who was married to another man. Eventually, Dorothea divorced her husband, lived with Schlegel, and then married him. Not surprisingly, contemporaries saw the relationship between Dorothea and Schlegel as the model for Schleiermacher's relation with Eleonore. Schleiermacher was drinking deeply of the countercultural, Romantic ethos, and, although distinctive in his religious commitments and churchly vocation, his life showed the signs of the circles in which he moved.

Pressure on Schleiermacher intensified as he was working on the *Speeches* and turning in the manuscript for the scrutiny of the governmental censor. The censor was Friedrich Samuel Gottfried Sack, preacher at the court church and an ecclesiastical official with whom Schleiermacher had a multileveled relationship. Sack was an old friend of Schleiermacher's uncle, Samuel Stubenrauch, and had befriended the young ministerial candidate already in 1790, arranging for his position as tutor to Count Dohna's children. Sack was also Schleiermacher's ecclesiastical supervisor and became censor as the chapters of the *Speeches* rolled in. One of Sack's central concerns with the *Speeches* was what he perceived as its pantheism. Schleiermacher calls his readers to toast Spinoza, whom he honors as one filled with the Holy Spirit. But to Sack, as to most folk, Spinoza was a dangerously radical thinker whose pantheism was tantamount to atheism. In fact, the philosopher Johann Gottlieb Fichte had lost his position at the University of Jena in the "atheism controversy" of 1799 for advocating a position that looked like Spinoza's. Sack's concern was most serious, and the pressure built.

Schlegel's *Lucinde* was published in 1799; it is "a glorification of true marriage," a celebration of "the happy communion of two people."[1] Marriage is affirmed, but only when it is a genuine and loving relation in which both partners find themselves completed by their union with the other. Because of *Lucinde*'s vigorous rejection of conventional Protestant understandings of marriage as a commitment that is to remain steadfast in spite of emotional fluctuation, it has often been identified as a celebration of "free love." So it was deeply criticized from the beginning. Nor was it helped by its form— "a chaotic mixture of disjointed ingenious insights, fairy tales, allegories, and tasteless autobiographical sketches and indiscretions."[2] At the time, this is not how it appeared to Schleiermacher, although his views changed in later years. He rose up to defend his friend Schlegel, Schlegel's love for Dorothea Veit, and *Lucinde*. In 1801 he published his *Confidential Letters on Schlegel's Lucinde*. This work was a defense of true love in which the spiritual and physical are united, in which the true mystery of human existence is encountered and the lovers are opened to the infinite. In the end, "Schleiermacher presented romantic marriage much more positively and clearly than Schlegel could,"[3] but, missing its subtle criticisms, Sack and much of the public saw the *Confidential Letters* only as a defense of the novel and of Schlegel's behavior. The pressure on Schleiermacher increased.

His relationship with Eleonore was in keeping with his general outlook at the time. Schleiermacher was smitten by Eleonore when they were introduced in 1799. Eleonore was neither brilliant nor beautiful; Schleiermacher was captivated by her "moral innocence" and became her defender against the "cold insensitivity" with which "her husband, a Lutheran minister, appears to have treated her."[4] In 1801 Schleiermacher went so far as to confront the Rev. Grunow about his treatment of Eleonore. Meanwhile Schleiermacher courted Eleonore publicly; they developed a deep love for one another, and Schleiermacher urged Eleonore to divorce her husband that she might be free to marry him.

In 1802 Schleiermacher bowed to the pressure and left Berlin for Stolp, a town near the Baltic Sea in Pomerania. There he served as court chaplain for two years. Cut off from the social life of Berlin, the time in Stolp was the most difficult and depressing of Schleiermacher's life. When in March

1803, Eleonore writes him saying she will not leave her husband, Schleiermacher was devastated. He continued to pursue her for two years and only then accepted the finality of her decision. Stolp was a cold and lonely place, and Schleiermacher had suicidal feelings.[5] It was only many years later that Schleiermacher came to an acceptance of what had happened. In 1819 he is reported to have said to Eleonore, "God has indeed made amends to us."[6] He was freed from his exile in Stolp only when he was called to Halle in 1804.

HALLE: *CHRISTMAS EVE DIALOGUE* AND NEW POLITICAL CONSCIOUSNESS

In Halle Schleiermacher came into his own as a preacher, professor, and scholar. When it appeared that Schleiermacher would accept an appointment at the University of Würzburg, the Prussian government stepped in and offered the position at Halle. There Schleiermacher was the first Reformed theologian on a previously all-Lutheran theological faculty. He also served as university chaplain. Redeker identifies a two-point agenda in the state's appointment of Schleiermacher to Halle: it hoped to make Halle the outstanding Prussian university by the appointment of brilliant, cutting-edge thinkers like Schleiermacher, and it wanted to take a step toward Lutheran and Reformed union by integrating the theological faculty.[7] With his reputation as one of the new breed of thinkers, moving beyond the Enlightenment, Schleiermacher encountered opposition from old guard rationalists, supernaturalists, and pietists. At Halle, he lectured on hermeneutics, ethics (both philosophical and Christian), dogmatics, and the New Testament. These lectures provided the basis for the later development of his theological and philosophical systems.[8]

In terms of theology, Schleiermacher's most significant work in the Halle period was *Christmas Eve: Dialogue on the Incarnation*.[9] This work represents a reorientation of Schleiermacher's thinking about theological method, more specifically about the relation between religion in general and Christianity in particular. The *Speeches* begin with and focus on religion and only secondarily move on to consider Christianity. With *Christmas Eve*, Schleiermacher alters his starting point; he begins with the particularity of Christian faith. Not only this, *Christmas Eve* opens up

> a new and positive stage in christological thinking. [Schleiermacher] began neither with ancient dogmas nor with ancient history, but with what every Christian experiences, and he sought to give an honest account of it that would not run away from the intellectual problems of the modern world.[10]

Gerrish notes three problems that Schleiermacher is able to resolve by establishing a new footing for Christology. *Christmas Eve* addresses the logical difficulties of traditional dogma (the view of Christ as two natures in one person), the issue of the uniqueness of Christ and the relation of Christianity to other religions (made acute by the Enlightenment elevation of the universal and denigration of the particular), and the issue of the historical reliability of the New Testament (the conflicting narratives of Jesus' life and teaching in the four Gospels).

The *Christmas Eve Dialogue* is just that—a conversation among friends about the meaning of Christmas; the conversation takes place in the parlor of a middle-class home on Christmas Eve. What emerges in the course of the dialogue is the insight that it is the experience of redemption, of new life in the Christian community—mediated, for example, by the celebration of Christmas itself—that creates and grounds faith in Christ. On the basis of this experience, Schleiermacher can see who Christ must be—the possessor of a unique and powerful consciousness of God in which Christians now share. This is a "Christology from below" that starts not with creeds or scripture, but with Christian experience. The three issues noted above are raised by various speakers and resolved by the turn to the experience of Christ and his unique God-consciousness.

> By pegging everything on the Redeemer's unique consciousness of God, Schleiermacher was able to claim, first, that Christ was not just one teacher of the common religion of humanity; second, that the Gospel story does not need to be infallible in all details if only it verifies and mediates the picture of him; and, third, that there is no need to conceive of God's presence in Christ as a conjunction of two natures.[11]

Christmas Eve's crucial turn to Christian experience—its theology "from below"—sets the stage for Schleiermacher's culminating theological works, but not before he is caught up in historical events and swept back to Berlin.

Up until 1806 Prussia had sat on the sidelines of the Napoleonic wars, but in that year, learning that Napoleon had secretly pledged to return Hanover to the English crown, Prussia confronted France and was soon at war. The Prussian armies were crushed at the battles of Auerstädt and Jena in October 1806, and the king was driven from Berlin to exile in Königsberg. The peace treaty at Tilsit in 1807 made Prussia completely subject to the French. Schleiermacher witnessed the humiliation of his country at firsthand as the Prussians were defeated in Halle. Schleiermacher's house was plundered, and he was forced to quarter French officers even after he had taken in friends left homeless by the occupation. The university was dissolved, and the church where Schleiermacher preached was used by the

French to store grain. Still Schleiermacher vowed to stay on; he worked on projects and located another pulpit from which he could preach into 1807, surviving on "potatoes and salt."[12]

RETURN TO BERLIN

Schleiermacher repudiated Napoleon as an aggressor and a dictator. When Halle was severed from Prussia in 1807 (handed over to Westphalia), he returned to Berlin. There he found some opportunities to teach. But, of more importance, he returned to the capital with a new political consciousness and commitments to the reform of the Prussian educational and political system and to liberation from the oppressor's domination. This new political consciousness, with its call for moral activity in the world, also made a mark on Schleiermacher's theology. Whereas the *Speeches* had emphasized the passive element in religion, the soul dissolved in a union with the universe, Schleiermacher's later theology gives significant place to the active, ethical expression of the faith: in addition to being personforming, faith is now seen to be community-forming, nation-forming, (human) race-forming, and even world-forming. This gives a decisive shape to Schleiermacher's philosophical and theological program and is especially evident in the *Philosophical Ethics* and *Christian Ethics*.

Utterly defeated in 1806, Prussia remained under French control until about 1812. In Schleiermacher's lifetime, the external military and political fortunes of Prussia began with the heights of Friedrich the "Great," fell to the depths of subjugation to Napoleon, and rose again in the latter portion of Friedrich Wilhelm III's rule. Schleiermacher was deeply connected with the Reform movement of 1807–19; consequently, his view of internal political fortunes of Prussia saw a pattern the inverse of the external fortunes. As so often happens, warfare opens a window for social and political change. The Reformers with whom Schleiermacher was connected viewed Prussia under Friedrich the "Great" as a "'machine state' in which the individual was to function as a cog in a mechanism."[13] Napoleon's conquest opens up a period of reform, a "Prussian springtime" as freedom and justice come out from the shadows. The period of reform begins to wane in 1814 with liberation from Napoleon and is altogether lost by 1819 when a period of repression and authoritarian high-handedness sets in.

In the midst of this military and political turmoil, 1809 was a banner year for Schleiermacher. In May he married the young widow Henrietta von Willich and became a husband and a stepfather. In the next month his appointment as pastor at Trinity Church in Berlin became official; he held this position until his death in 1834. In July of that same year he was appointed as a professor of theology at the newly formed University of

Berlin, which then opened its doors in the fall of 1810 with Schleiermacher as the first dean of the theology faculty.

In marrying Henrietta von Willich, Schleiermacher took a wife almost twenty years his junior. Henrietta's first husband, Ernst von Willich, had become Schleiermacher's closest friend after the latter's break with Friedrich Schlegel. Henrietta was only fifteen when she was betrothed; at seventeen she became a mother, and at nineteen a widow. Schleiermacher had shared in the couple's marriage through letters full of affection, and Henrietta looked upon her future husband as a father figure. The pronounced difference in their religious sensibilities is indicated by Henrietta's preference for the sermons of Schleiermacher's Lutheran colleague at Trinity Church and her trust in the visions and predictions of the spiritualist, Mrs. Fischer. Redeker notes that Schleiermacher and Henrietta were "each . . . devoted to the other in his or her own distinct way," and that Schleiermacher allowed Henrietta to take Mrs. Fischer and her children into their household, though he disapproved of her consultation with spirits "because he loved his wife and because he respected the independent development of individuality in his wife as well as his children."[14] In his later life and thinking, Schleiermacher turns away from his earlier Romantic views of marriage toward more conventional practice and understanding; as he does so he continues his respect for the other's individuality. This respect for individuality was at odds with the dominant view and practice of the time. In addition to Henrietta's two children to whom Schleiermacher became stepfather, the couple had four children of their own. The only son, Nathaniel, died at age nine, bringing tremendous grief to the couple.

PUBLIC FIGURE IN BERLIN

Schleiermacher's greatness as a public figure and the honor given him by Berlin at his death derives from his achievements in three distinguishable but interrelated arenas: the political, the ecclesiastical, and the academic. He held positions as preacher and professor from 1809 until his death, and it was from the pulpit and classroom that he took some of his most significant social-political stands. Schleiermacher's return to Berlin and political activity positioned him, geographically and in terms of political connections, for the offices he gained in 1809. Similarly, one of his greatest achievements in the academic realm—his contributions to the founding of the University of Berlin—came as a direct result of a governmental post he held in the Ministry of the Interior. Also, the Prussian church being tightly reined by the government (especially after 1819), ecclesiastical issues were through and through political. So the controversy over the church's liturgy,

1822–29, in which Schleiermacher led resistance to the order of worship prescribed by the king, was inseparably ecclesiastical and political.

In 1807 Schleiermacher made a secret trip to eastern Prussia at the behest of leaders in Berlin agitating for an uprising against Napoleon. On this trip, Schleiermacher carried messages to exiled government officials and had an audience with Queen Louise and Princess Wilhelmina. Then in 1808 he was appointed to the Interior post working in the Department of Public Instruction, which was working to restructure the educational system and make it available to more than the children of the nobility. He held this position until 1814, and it was from here that Schleiermacher contributed to the formation of the new university. The years 1813–14 were filled with hope for the Reformers: Napoleon was in retreat, Prussia had joined the attack on the French, and Friedrich Wilhelm had promised a constitution that was to mean a significant reordering of Prussian life. In these same years, Schleiermacher worked as editor of the *Preussische Zeitung*, a reform-minded newspaper that was regularly critical of the government, particularly of any compromise with Napoleon. Although Schleiermacher was not a politician by vocation, he was an active participant in this arena; he was always on the side of reform and often at odds with conservative and reactionary political forces.

Schleiermacher's greatest impact on his contemporaries, politically and in other arenas, was arguably from the pulpit. He preached weekly from 1790 until his death in 1834 and had "a charismatic ability to sway a whole congregation through fervent delivery and profound wrestling with many of the most vital religious questions troubling people of the day."[15] Perhaps the most moving and significant sermons were preached in Berlin during the quest for liberation from Napoleon. The sermon sending student volunteers off to join the army communicated a profound sense of God's action in history: the fall of Prussia is the judgment of God on the nation's pride and moral dissolution and the call of God is for sacrificial action on behalf of the humiliated country. The impact of Schleiermacher's sermons during his lifetime was not confined to those who heard him; seven collections of sermons were published before his death, and they gained a wide readership.

Although Schleiermacher's work in preaching was his most visible ecclesiastic work, his role was not limited to this. He was Senior Pastor at Trinity Church, with its membership of some 12,000 persons, and oversaw the practical life of the church. This included everything from janitorial service and building repair to teaching confirmation classes and relief programs for the poor. Schleiermacher was also involved at the synodical level; in 1817, at the time of the king's push for a union of Lutheran and Reformed churches, Schleiermacher was the Presiding Officer of the Synod of Berlin. Schleiermacher favored the union and considered himself a theologian of the union (Evangelical) church, but he resisted the imposition of the union by royal fiat. He defended the union in print against conservative Lutheran critics even as he affirmed the church's independence from state interference. Conflict with the Prussian government came to a head with the liturgical dispute (*Agendestreit*) of 1822–29. Although he ultimately lost the battle, in this ecclesiastical realm as in the political realm, Schleiermacher resisted the king's drive for increased control over Prussian life. He exercised his pastoral role in accordance with his convictions and was able to hold out against royal pressure for seven years.

Schleiermacher's several great achievements in the academic world need to be seen in the context of the larger intellectual and cultural movement in which he participated. This movement established a new approach to the study of human historical and cultural life. It emerged out of a synthesis of Romanticism and Critical Idealism and is represented in philosophy by Fichte, Schelling, and Hegel, and in philosophy and theology by Schleiermacher. Characteristic of this movement in its philosophical expressions is agreement that Kant has sounded the death knell for traditional metaphysics, and a move beyond Kant to a new metaphysical vision built on an analysis of the dynamics of consciousness or spirit. The analysis of spirit provides a bridge in these thinkers that enables them to overcome Kant's *phenomenal/noumenal* divide and move from subjectivity to objectivity. There is a movement in these thinkers from a transcendental moment (the analysis of spirit) to an objective historical moment (analysis of the positive, historical manifestations of spirit and how these manifestations give expression to the eternal and universal). These thinkers

> were struggling against the same enemies, the rule of eudaimonism, of mere "understanding" (i.e., the rigid or "hard and fast" abstract thought of a formal deductive system, which fixes and defines in such a way as to exclude fluidity and movement, and thus life). They . . . sought a unitary view of the world and culture, and a movement beyond subjectivity to the objective, to the eternal and the universal."[16]

Characteristic of this new intellectual movement is its view of the manifestation of the ideal in history. Here there is a balance between a unitive vision of knowledge that has a consciousness, self-awareness, and attention to the particularities of historical life as the arena in which truth is to be found. This is also characteristic of Schleiermacher's intellectual approach and achievement. It can be seen in his influential vision for the new University of Berlin, in his hermeneutics, and his founding of the new Protestant theology.

Schleiermacher was not part of the first committee commissioned to plan the University of Berlin. In 1808 on his own initiative, he published an essay on the idea of a German university. This led to his inclusion in the work;

quickly he became Wilhelm von Humboldt's chief collaborator in making the university a reality. Balance between the philosophical vision of a universal and coherent system of human knowledge and attention to historical particularity is the hallmark of Schleiermacher's view, and it becomes incarnate in the new university. The philosophical vision of the interconnection of all knowledge was to pervade all departments of the university; at the same time, Schleiermacher championed such practical and particular fields as theology, medicine, and law against critics like Fichte, who saw no room for them in a true university. Schleiermacher also insisted on the interconnection between research and teaching and on the university's freedom in both fields from state censorship. His vision of the university was the beginning of his contribution: Schleiermacher helped select the original theology faculty, was dean of theology four separate times, and taught an impressive array of courses in philosophy and theology. In philosophy he taught dialectics, ethics, psychology, pedagogy, aesthetics, and hermeneutics; in theology he taught dogmatics, ethics, exegetical theology, church history, and practical theology. All this he did in addition to his work as pastor of Trinity Church and his other involvements.

Schleiermacher is regularly identified as the founder of modern hermeneutics. In his teaching career he accomplished what he had set out as a goal in his first lecture course at Halle—to raise hermeneutics to the level of a genuine science.[17] Central to Schleiermacher's hermeneutics is the conviction that a text is the production of a living human being and that to listen to the text and intuitively grasp its inner logic is like a conversation with another person. Hermeneutics is not about mining kernels of truth from a text, but it is a living encounter in which it is possible to understand the text even better than its author did. This kind of genuine understanding requires that one know the language and the denotation and connotation of its words intimately and that one imagine oneself into the situation of the author. Then one works to grasp both the sense of the words in their broader, general meaning and in the creativity and individuality of their use by the author. This makes possible a grasp of the parts and the whole of the text in their interconnection and the achievement of a genuine (but never final or absolute) understanding of the text. Here is an approach to hermeneutics that transcends those of Protestant Orthodoxy and Enlightenment Rationalism: the text is seen as the product of a historical human being, and all the tools of historical and human analysis are brought to bear on the text, which is a living witness of human reason in the world. The transcendental moment in Schleiermacher's hermeneutics can be seen in his presupposition that understanding is possible because reason or spirit is operative in the author as it is in the interpreter, and historical moment is evident in the careful textual and contextual work necessary to the hermeneutical task.

Schleiermacher's translation of Plato also evidences his participation in the new approach to historical life. It is also a working example of Schleiermacher's hermeneutical work and a demonstration of what his approach can achieve. Redeker sees the work with Plato as the key to Schleiermacher's transition from Romanticism's emphasis on "subjectivity" and "confession" to an emphasis on what is objective in human historical life.[18] Schleiermacher worked at the translation of the Platonic corpus for almost thirty years. The project had been begun with Friedrich Schlegel, but was soon left to Schleiermacher alone. Between 1804 and 1828 he published translations of all of Plato's works, except the *Timaeus* and the *Laws*. Schleiermacher's work remains the standard for Plato translation into German. By means of careful attention to the Platonic texts and discernment of their inner logic, Schleiermacher hypothesized a chronology of the works and a view of the development of Plato's ideas. The outcome was a breakthrough in understanding Plato: for the first time in centuries a view of Plato was put forth that was not colored by the Neo-Platonism that had been dominant for centuries. Schleiermacher attained an interpretation of Plato grounded in the texts and developed an understanding of Plato with which subsequent interpreters have had to reckon ever since. Here we have a concrete instantiation of Schleiermacher's engagement in the hermeneutical task and the depth of understanding he was able to achieve.

Schleiermacher's work as a member and organizer of the Berlin Academy of Sciences is another important outlet in which he develops and shares the new approach to historical life. The academy was the most prestigious intellectual organization in the German-speaking world of the time. Intellectual achievement was highly valued in Prussian culture; it was a source of Prussian strength in its bid to survive Napoleon. After Prussia's defeat by French forces, Friedrich Wilhelm III said that Prussia must make up for physical loss with intellectual gain. Schleiermacher was a member of the academy's Philosophical Division from 1810 and its permanent secretary from 1814. He gave an impressive number of papers to the academy, especially in the areas of philology and philosophical ethics, and his work in this context was crucial to the new approach to history that led beyond Supernaturalism, Rationalism, and Kant to the heady new vision of spirit or reason manifest in history, bringing together the transcendental and historical moments.

The preponderance of Schleiermacher's work in philosophy and some of his work in theology is available to subsequent generations only on the basis of works pulled together and published by his students after his death. This is true of the *Dialektik*, the *Hermeneutics*, the *Philosophical Ethics*, and the *Christian Ethics*. These volumes are helpful as they enable us to gain a sense of Schleiermacher's work in these areas, even though Schleiermacher himself did not prepare them for publication. That he understood himself preeminently as a theologian among the academic disciplines in which he labored is evident from the effort he put into publication of his theological volumes. The two great theological works from his mature Berlin period were published in two distinct editions: *The Christian Faith* in 1822 and 1831, and the *Brief Outline on the Study of Theology* in 1811 and 1830. History knows Schleiermacher as a theologian on the basis of these works, together with the *Speeches*.

BRIEF OUTLINE ON THE STUDY OF THEOLOGY

The *Brief Outline*, originally published in 1811, sets forth Schleiermacher's understanding of theology as a discipline, including its *raison d'être* and the way in which its constituent subdisciplines relate to each other. Although it is an abstract and encyclopedic work, real life is its focus. The *Brief Outline* conceives of theology as an organic whole in the service of the church. For Schleiermacher the practical concern for the maintenance and growth of the church as a community of faith holds the theological disciplines together. For theology to be genuine, it must arise out of Christian faith, out of commitment to the church. Its ultimate goal is to express, purify, and expand the life of faith in the church. So theology is a practical and teleological discipline existing in a circular relation with the church and its faith. The church is at once the ground and goal of theology: theology arises out of the church and seeks to contribute to its ongoing life by means of careful and critical reflection on faith in its historical manifestations. Practical theology, then, is the "crown and goal" of all the theological disciplines, for it connects most directly with the life of the church, delineating methods to be employed for leadership.

This elevation of the practical character of theology is one of the great insights of the *Brief Outline*. The other is the recognition that Christian theology is and must be through-and-through historical. Schleiermacher recognizes in a new way the historical character of faith and theology. Faith and theology exist only in history, only as mediated by real people in specific times and places. There is no way to get beyond or behind historical manifestation and grasp a Platonic essence of the faith. Theology is always historically conditioned and grounded in historical particularity. Historical theology, then, is the core of theology, including biblical disciplines, church history, and dogmatics. Dogmatics is considered historical because it attempts to set forth doctrine valid in and for the present historical moment. Historical theology provides a foundation for practical theology, because leadership in the church must be built on awareness of the past and present situation of the church. Leadership that is unaware of the tradition lacks rootedness and integrity. This is the signal contribution of the *Brief Outline*: its insight into the historical character of theology and the relativity and modesty that must therefore accompany theological claims.

If practical theology is the crown and goal and historical theology the core, philosophical theology provides a place to begin. The tripartite division of the *Brief Outline*, in ascending order, is philosophical, historical, and practical theology. Philosophical theology is a "critical discipline" that mediates speculative and empirical elements of knowledge. It provides a starting place for theological work by identifying the distinctive character of Christianity and related concepts that can then be employed and tested in the actual work of historical theology. It does not attempt to ground or prove theological knowledge by demonstrating how it follows from some highest knowledge arrived at speculatively. Rather, it presumes the existence of theological knowledge and identifies "working definitions" of key concepts that can then be employed and tested in historical theology, the main body of the theological disciplines.

In the main, Schleiermacher conceives of theology as a "positive" or "empirical" science; philosophical theology as a critical discipline combines the "positive" pole of knowledge and its relative opposite, the "speculative" pole. The primary task of philosophical theology is to identify in a preliminary way the "essence or idea of Christianity" and other concepts needed for the explication of Christianity. To do this, philosophical theology attends to the historical chronicle, gaining an overview of the course of Christianity, without great attention to detail. Philosophical theology also works from a standpoint "above" or at least "outside of" Christianity. Borrowing from philosophy of religion, it works to identify the distinctiveness of Christianity also by means of comparison with other religious traditions. Historical theology then tests and verifies the proposals of philosophical theology to see how they hold up when employed in careful scrutiny of Christian history. In this way, historical theology is the "verification of philosophical theology," even as it is the "foundation of practical theology."[19] Historical theology provides the bridge between philosophical theology, where the scientific interest dominates, and practical theology, where the practical interest dominates. Schleiermacher's view of theology comprises these three moments: the philosophical, which identifies concepts in a preliminary way, the historical, which tests and verifies the results proposed by philosophical theology and develops more extensive material for the practical moment, which culminates the process.

Schleiermacher's vision of the purpose and divisions of theology has exerted enormous influence on seminary education in Europe and North America. Recent discussions[20] attest to the *Brief Outline's* continuing influence; it remains the starting point for revisions of the structure and character of theological education. In its original context, the *Brief Outline* provided a coherent vision of theological education, attentive to the academy and oriented toward the church. It reconceived of theology in a way that gave it a functional goal—the upbuilding of the body of Christ—appropriated the growing historical consciousness into theology, and gave theology a relation to and place within a larger architectonic of all knowledge. Thus the *Brief Outline* needs to be included as one of the works by which Schleiermacher inaugurated a new era in Protestant theology.

THE CHRISTIAN FAITH

Although the *Speeches*, *Christmas Eve Dialogue*, and *Brief Outline* are works of significance, it is Schleiermacher's magnum opus, *The Christian Faith*, that decisively opens up a new era in theology, the "New Protestantism" as Troeltsch calls it. This work is a full-scale dogmatics comparable to Thomas's *Summa Theologiae* or Calvin's *Institutes of the Christian Religion*. It is dogmatics in a new key as it lays out in a programmatic way a theology from below, a theology whose touchstone is faith as experienced by contemporary Christians. The German title of *The Christian Faith*, "Glaubenslehre," signifies this new orientation, for the term means doctrine or teaching of the faith. Schleiermacher begins not with the dogmas of the church, but with the experience of faith. His attempt is to explicate Christian faith as humanly experienced, eschewing what he considers metaphysical speculation.

Schleiermacher's theological achievement is, above all, this rendering of theology in experiential, "naturalistic" this-worldly terms. This is indeed a theology "within the limits of piety alone,"[21] in the words of Gerrish. The essay from which this phrase comes explores how Schleiermacher appropriates and transforms John Calvin's focus on piety. In Schleiermacher, piety becomes not only the touchstone for authentic theology as it had been for Calvin, but also a limiting principle beyond which theology may not go. *The Christian Faith* argues that claims about origins (e.g., of the world or of sin) and about the future (especially traditional Christian eschatological claims) are not, properly speaking, theological claims, for they go beyond what can be known on the basis of Christian piety or feeling. Theology is to explicate the contents of Christian piety, and although claims about God and the world can be made, most fundamental theology deals with states of consciousness. Claims about God and the world have a secondary, derivative status. With Calvin, theology's focus remains on the pious affections. New here is the limit placed on the scope of theological claims. Theology is reconceived in terms that are strictly experiential, naturalistic, and this-worldly.

This reconception of the scope of theology's claims moves beyond the impasse between the supernaturalism of Orthodoxy and Pietism and the flat naturalism of Enlightenment theology. *The Christian Faith* establishes a new way of doing theology that fits neither previous Orthodoxy nor Rationalism. This is evident in the treatment of the church. It is neither Orthodoxy's "divinely instituted custodian of infallible truths"[22] nor Rationalism's voluntary association of like-minded individuals. Instead, the church is a living organism, inspired by God to be sure, but caught up in the flux of social and historical life like every other human movement or institution. This conception of the church as a living organism resonates with New Testament images like the branches of the one true vine or the body of Christ. The church is a true community of persons united by a common spirit that is more than the individuals who make up the community. The common spirit of the church is the Holy Spirit, who is at once the source of the community and who is made known in and through the community. This community can be comprehended and analyzed as a human historical product by theologians and "outside" critics. Its theological significance is experienced by believers who know the new and higher life in Christ, mediated by the community and its common Spirit, the living spirit of Jesus. Even Karl Barth, no friend of Schleiermacher's theology, recognized it as "predominantly and decisively of the Holy Spirit."[23] *The Christian Faith* sets forth a theology of the church and the Spirit in which both are reconceived; this is a "revisionist" theology that shares characteristics of both Orthodoxy and Rationalism, but is reducible to neither.

One characteristic of Schleiermacher's "revisionist" theology is its "radical conservatism." *The Christian Faith* is conservative in its sense of continuity with the tradition of the church, particularly with the Protestant Reformation. Traditional theological concepts are not cast off; instead, they are subject to a new interpretation. This is the radical aspect, for the new interpretation often reshapes the old concept, making it almost unrecognizable.

Schleiermacher's reorientation of theology—his move to reconceive theology in "natural," experiential, this-worldly terms—is perhaps most evident in the Christology of *The Christian Faith*. Building on the work of *Christmas Eve*, it begins not with traditional dogma nor with the New Testament picture of Jesus, but with the contemporary Christian's experience of salvation. Schleiermacher starts with the new and higher form of life that the believer receives in and through the Christian community, and then moves backward, tracing the line that leads to the origin. The immediate source of the experience of salvation is the Christian community. The community has its own history; in turn, it attributes all its power to its founder, Jesus Christ, and his Spirit that vivifies the community still. Jesus is the crucial historical source of the new life experienced by the believer. Behind this, Schleiermacher sees the plan and purpose of God.

Schleiermacher's method, then, is to consider who Jesus must have been in order to communicate this new and higher life to believers through the medium of the church. He concludes that Jesus must be the possessor of a unique and unblemished consciousness of God. Schleiermacher cannot arrive at an understanding of Christ as the incarnation of the second person of the Trinity as traditionally understood, nor at the Chalcedonian formula—"two natures in one person." Such claims are beyond what persons can legitimately know. But as the ultimate source of the reality of salvation in believers' lives, Jesus must be perfect in his God-consciousness. He is the perfection of humanity (in terms of relation to God) and the culmination of God's intention for humanity. Here we come across the one remaining "supernatural" element in Schleiermacher's otherwise seamlessly "naturalistic" system. Jesus, the new Adam, is inexplicable in terms of his historical context, for he was born into a world of sin. He transcends his context in the sinless perfection of his God-consciousness. Christ is not absolutely supernatural, for he incarnates what God had intended for humanity from the beginning (and what in theory is possible for any human being—a perfect consciousness of God), but he is relatively supernatural in that he cannot be explained by the world that shaped and nurtured him. So, even as devotion to Christ as the unique and perfect Redeemer remains central to *The Christian Faith,* the person and work of Christ is significantly reconceived. This is theology that doesn't fit with previous frameworks; yet it retains a claim to be distinctively Christian far beyond what Enlightenment theology attained.

Another prime example of a traditional concept subject to serious reconsideration is *The Christian Faith*'s treatment of "reprobation," the idea that some folk are destined by God for eternal damnation. In the first place, Schleiermacher has reservations about notions of life after death. Strictly speaking, they transcend the limits imposed on theological reflection by piety. "Eternal life" understood as individual immortality goes beyond what Christian consciousness can know into a speculative realm. Schleiermacher's focus is on the experience of faith in this world, and strictly speaking, theology is to be limited to actual experience.

That Schleiermacher addresses the issue of reprobation at all signals his own Reformed self-understanding. Who but one shaped by the Reformed tradition takes up and wrestles through this issue? Schleiermacher considers reprobation in his reflection on "election," which is based solely on divine favor. In dealing with reprobation, one must avoid the opposing errors of Pelagianism, on the one hand, and a view of God as capricious, on the other. Schleiermacher's reinterpretation of the doctrine proposes a middle way that rejects any eternal reprobation and insists it can refer only to those who have "not yet" been regenerated in Christ. The problem with traditional views is their "atomistic" character, their focus on individuals. Viewed in light of God's care for all of humanity, reprobation can have only temporal and this-worldly meaning, referring to those not yet drawn in.

Implicit here is a kind of faithfulness to the (Reformed) tradition that refuses to jettison traditional concepts altogether even when they transgress Schleiermacher's theological method. So the "radical conservatism" of *The Christian Faith* engages traditional understandings and claims the freedom to appropriate those concepts in new and surprising ways.

The theological program of *The Christian Faith* affirms a view of Christian existence with a sharp focus on this world. Eschatological themes are minimized almost to the point of disappearing; life is no longer viewed as a pilgrimage to a "better place," but is affirmed for its intrinsic significance—for the possibility of relation to and consciousness of God in the present and the difference this can make here and now. One effect, then, of Schleiermacher's this-worldly reorientation of theology is a new valorization of history, of life in this world. As a result, Christian ethics attain a heightened significance. The topic of Christian ethics—how Christians as communities and as individuals are to live out the faith in daily life—is crucial to a theology that wants to lift up its this-worldly significance. How to live out the faith comes into sharp focus as an eschatological orientation with its temptation to escapism is all but disallowed. We might even say that ethics replaces eschatology as the culmination of the theological system. In this way also, then, *The Christian Faith* points beyond itself to its completion in the *Christian Ethics*. There we discover a vision of the Christian life, grounded in pious apprehension of God's grace in Christ and concerned for the upbuilding of the church and the transformation of the world. Having glimpsed something of Schleiermacher's life and achievement, the main task of this book is before us—to analyze Schleiermacher's ethical vision as it illumines and is illumined by scenes from his life.

NOTES

1. Martin Redeker, *Schleiermacher: Life and Thought,* trans. John Wallhausser (Philadelphia: Fortress Press, 1973), 64.
2. Ibid., 65.
3. Ibid.
4. Albert L. Blackwell, *Schleiermacher's Early Philosophy of Life: Determinism, Freedom, and Phantasy* (Chico, Calif.: Scholars Press, 1982), 171.
5. Ibid., 265–68.
6. Friedrich Schleiermacher, *Aus Schleiermacher's Leben: In Briefen,* 4 vols., ed. Ludwig Jonas and Wilhelm Dilthey (Berlin: Georg Reimer, 1860–63) 1:138, as quoted in Blackwell, 271.
7. Redeker, 78.
8. Ibid., 79.
9. Friedrich Schleiermacher, *Christmas Eve: Dialogue on the Incarnation,* trans. Terrence N. Tice (Richmond: John Knox Press, 1967).
10. B. A. Gerrish, *A Prince of the Church: Schleiermacher and the Beginnings of Modern Theology* (Philadelphia: Fortress Press, 1984), 49.

11. Ibid., 50.

12. Redeker, 87.

13. Hajo Holborn, *A History of Modern Germany*, 3 vols. (New York: Alfred Knopf, 1959–69), vol. 2 (1648–1840), 393.

14. Redeker, 211.

15. Keith W. Clements, "Schleiermacher, A Life in Outline," in *Friedrich Schleiermacher: Pioneer of Modern Theology* (London and San Francisco: Collins, 1987), 32. See also F. D. E. Schleiermacher, *Hermeneutics: The Handwritten Manuscripts*, ed. Heinz Kimmerle, trans. James Duke and Jack Forstman (Atlanta: Scholars Press, 1977).

16. Claude Welch, *Protestant Thought in the Nineteenth Century* (New Haven and London: Yale University Press, vol. 1, 1972; vol. 2, 1985), 1:91–92.

17. Redeker, 48.

18. Ibid., 184.

19. Friedrich Schleiermacher, *Brief Outline on the Study of Theology*, trans. Terrence N. Tice (Richmond: John Knox Press, 1970), 26.

20. Cf. Edward Farley, *Theologia: The Fragmentation and Unity of Theological Education* (Philadelphia: Fortress Press, 1983); Don S. Browning, *A Fundamental Practical Theology* (Minneapolis: Augsburg Fortress Press, 1991); and David H. Kelsey, *Between Athens and Berlin: The Theological Education Debate* (Grand Rapids: Eerdmans, 1993).

21. B. A. Gerrish, "Theology Within the Limits of Piety Alone: Schleiermacher and Calvin's Notion of God," in *The Old Protestantism and the New: Essays on the Reformation Heritage* (Chicago: University of Chicago Press, 1982), 196–207.

22. B. A. Gerrish, *Tradition and the Modern World: Reformed Theology in the Nineteenth Century* (Chicago: University of Chicago Press, 1978), 40. See also pp. 52 and 68–69, where Gerrish indicates how Schleiermacher transcends and synthesizes the Protestant orthodox and sectarian views of the church.

23. Karl Barth, *The Theology of Schleiermacher*, ed. Dietrich Ritschl, trans. Geoffrey W. Bromiley (Grand Rapids: Eerdmans, 1982), 278.

3

SCHLEIERMACHER AMONG THE MORAVIANS AND THE *CHRISTIAN ETHICS* AS AN ETHICS OF PIETY

In a life that included more than its share of crises, that of 1787 is arguably the great crisis of Schleiermacher's life. The future pastor and theologian was asked to leave the Moravian seminary, and for a time it appeared that he might be abandoned, emotionally and financially, by his pastor father—his only living parent by then and the person on whom he was economically dependent. In the end, Schleiermacher does break with the Moravians and their brand of Pietism, after having been nurtured and shaped in their schools for four years of residential education. The break is decisive, and in this act, Schleiermacher claims an identity for himself that sets him on the path to becoming the founder of a new epoch in Protestant theology. And yet, even as he breaks with the narrowness and authoritarianism of Pietism, he carries forward something of the Moravian sensibility, especially as piety remains the touchstone of his theology.

The topic of this chapter is Schleiermacher's relation to the Moravian version of Pietism[1] and the importance of piety in his theological system, especially in his *Christian Ethics*. Christian piety is the center around which the *Christian Ethics* revolves: for Schleiermacher Christian ethical action is grounded in piety or the religious self-consciousness, and a key goal of Christian action is the purification, expansion, and expression of piety. The *Christian Ethics* is an ecclesial ethics of piety. In terms of Schleiermacher's personal relation to Pietism, there is something of a Kierkegaardian "double movement of infinity"—an early identification with the Moravians, followed by a deep alienation to the point of a radical breaking of relationship, and then a "second naïveté" in which Schleiermacher reclaims a chastened sense of piety, reinterprets it in a this-worldly and naturalized way, makes it central to his theology, and identifies himself as a "Moravian of a higher order."

PIETISM IN THE SCHLEIERMACHER FAMILY

The relations among grandfather Daniel Schleiermacher, son Gottlieb, and grandson Friedrich would make for an interesting study using family systems theory. For the purposes of a chapter with its focus on Pietism and piety, the relation of the three generations of Schleiermacher pastors to pietistic forms of Christianity is noteworthy. Daniel was a Reformed pastor who was involved with the Elberfeld sect, a radical Reformed pietist group that called itself the "Children of Zion." The sect was led by Elias Eller, acclaimed as prophet by the group; his wife, Anna, called the "Mother of Zion," was believed to be clairvoyant. Together, they predicted the coming of the new Zion and eventually ran afoul of local church authorities.[2] Suspicions of Daniel arose as a result of his involvement; he was even charged with witchcraft and sorcery, and his wife and son (Gottlieb) were forced to testify against him.[3] Eventually he fled into Holland, where he repented of his earlier mistakes, took a position as an elder in the Reformed church there, but preached no more. Gottlieb had followed his father into the sect; by the age of nineteen he was its second-ranking preacher. His father's demittal in 1749 and subsequent flight was obviously a crisis for Gottlieb. He too rejected the sect and was drawn to rationalistic and skeptical theology, though he, too, functioned as a Reformed pastor. In 1778, under the influence of the Moravians, he had his awakening and became committed to a pietist version of Christianity. So it was that the education of Friedrich, together with that of his sister Charlotte and brother Karl, was given over to the Moravians, not least because of their parents concern for their eternal salvation.[4]

Concern for the personal appropriation of salvation through conversion and rebirth was the hallmark of Pietism. It is without doubt the most significant movement in the Protestant world of the seventeenth and eighteenth centuries. It found parallels in the other religious groupings in Europe in that period—Jansenism in the Roman Catholic church, Wesley's Evangelical Revival in Britain, and Hasidism among Jews. All these were movements of religious renewal.[5]

Pietism is best understood as a renewal movement within the church. Reacting against perceived indifference in personal faith and morality and an unnecessary doctrinal rigidity, it sought to instill living faith and moral earnestness in people through nurture and accountability. The "pioneer of Pietism" was Philip Jacob Spener (1635–1705), who published his classic, *Pia Desideria* ("pious desires") in 1675.[6] Spener outlined a program of reform that was directed at the princes, pastors, and lay people. He was critical of indifference toward the faith, moral laxity, and an overemphasis on pure doctrine, to the detriment of living faith. Although he claimed his Lutheran identity proudly and saw a place for orthodox standards, he was concerned that the argumentative preaching of pure doctrine did not edify people. Spener also shifted his theological center from the Lutheran accent on "justification," the forgiveness of the sinner, to "regeneration," the birth of the new life of faith. This accorded more closely with his concern for the personal appropriation of faith that manifests itself in moral living.[7]

The vehicle of pietist reform, the responsibility for accomplishing nurture and accountability, was lodged in particular communities. The distinctive mark of Pietism was its development of small groups of believers who gathered together for prayer, study of the Bible, and mutual admonition. These groups, called *collegia pietatis*, were distinctive in being lay-led and thereby making real the "priesthood of all believers" in an effective way. This indicates the practical orientation of Pietism; it was not primarily a movement of theological construction or critique, but was rather aimed at the transformation of the church as it lived out the faith. Directly and indirectly, Pietism exerted enormous influence on the life of the church. Directly it did so through its development of communities and practices dedicated to renewal of faithful living. Indirectly it did so through its impact on individuals who, though they ceased to identify unreservedly with Pietism, yet carried with them important pietist themes. Among this latter group were figures such Kant, and of course Schleiermacher himself.

The Moravian form of Pietism that Schleiermacher encountered fits the above description in terms of its emphasis on a personal piety and on structured communal life for nurture and accountability. At the Moravian school at Niesky from 1783–85, Schleiermacher experienced community worship four times daily as well as monthly confession and communion. In addition, the relation of teacher to student was individualized with attention to cultivation of the latter's intellectual and spiritual gifts. The Moravian movement had been shaped decisively by Count Ludwig von Zinzendorf, who gave a Lutheran cast to Pietism, emphasizing justification and lacking the focus on sanctification of many pietist groups.[8] Unlike some other forms of Pietism—for example, that of Halle with its emphasis on a powerful conversion experience and the ongoing penitential struggles of the Christian life—the Moravians focused on salvation given freely out of God's steadfast love and the joy of personal communion with the Savior. There was a kind of mysticism here, a cultivation of the religious imagination that never left Schleiermacher.

SCHLEIERMACHER AT NIESKY AND BARBY

The Moravian version of Pietism also had a monastic cast to it, including a sectarian sensibility that felt the need to withdraw from the evil world where the true life of faith was ever in danger of corruption. With this went a form of asceticism at Niesky: students there were all male; girls like Friedrich's sister Charlotte attended a separate institution. The personal lives of the students were heavily structured and supervised; "worldly" pursuits such as swimming, skating, card playing, and board games were prohibited. The aim of this structure and regimen was to turn students away from the "world" and toward the cultivation of the inner life of piety.

Schleiermacher was happy in his time at Niesky and at one with the religious sensibilities in which he was immersed. He also received a good education there, especially as the students were given much freedom to pursue their own interests. Schleiermacher loved botany and mathematics, and he gained good language skills in Greek, Latin, Hebrew, and English. He built on the foundation laid by the earlier tutelage of his mother and blossomed as a young scholar.

In contrast to the happy time at Niesky, Schleiermacher's experience at the seminary at Barby was marked by the oppressive narrowness against which he was to rebel. Stifled by the intellectual and spiritual narrowness of the school, Schleiermacher and a small group of other like-minded students took their education into their own hands. The group began a covert reading operation; they read Kant's *Prolegomena* and poetry and novels of a humanist inclination—very much at odds with the piety of the seminary. Among the works they smuggled in was Goethe's heroic novel, *The Sorrows of Young Werther*, which had been published in 1774. The novel affirmed the sense of social alienation felt by many young people and inspired them to develop their own inner lives. The likely effect on Schleiermacher and his friends was just that; it reinforced their alienation from the powers-that-be at the seminary and their determination to cultivate their own inner lives in an autonomous fashion.

In Schleiermacher, the struggle against the authorities and for autonomous self-cultivation developed together with a deep sense of alienation from the inherited theological tradition. Eventually this led the seminary to ask Schleiermacher to leave; he did so in the spring of 1787. Before he left, Schleiermacher and his group had been severely disciplined and forbidden to continue their independent studies. As Schleiermacher explained in a letter to his father (January 21, 1787), doubt had captured his heart:

> I cannot believe that He, who called Himself the Son of Man, was the true, eternal God: I cannot believe that His death was a vicarious atonement, because He never expressly said so Himself; and I cannot believe it to have been necessary, because God, who evidently did not create men for perfection, but for the pursuit of it, cannot possibly intend to punish them eternally, because they have not attained it.[9]

Here we see Schleiermacher denying three theological pillars deemed crucial by Orthodoxy and Pietism alike: the divinity of Christ, atonement necessarily accomplished through Christ's death on the cross, and eternal damnation as the destiny for unbelievers. He never recants these youthful denials, but eventually finds a way to reconstruct Christian theology without them.

The subsequent correspondence between father and son is heart wrenching. Each is filled with sorrow because of the misery he is inflicting on the other, each expresses deep affection and concern for the other, and each holds his theological ground. Friedrich asserts that his doubt has "deep roots"[10] and will not be easily overcome; Gottlieb, for his part, responds with entreaty, admonition, and prayer. His response of February 6, 1787, is typical:

> Turn back, my son, turn back! Human virtue is not to be perfect, but to turn back speedily from the path of error. O Lord Jesus, Shepherd of the human race! bring back to Thyself Thy straying lamb![11]

Friedrich never does turn back, but neither does he abandon utterly what his father and the Moravians hold dear. Instead, he takes his doubt with him to the study of theology at Halle. And after a period of wilderness wandering—actually years of intense intellectual endeavor—he makes his way to a new land, unlike any he had known before. It is without doubt a Christian land, but with a new and different way of figuring what it means to be Christian.

In the end, Schleiermacher's own theological construction retains a strong *formal* parallel to the Pietism that had molded him in his formative years. Piety—the personal, experiential sense of God made known through the community indwelt with the spirit of Christ—is the touchstone of Schleiermacher's theology, including his ethics. This is also evident in his view of the church, which retains overtones of the pietist focus on an intimate community sharing a life of worship and nurture and bound together in a strong sense of common purpose and mission. At the same time, there is a profound *material* divergence as Schleiermacher rejects the Supernaturalism of traditional theological understanding. Devotion to Christ the Redeemer remains at the very heart of Schleiermacher's theology, but it is Christ recast in naturalistic terms, limited to what is known through the experience of faith in the community.

Schleiermacher's theology has, deservedly, been called a "theology within the limits of piety alone;"[12] Christian consciousness or piety is a prime source for and limit to theological reflection. Schleiermacher's understanding of piety in *The Christian Faith* identifies the essence of piety as the "feeling of absolute dependence." If that is the essence of piety, what place can there be for an ethical impulse or ethical action in relation to piety? An answer to this question requires a careful examination of Schleiermacher's conception of Christian piety, as we have it in *The Christian Faith* and the *Christian Ethics*.

Schleiermacher's most common account of the unity-in-difference relationship of dogmatics and ethics is that Siamese twins have been surgically separated for the sake of the "weaker" sibling's health. In this the surgical reports of *The Christian Faith*, *Christian Ethics*, and *Brief Outline* agree. But even as the *Ethics* concurs in this report, it forges on to a more deeply grounded understanding. Early on, the *Christian Ethics'* "General Introduction" affirms that "we must prove that Christian teaching can be nothing other than, on the one hand dogmatics, and on the other hand, ethics."[13] The analysis must reach the point where it can "ground the matter from the inside outwards (*von innen heraus*)."[14]

PIETY IN THE *CHRISTIAN ETHICS*

How is piety understood in the *Christian Ethics*? And how does this compare with the more familiar presentation in *The Christian Faith*. Schleiermacher's approach to this consideration of piety is indirect in the *Ethics*. The question that sets the whole discussion in motion is posed on page 3, an "indication" of an answer arrives on page 15, and the final resolution only on page 24. This is indicative of Schleiermacher's lecture style: he circles around the issue, drawing ever nearer to the center and finally arriving at a decisive conclusion.

Schleiermacher insists that theology is scientific in form in order that it may better serve "the spread of Christianity."[15] As in the *Speeches* and *The Christian Faith*, Schleiermacher is careful to distinguish piety from theology; the latter is only a developed representation of "that which makes a person a Christian."[16] Having affirmed this distinction, Schleiermacher proceeds to ask rhetorically about the nature of "that which makes a person a Christian." "Is it knowledge? Of course! It is a way of acting? That too."[17] But this requires refinement. For "that which makes one a Christian" is piety, and piety cannot be identified with knowledge or action, either individually or in combination. Schleiermacher argues that a person could comprehend a concept (e.g., the concept of "God") involved in Christian faith and still lack the inward disposition of piety. Similarly, one could act in a manner that appears to be in accord with Christian morality while lacking the appropriate inward disposition. Now Schleiermacher can draw the strands together and indicate how the inner/outer and action/knowledge distinctions relate to the nature of piety itself. He asserts:

> In the condition of piety these two elements are essentially bound together; on the one hand, interest in the religious object, which interest this object's concept calls forth in differing measures; on the other hand, impetus, ορμή, impulse, which certainly must express itself in action, but in different measures. These two elements in their pure identity are the actual origin which constitutes the condition of piety.[18]

The "object" of religious interest and that which propels one to action is, of course, God. Now the distinction between dogmatics and ethics follows easily: dogmatic propositions are those that, in terms of content, "express the relationship of persons to God as interest," whereas ethical propositions are those that "express the same thing in terms of inner impetus."[19] The tasks for these disciplines are formulated in terms of questions:

> **For dogmatics**—"What must **be** on the basis of religious self-consciousness?"
> **For ethics**—"What must **become** on the basis of religious self-consciousness?"[20]

Piety is seen under a double aspect; it consists in impulse and interest, giving rise to action and knowledge, respectively; these latter in turn are brought to conceptual precision and systematic coherence by ethics and dogmatics. As is often the case with Schleiermacher, this series of relationships is susceptible of a neat schematization. The Schleiermacherian system is almost always consistent, with connections and distinctions carefully drawn. We suggest the following schema:

Element of Piety	Mode of Expression	Systematizing Discipline
Impulse	Action	Christian Ethics
Interest	Thought	Christian Dogmatics

It is the case that in Schleiermacher's theology, the system, the whole is of utmost importance. Distinctions are made: for example, between consciousness of sin and consciousness of grace; or between the "religious self-consciousness presupposed by and contained in every Christian religious affection" and Christian self-consciousness proper; or between mind and will as components of the human spirit (*Gemüth*). In each case the distinctions are important, but to focus on one element and ignore the other is to misinterpret Schleiermacher. The point *is* the system: polar opposites balanced against each other; the two sides of the one coin seen as a whole. So piety is seen here as interest and impulse; Christian theology as dogmatics and ethics. The *Christian Ethics* claims that the division into ethics and dogmatics is grounded in the nature of piety itself.

PIETY IN *THE CHRISTIAN FAITH*

But how does the view of piety in *The Christian Faith* compare with the notion of piety in the *Christian Ethics*? Many interpreters of Schleiermacher are tempted to derive their reading of *The Christian Faith* exclusively from Part I, "The Development of that Religious Self-Consciousness which is always both presupposed by and contained in every Christian Religious Affection."[21] There the essence of piety is identified as the immediate self-consciousness of absolute dependence; this seems to correspond but poorly with the notion of piety in the *Christian Ethics*. Piety, identified with absolute dependence, would suggest pure passivity on the part of the pious individual; this is not in accord with the active element of piety indicated in the *Christian Ethics*. In this connection one is reminded of Hegel's gibe that if absolute dependence expresses the true nature of religion, then a dog would be the best of Christians.

The problem is that this view represents an utter misreading of the nature of Christian piety as understood in *The Christian Faith*, even as it is developed in Part I. Schleiermacher says that piety "considered purely in itself" is feeling, but it stands in close connection with moments of knowledge and action. "[I]ndeed, it is the case in general that the immediate self-consciousness is always the mediating link in the transition between moments in which Knowing predominates and those in which Doing predominates."[22] These three moments of human experience are distinguishable, but not ultimately separable: "There are both a Knowing and a Doing which pertain to piety, but neither of these constitutes the essence of piety."[23] In its essence, piety is a modification of feeling, but this feeling stands in intimate and inseparable relation to action and knowledge. Here at the most fundamental level—in a discussion of the "essence" of piety—the door to the room where ethics lives has been opened a crack. The possibility of a religious ethics is first suggested here as feeling provides a mediating link to moments of action.

The door is opened more widely in paragraph 5. Schleiermacher affirms that the feeling of absolute dependence always occurs in conjunction with the feeling of reciprocal influence between self and world. That is to say, although the feeling of absolute dependence is absolutely simple and always self-identical, it always coexists with the self-consciousness actively or passively related to the world. This becomes particularly important when Schleiermacher considers the nature of individual religions; he affirms that there is a determination of the religious self-consciousness at the level of reciprocity that gives the individual religion its particular character.

In every individual religion the God-consciousness, which in itself remains the same everywhere on the same level, is attached to some relation of the self-consciousness in such an especial way that only thereby can it unite with other determinations of the self-consciousness; so that all other relations are subordinate to this one, and it communicates to all others its color and tone.[24]

Schleiermacher introduces the notion of aesthetic and teleological religions in paragraph 9. The feeling of absolute dependence remains the same in all religious traditions; it combines with the elements that vary from religion to religion. The character of a particular religious tradition is shaped by its historical origin, the material specification given its piety, and the manner in which it relates active and passive moments to each other; all of these elements relate to the reciprocal level of consciousness, the level at which the self experiences relative freedom and relative dependence in relation to the world. Thus, any religious tradition is colored decisively by its concrete origin and its directionality. Religious feeling is mediated in and through the finite world, and that which mediates the feeling of absolute dependence becomes a part of piety itself. The key determination relating to ethics is whether a particular religion is identified as aesthetic or teleological.

In sum then, feeling exists on two levels. On the fundamental level, abstracted from religious self-consciousness, feeling is determined as absolute dependence, the entire world being passive in the face of divine causality. On the worldly, finite level, feeling is determined by reciprocity among finite agents. An individual religious tradition involves particular determinations at the finite level, in combination with the feeling of absolute dependence. Feeling is a mediator between different moments of human consciousness; action and knowledge have an immediate connection with feeling. This is so "inasmuch as the stirred-up feeling sometimes comes to rest in thinking which fixes it, sometimes discharges itself in an action which expresses it."[25] Sorting out these levels of feeling and the relationship of feeling to other human capacities (action and thought) indicates how the impulse to ethical activity is grounded in Christian piety.

The Christian Faith identifies Christianity as a teleological religion. A teleological religion is characterized by "the passive states . . . [arousing] the feeling of absolute dependence in so far as they are referred to the spontaneous activity."[26] In teleological religion, religious emotions "appear as simply means for evoking the totality of . . . active states."[27] Religious feeling is marked by "a predominating reference to the moral task. . . . In Christianity all pain and all joy are religious only in so far as they are related to activity in the Kingdom of God."[28] The polar opposite of teleological religion is aesthetic religion, exemplified most clearly in Greek polytheism.

Here the directionality of moments in human consciousness is from the sense of activity that comes to rest in passivity, this sense then being taken up into the feeling of absolute dependence. This move from the feeling of activity to that of passivity in one's relations to the world is "a result of those relations which exist between the subject and all the rest of existence."[29] The directionality of moments of consciousness is the crucial difference here: in aesthetic religion the movement is from activity to passivity—the religious goal is feeling itself.

In terms of Schleiermacher's understanding of piety, then, it is the teleological character of Christian religious consciousness that grounds the ethical moment and thereby, at the level of reflection, the discipline of ethics as a part of theology. The ethical moment is an essential characteristic of Christian piety.

> In view of the teleological character of Christianity we can conceive of no completely developed moment of religious experience which does not either itself pass over into some activity or in a definite way influence activities already going and combine with them.[30]

This being the case, the impulse to ethical action and action itself are essential to Christian piety; it cannot exist without concurrent impulse and activity. At the theological level, this means that ethics is the necessary complement to dogmatics. Schleiermacher warns that even if ethics is not included within dogmatics,

> we should nevertheless always keep in mind the fact that to a system of doctrine, of whatever form, there essentially belongs also a system of Christian morals developing in harmony with it.[31]

By dissecting Schleiermacher's conception of Christian piety in this manner, we can thereby identify its constituent elements. Christian piety comprises absolute dependence—its abstracted, foundational, self-identical feeling; a teleological orientation—a generic quality it shares with other religions of this type; and that which is distinctively Christian—its historical origin in Jesus of Nazareth and its material specification as consciousness of sin and grace. So, clarity about piety's constituent elements and their interrelationships can be obtained by carefully attending to the whole of Schleiermacher's system and the interrelation of its constituent parts. *The Christian Faith* identifies the teleological character of Christianity and shows that the drive to activity is essential to Christian piety itself. Slight differences of language cannot obscure how this corresponds to the view of piety in the *Christian Ethics* and its identification of piety's "interested" and "impulsive" elements. But in both cases Christian piety includes an element of impulse toward ethical activity. Schleiermacher is quite clear about the elements that constitute Christian piety: absolute dependence, redemption in Christ, and impulse to ethical activity.

Piety is the ultimate ground for Christian theology: both dogmatics and ethics. The argument of the *Christian Ethics* is that only when ethics is grounded "inwardly," that is, by piety, has one arrived at the most basic reason for the division of theology into dogmatics and ethics. Christian piety includes a particular determination of the disposition, an impulse to ethical action. This impulse gives rise to action and is the ground for Christian ethics as a discipline. So it is also clear that just as *The Christian Faith* is a theology of piety, the *Christian Ethics* is an ethics of piety. Piety provides the ultimate ground for Christian ethical action, and at the level of theological reflection, for Christian ethics.

DESCRIPTIVE METHOD IN THE *CHRISTIAN ETHICS*

Because ethics is grounded in Christian piety, its method and form are defined by piety. Schleiermacher claims that Christian ethics achieves its true form and method only when it adopts a descriptive approach. He rejects an ethics of duty or an imperative ethics as inadequate for Christian purposes because of Christian ethics' ground in piety. A descriptive approach is appropriate for Christian ethics because the primary task is to describe what is already present, what is given. For Schleiermacher, piety is given, theologically speaking and methodologically speaking. Theologically speaking, piety is given because it is the result of divine grace; it is a gift. Methodologically speaking, piety is given because it is presupposed; it is the starting point for dogmatics and ethics; it is the given subject matter of both disciplines. The primary task for Christian ethics is to describe the impulses to action that are an element of piety and the actions themselves that arise from these pious impulses.

The descriptive method of the *Christian Ethics* derives from its grounding in piety. The method of Christian ethics

> must be the representation of communion with God as determined by communion with Christ, the redeemer, in so far as this is the impulse for every action of the Christian; it can be nothing other than a description of those ways of acting which arise from the rule of the Christianly determined religious self-consciousness.[32]

The *Christian Ethics* is an ethics of piety, in the first place, because piety is its ground and because piety determines its descriptive method.

PIETY AND THE STRUCTURE OF THE *CHRISTIAN ETHICS*

Schleiermacher also asserts that the structure of the *Christian Ethics* derives from piety. Schleiermacher notes that the rule of piety in the self-consciousness of the Christian is never perfect, never complete. It is always in a process of becoming. This being so, there is a continual oscillation between the rule of the higher self-consciousness, or spirit, and the lower self-consciousness, or flesh. The goal is not that the flesh be destroyed, but that it become the tool or agent of the spirit. There is an ongoing struggle between spirit and flesh as the spirit seeks for domination. In Christian consciousness, those moments in which the flesh gains ascendancy are felt as pain, and those in which the spirit gains ascendancy are felt as pleasure. These feelings of pain and pleasure give rise to different forms of action. When pain results from the ascendancy of the flesh over the spirit, the higher self-consciousness responds with an impulse to overcome this negation; this is an impulse to a restoring or purifying action. When pleasure results from the ascendancy of the spirit over the flesh, the higher self-consciousness responds with an impulse to continue and expand this rule of the spirit; this is an impulse to a broadening action. These two forms of action Schleiermacher calls "effectual actions" because they seek a change in the spirit-flesh relation, either a reduction of the power of the flesh or an elevation of the power of the spirit.

In addition to the Christian self-consciousness being determined as pain or pleasure, there is a third possibility. This is a moment of relative contentment in which the rule of the spirit is constant and no change in state is sought. Such a condition can give rise to action, but not an effectual action. Rather, such a condition gives rise to what Schleiermacher calls a "representational" action. Such an action seeks no change in an inward state; it seeks only to express or represent the inward state by means of an outward representation. The aim of such an action is that the inward state be remembered by the individual experiencing it or that it be communicated to another person. These are the three forms of action grounded in Christian piety, and these three types of action provide the structure for the *Christian Ethics*: Schleiermacher's distinction between effectual action (including both purifying and broadening actions) and representational action provide the rubrics by which the *Christian Ethics* is structured.

This makes it clear that the *Christian Ethics* is also an ethics *for* piety. These actions are grounded in piety, and they seek the restoration, the expansion, and the representation of piety. Piety is not only the ground of these actions; it is also their goal as they seek to purify, expand, and express piety. The focus is on what might be called the "inward" mission of the church. It works to celebrate and strengthen the piety of those within the community and invite others to come in. On the other hand, the church also relates to the world outside; it has a corresponding "outer" mission. So, the complete structure of the *Christian Ethics* is formed by crossing these three kinds of action with the two "spheres." Schleiermacher distinguishes the "inner" sphere, or the church, from the "outer" sphere, the society, the "not yet church." A sixfold division results: each type of action is analyzed as it exists in the inner sphere and in the outer sphere.

The Structure of Schleiermacher's *Christian Ethics*

	Purifying Action	Broadening Action	Representational Action
Inner Sphere The Church	Church Discipline Church Reform	Christian Education Missions Family: Child Rearing	Worship: Narrow— Household & Public Broad—Virtue in Daily Life
Outer Sphere Society	Criminal Justice International Relations Warfare & Colonization	Education Labor & Industry Commerce	The Arts Social Relations

Even a cursory consideration of the issues considered in the inner sphere reveals that they are defined by the distinctive nature of the church as a community of Christian piety. Thus, under the restoring action Schleiermacher considers ecclesiastical discipline of individuals, the discipline of children in the family, and reformation of the church when it has fallen into error. All these actions aim at restoration of piety—the rule of spirit over flesh. Broadening action includes an analysis of marriage and family and the ecclesiastical functions of education and missions. The aim here is an increase of piety among individuals and communities currently in the church and piety's spread to individuals and communities not yet under its sway. Representational action takes up public and household worship and also worship "in the broad sense," which is the expression of the Christian virtues of chastity, patience, forbearance, and humility in daily life. The aim is piety's outward and public expression. As the enumeration of these topics makes clear, this is an ethics for piety; the issues addressed derive from the dynamics of the life of piety, and the goal is to further piety.

That the *Christian Ethics* is an ethics of and for piety is evident in Schleiermacher's claim that "the instructions [*Vorschriften*] of Christian ethics must be descriptions of the actions of Christ."[33] Christ is the origin and model for Christian action; Christian action participates in and furthers the perfect God-consciousness manifest in Christ. "All actions of Christians are either completions of the church-forming actions of Christ, the reception of Christ's action, or continuations of it; in either case therefore they are a continuous realization of the relationship established between Christ as the redeemer and the human race as the redeemed."[34] The uniqueness of Christ resides in his God-consciousness and his ability to express it such that others will participate in it. Christian action mediates the ongoing presence of Christ; Christian action originates in the perfect piety incarnate in Christ and seeks the expression and increase of that piety. Thus ethics as a description of Christian action is, in the first place, an ethics of and for piety.

Our final characterization of the *Christian Ethics* will be that it is an ecclesial ethics of piety *and* a transformative theology of culture. At this point we simply note the areas and issues of cultural, social, and political life that the *Christian Ethics* considers. The question posed in this consideration of the "outer sphere" is how Christian individuals and the Christian community are to relate themselves to the wider society. The discussion of purifying action in the outer sphere concerns itself with the criminal justice system, international relations (especially war and the criteria for considering a war just), and relations between the state and tribal groups (a pressing issue in a day of colonization). The purifying action in the outer sphere, then, deals with the Christian relation to law, domestic and international. The broadening action in the outer sphere concerns the state as the custodian of "talent and nature formation," that is, with questions of education, industry, and commerce. Schleiermacher here indicates concern over the mechanization of industry and consequent dangers this poses to workers as they are reduced to the status of machines. Schleiermacher also takes up here issues of church-state relations. Finally, regarding representational action in the outer sphere, Schleiermacher analyzes what he calls "general social representation." This includes the whole gamut of artistic and cultural expression from poetry and theater to music, painting, and sculpture. Schleiermacher also considers language, especially as it is a symbol of national differences. In reflecting on this broad range of human culture from the penal system to artistic expression, the issue is always how the Christian individual and community approach this vast array of phenomena. The phenomena are given; the Christian must decide how to relate to them—whether to abstain from a given realm of cultural life altogether, accept it as it is, or seek its transformation by means of the Christian principle.

In Schleiermacher's own work as a scholar, the realm of cultural life outside of the church that claimed enormous attention from him was the intellectual life of the academy. Within the academy he gave particular attention to the discipline of philosophy. He gave lecture courses on a wide array of philosophical topics including dialectics, hermeneutics, and ethics. He had his own philosophical system, which raises the question of how he worked out the relation between his philosophy and his theology. We will consider in particular the relation between his work in philosophical ethics and his *Christian Ethics*.

In terms of Schleiermacher's life, the relation between philosophy and theology is illumined by his personal, professional, and ideological relation with his contemporary, G. F. W. Hegel. The relation between the two renowned professors at the University of Berlin was fraught with disagreement, even hostility. The division between them defined the Prussian intellectual world of the decade before their deaths in the early 1830s. Hegel and Schleiermacher felt a world apart; their differences seemed to both of them irreconcilable.[35] To the question of the relation between the two towering intellectuals and the related issue of Schleiermacher's view of the relation between theology and philosophy, we turn next.

NOTES

1. Currently there is no scholarly consensus as to what constitutes Pietism. Some scholars, such as F. Ernest Stoeffler in his two-volume work *The Rise of Evangelical Pietism and the German Pietism of the Eighteenth Century* (Leiden: Brill, 1973), cast a wide net and include English Puritanism as a manifestation of Pietism. Stoeffler's work is the most detailed English language work on Pietism, but it is now outdated. German scholars tend to work with a narrower definition of Pietism. An important recent interpretation of Pietism is that of Johannes Wallmann in *Der Pietismus*, Vol. 4 in *Die Kirche in Ihrer Geschichte* (Göttingen: Vandenhoeck & Ruprecht, 1990) and "Was ist Pietismus?" *Pietismus und Neuzeit* 20 (1994): 11–27. Wallmann's characterization of Pietism emphasizes devotional Bible reading; gathering in small groups for prayer, study, and mutual admonition; and chiliastic expectation as the key marks of the movement.

2. Johann F. G. Goeters, "Der reformierte Pietismus in Bremen und am Niederrhein im 18. Jahrhundert," in *Der Pietismus im achtzehnten Jahrhundert*, edited by Martin Brecht and Klaus Deppermann (Göttingen: Vandenhoeck & Ruprecht, 1995), 411–19.

3. Martin Redeker, *Schleiermacher: Life and Thought*, trans. John Wallhausser (Philadelphia: Fortress Press, 1973), 6.

4. F. W. Kantzenbach, *Friedrich Daniel Ernst Schleiermacher* (Reinbek bei Hamburg: Rowolt Taschenbuch Verlag GmbH, 1967), 13.

5. Cf. Ted Campbell, *The Religion of the Heart* (Columbia: University of South Car-

olina Press, 1991) for an interpretation of these various movements belonging together as "heart religion."

6. Philip Jacob Spener, *Pia Desideria*, trans. Theodore G. Tappert (Philadelphia: Fortress Press, 1964).

7. Cf. Wallmann, *Der Pietismus*, 36–58, who identifies the true beginning of Pietism with Spener rather than Johann Arndt, as some other interpreters do.

8. For this reason, some interpreters argue that the Moravians ought not be seen as pietists at all. Cf. Dietrich Meyer, "Zinzendorf und Herrnhut," in *Der Pietismus im achtzehnten Jahrhundert*, edited by Martin Brecht and Klaus Deppermann (Göttingen: Vandenhoeck & Ruprecht, 1995), 5–106.

9. *The Life of Schleiermacher, as Unfolded in His Autobiography and Letters*, trans. Frederica Rowan, vol. 1 (London: Smith, Elder & Co., 1859), 46.

10. Ibid., 47.

11. Ibid., 53.

12. B. A. Gerrish, "Theology Within the Limits of Piety Alone: Schleiermacher and Calvin's Notion of God," in *The Old Protestantism and the New: Essays on the Reformation Heritage* (Chicago: University of Chicago Press, 1982), 163–78. Here it is important to note an important difference regarding the use of the term "piety" (*Frömmigkeit*). Following Schleiermacher's usual usage in *The Christian Faith*, "piety" connotes for Gerrish the essence of religion, abstracted from Christian faith—the feeling of absolute dependence. Without question, this is the usual reference that the term has in the Introduction and Part I of *The Christian Faith*. My own use of "piety" refers to "Christian piety," and thus to the whole scope of Christian consciousness. Schleiermacher does use "Frömmigkeit" in this way in *The Christian Faith*, edited by H. R. MacKintosh and J. S. Stewart (Edinburgh: T. & T. Clark, 1928), e.g., 64.2 (pp. 266–68) and 78.2 (p. 323). "Christian piety" is also the connotation of "piety" throughout the *Christian Ethics*.

13. Friedrich Schleiermacher, *Die christliche Sitte nach den Grundsätzen der evangelischen Kirche im Zusammenhange dargestellt*, ed. Ludwig Jonas in *Sämmtliche Werke*, div. 1, vol. 12 (Berlin: G. Reimer, 1943). Hereafter referred to as the *Christian Ethics*.

14. Ibid., 15. See Hans-Joachim Birkner, *Schleiermachers Christliche Sittenlehre im Zusammenhang seines Philosophisch-Theologishen Systems*, Theologische Bibliothek Töpelmann, edited by Kurt Aland et al. (Berlin: Alfred Töpelman in 1964), 67, where the distinction is between the grounding of the separation of dogmatics and ethics in Friedrich Schleiermacher, *Brief Outline on the Study of Theology*, trans. Terrence N. Tice (Richmond: John Knox Press, 1970), and that found in both *The Christian Faith* and the *Christian Ethics*. Birkner says, "Schleiermacher's *Christian Faith* and also his *Christian Ethics* show that for him the difference between [these two disciplines] is not just technical as it appears to be in the *Brief Outline*, but rather it is grounded 'from the inside outward' (*Ethics*, 15). The thematic differentiation of *Christian Faith* and *Ethics* has its ground in the pious self-consciousness itself." Our analysis of piety as grounding the distinction between dogmatics and ethics follows the suggestions of Birkner, 67–71.

15. *Ethics*, 16.

16. Ibid., 10–11. Schleiermacher says that "the innermost element, underlying thought and speech is certainly consistent, identical, but this does not allow of outward expression." 17.

17. Ibid., 10–11.

18. Ibid., 22.

19. Ibid., 19.
20. Ibid., 23.
21. Some succumb to this temptation. E.g., Ronald F. Thiemann, "Piety, Narrative, and Christian Identity," *Word and World* 3, no. 2 (Spring 1983): 148–59.
22. *The Christian Faith*, 8.
23. Ibid.
24. Ibid., 47.
25. Ibid., 10–11.
26. Ibid., 41.
27. Ibid.
28. Ibid.
29. Ibid.
30. Ibid., 232.
31. Ibid., 124.
32. Ibid., 32–33.
33. Ibid., 75.
34. Ibid., 74–75.
35. Hajo Holborn, *A History of Modern Germany*, 3 vols. (New York: Alfred Knopf, 1959–69), vol. 2 (1648–1840), 493.

4
PHILOSOPHY AND THEOLOGY IN SCHLEIERMACHER'S *ETHICS*: THE CONTRAST WITH HEGEL

In 1818 G. W. F. Hegel joined the faculty of the University of Berlin as professor of philosophy. By then he was already renowned as the leading light in the movement of Speculative Idealism, having published his magnum opus *The Phenomenology of Spirit* in 1807, his *Encyclopedia of the Philosophical Sciences* in 1817, and the *Science of Logic* in the years 1812–16. Schleiermacher was among the members of the Berlin faculty who voted in favor of Hegel's appointment; this was significant, for Schleiermacher's valued colleague in biblical studies, W. M. L. de Wette, was opposed to Hegel's appointment. De Wette wanted the position to go to his former teacher, J. F. Fries. After Hegel's arrival, he and Schleiermacher were colleagues until the former's untimely death in 1831.

The similarities in the biographies of Schleiermacher and Hegel are noteworthy. Both were the sons of middle class German families. Both attended seminary and, finding the theology taught by their instructors insufferable, created alternative educational paths with fellow students. Hegel attended the seminary in Tübingen from 1788–93. There he formed a close friendship with Friedrich Schelling and Friedrich Hölderlin, and the threesome immersed itself in Enlightenment literature. Schleiermacher and Hegel were also similar in gaining early employment as tutors for the children of wealthy families; each studied Kant on his own and wrote youthful essays while working as a tutor. Professional experience for both included a stint as a newspaper editor. Hegel edited a paper in Bamberg in 1807–08, and both had firsthand experience of Napoleon's defeat of the Prussian army in 1806. Hegel was teaching at the university in Jena when the French army won its climactic battle there in 1806. Like Schleiermacher in Halle, Hegel chose to leave the town where he had been teaching after the French occupation made life difficult in the extreme.

The love lives of Hegel and Schleiermacher also exhibit remarkable parallels. Both had illicit love affairs as young men. Schleiermacher's love for the married Eleonore Grunow was scandalous in the Berlin of his day; Hegel fathered a child by the wife of his Jena landlord. His son Ludwig was born in 1807 and later raised in Hegel's family when the philosopher married Marie von Tucher in 1811. Like Schleiermacher, Hegel married a woman who was much younger than he and who had aristocratic connections. Marie was twenty to Hegel's forty-one; Schleiermacher was also forty-one when he married; his bride Henriette von Willich was twenty-one. Both men had children with their wives and were survived by them.

More important than these striking biographical parallels are the similarities in their intellectual projects. Both Schleiermacher and Hegel were key participants in a period of creativity and insight that is among the most significant in the history of the western European world.[1] The epoch of 1770–1830 witnessed an outpouring of philosophical and artistic expression in the German states that plumbed the depth of human consciousness in remarkable new ways. Luminaries of this period included Lessing, Herder, Goethe, Beethoven, Schiller, and Kant, the Romantic poets and writers (e.g., the Schlegel brothers, Novalis, Kleist, Hölderlin, and Jean Paul), the philosophy of Speculative Idealism (Fichte, Schelling, and Hegel), as well as Schleiermacher's pioneering work in theology. Schleiermacher and Hegel were key figures in the latter half of the epoch.

Both Schleiermacher and Hegel worked at the interface of philosophy and theology, and the noteworthy similarities between them extend to the goals they had for their work. Having gained a deep understanding and appreciation for Kant's philosophy and been inspired by Romantic insights and sensibilities, each in his own way moved theology and philosophy to a new level of construction. Objectives of their respective programs on which they agree and which were central to their systems of thought include the following: a revised understanding of Christian theology that goes beyond Orthodox and Enlightenment views, a desire to reconcile the subjective and objective poles of Kant's thought, a reconciliation also of philosophical and religious thinking, an appropriation of the thoroughly historical character of human life, and the fervent wish that their respective work would reshape the German cultural and political world.

IDEATIONAL, PROFESSIONAL, AND PERSONAL DIVERGENCE

Given all this similarity of experience and intellectual orientation, one might well expect that Schleiermacher and Hegel would have enjoyed a congenial relationship during their years together in Berlin. But such was not the case. Rather, at ideational, professional, and personal levels, the relationship between the two great thinkers was marked by divergence and tension. In the first place, it should be noted that Schleiermacher's vote for Hegel's appointment to Berlin was made with qualified enthusiasm. From early on, Schleiermacher was highly critical of Speculative Idealism, and his vote for Hegel was at least as much a vote against Fries.[2]

The relationship between Schleiermacher and Hegel is complex and many-sided; it defies easy characterization.[3] Crouter indicates three specific points of disagreement and tension between the two. In the political arena, Schleiermacher was favorably disposed toward the student organizations at the universities (*Burschenschaften*), seeing them as furthering reforming ideals. Hegel was much more critical of the students for what he saw as dangers of extremism and subjectivism. The second point of tension concerned Schleiermacher's role in excluding Hegel from the prestigious Berlin Academy of Sciences. Schleiermacher argued that the academy's focus on philological and historical sciences was incompatible with speculative philosophy. Hegel responded by starting an alternative scholarly society. "The rival groups of scholars functioned as formal barriers between the two thinkers and were a continuous source of friction."[4]

The third area of tension and disagreement gets at the crucial ideational differences between Schleiermacher and Hegel. In 1821 Hegel offered his first lectures on the philosophy of religion, the same year that Schleiermacher published the first volume of the first edition of his *Christian Faith*. Crouter says that Hegel was "vitally disturbed" by Schleiermacher's position; in fact, he wanted to put Schleiermacher's theology "out of business."[5] Then in 1822 Hegel contributed a foreword to a book on religion by his former student H. F. W. Hinrichs.[6] This work appears to be the only one by either Hegel or Schleiermacher in which the position of the other is confronted directly. Even here Hegel does not name Schleiermacher, although the allusions to the ideas of his Berlin colleague are unmistakable.

What, then, are the crucial ideational differences between Schleiermacher and Hegel? To offer a summation of those differences in the small amount of space available here borders on the absurd. The complexity of each of their systems is staggering. Nonetheless, we can focus on one important issue between the two—the status and role of philosophical speculation in their respective systems. For Hegel, the issue comes into focus as he conceives of the relation between feeling and reason, on the one hand, and religious representation (*Vorstellung*) and philosophical conception (*Begriff*), on the other. For Schleiermacher, the central issues get framed differently. In his system, the distinction between religious feeling and theological reflection on that feeling is crucial. Also important is the relation between theology and philosophy as distinctive disciplines. Although both thinkers arrive at revisionist constructions of theological claims, the ways in which their respective systems are envisioned make comparison complex. It is very easy for Schleiermacher and Hegel to talk past each other and difficult to engage both in a way that doesn't privilege one system over the other.

Acknowledging the risk of oversimplification, our approach will be to consider each thinker on his own terms and then draw the differences between them in broad strokes. This analysis then sets the stage for a consideration of the place of the *Christian Ethics* in Schleiermacher's overall system of philosophy and theology and the way he envisions the relationship between philosophical ethics and Christian ethics. The relationship between philosophy and theology in general and that between the corresponding forms of ethics is important in Schleiermacher's system. Unfortunately for the purposes of our comparison, a distinction between theology and philosophy is not crucial in Hegel's work. In his system, crucial distinctions are rather those between feeling and reason, on the one hand, and religious representation and philosophical concept on the other. Not sharing the key concepts and distinctions, a direct comparison of the two systems is made difficult. Still, by examining their systems side by side, we can gain important insight into the structure and character of Schleiermacher's *Christian Ethics*.

HEGEL ON PHILOSOPHY AND THEOLOGY

For Hegel, the real is the rational and the rational is the real. This means that for him feeling, as a representative of subjectivity, is imbued with reason and includes its other, objectivity, within itself. If feeling does not include reason within itself, such feeling must remain at the level of "animal feeling"—thus Hegel's conclusion that in Schleiermacher's approach, a dog is the best of Christians.[7] Where Schleiermacher posits a pre-reflective consciousness as sheer immediacy or union in which the self is absorbed by the universe, Hegel asserts a mediated immediacy, a sense of unity-in-difference as the self exists both differentiated from and unified with the other. Hegel claims that "reason is a ubiquitous and never-ceasing feature of [human] experience.... His point is that reason cannot be systematically excluded from the deepest and holiest moments of our experience."[8]

Similarly for Hegel, there exists a coincidence of religious representation and philosophical concept. In terms of content, they are identical, though in terms of form a distinction remains, hence a unity-in-difference relationship. For Hegel, the assertions of Christianity, particularly the doctrines of incarnation and the Trinity, are identical to the results of a philosophical or speculative analysis of consciousness or spirit. In consequence of this, Hegel asserts the absoluteness of Christianity and claims that the doctrines of incarnation and the Trinity disclose the nature of ultimate reality. But he does so in a way that finally subordinates these theological claims to philosophy at the level of the forms in which they are expressed. The claims of faith, expressed in terms of representation (*Vorstellung*) indicate how Absolute Spirit objectifies itself in an other (both the second person of the Trinity and the world) and then moves to reconciliation with the other. Conceptually, this can be expressed as a movement from unconscious identity to differentiation to conscious unity. The real, the rational, is disclosed in this self-unfolding of spirit in the movements of history, and together the doctrines of the Trinity and incarnation express this at the level of religious representation.

Philosophy attains to a kind of formal superiority in Hegel's thought as the representational truths of Christian doctrine are rendered in conceptual (*begrifflich*) terms. This is true, although there is, as noted above, a unity-in-difference relation between religious representation and philosophical concept. The theological doctrines of the Trinity and incarnation are true and unsurpassable in terms of content for Hegel, but are "expressed in less than adequate form." So there is a need for a "speculative redescription of Christian theology." The "moments" in the dynamics of Absolute Spirit, conceptually expressed, are pure thought, representation, and self-consciousness.[9] For Hegel, this conceptual level of expression is formally superior to expression at the level of representation. Thus philosophical expression gives religious representation its "fully adequate form and [brings] into view its rational necessity."[10] At this formal level, then, philosophy transcends representation and brings it to completion.

So although Hegel reclaims the doctrines of the incarnation and the immanent Trinity in a way that Schleiermacher does not, Hegel does so in a way that subordinates theology to philosophy, at least in terms of the form in which truth is expressed.[11] On the other hand, Schleiermacher insists that speculation has no place in theology. He bases his system on the pious feelings of absolute dependence and redemption in Christ and ends up with reinterpretations of the doctrines of the incarnation and the (immanent) Trinity that do not attain to the speculative heights of earlier Orthodoxy or Hegel. Jesus, who manifests redemption by means of his perfect God-consciousness, is not the incarnation of the second person of the Trinity, though Schleiermacher can speak of Jesus' perfect God-consciousness as the "a veritable existence of God in him."[12] And the Trinity to which Schleiermacher attains is an economic Trinity of God, Christ, and Spirit. Although the content of Schleiermacher's theological construction is in this way more modest than Hegel's, he does not subordinate theological claims in terms of their form to a higher, speculative expression, but instead develops his theology (both dogmatics and ethics) founded in the life and experience of the community of faith and meant to further the mission of that community. Schleiermacher's theology is theology of and for the church.

THE *CHRISTIAN ETHICS* ON PHILOSOPHY AND THEOLOGY

This is especially the case with his *Christian Ethics*. But like Hegel, Schleiermacher works both sides of the aisle: he develops his own philosophical system alongside his theology. Returning to the *Christian Ethics*, the task now is to sort through where Christian ethics fits in Schleiermacher's overall system and how it conceives the relation between philosophy and theology. More specifically, the focus is on the relation between philosophical ethics and Christian ethics. How does Schleiermacher differentiate the two forms of ethics from each other, and is Christian ethics distinctive? And does he place theology in a position in some ways over philosophy, as would be expected?

The *Christian Ethics'* "General Introduction" contributes the only detailed discussion of the relation between Christian ethics and philosophical ethics in the whole corpus of Schleiermacher's work. Schleiermacher claims that as regards content Christian ethics and philosophical ethics are "completely the same," and as regards form they are "completely different."[13] It is a statement such as this that seems to support Poul Jorgensen's claim that the *Christian Ethics* is nothing but a translation of philosophical ethics into Christian language.[14] Is there nothing distinctive about the content of Christian ethics?

But this statement must be considered in its context, and caution is in order—for two reasons. The first has to do with the nature of our text. The *Christian Ethics* is a compilation of lectures, edited and published only after Schleiermacher's death. And his distinctive style of lecturing militates against taking any one statement as the definitive representation of his position. Schleiermacher's explicit statements about the relation of Christian and philosophical ethics require "considerable, and careful, explication."[15] Schleiermacher's lectures had a lively, engaging style that involved his hearers in the process of thought. Schleiermacher did not present his own view in deductive fashion; rather, he began with the presuppositions of his hearers and weighed strengths and weaknesses until his own position was characterized.[16] This means, above all, that individual statements must not be taken out of context and absolutized. Because of the way that he unfolds his position in the course of lecturing, drawing students along as he develops his position ever more exactly, it is the process of thought and not fixed formulae that is crucial. Birkner is explicit in noting that this applies particularly to Schleiermacher's view of the relation between philosophical ethics and Christian ethics as we have it in the *Ethics*.[17]

Caution is necessary, in the second place, because there is a significant difference between Schleiermacher's view of the relation between Christian and philosophical ethics as we have it in the *Christian Ethics* and the actual relation between his own Christian ethics and his own philosophical ethics. In the "General Introduction," Schleiermacher is talking about the relation between Christian and philosophical ethics as it exists *in principle*. The actual relation between Schleiermacher's own works in the two types of ethics, the relationship that exists *in fact*, is significantly different from, though not necessarily in contradiction to, this *in principle* relation.

The claim that, as regards content, Christian ethics and philosophical ethics are completely the same refers to the *in principle* relation between the two forms of ethics.

One indication that the discussion in the *Christian Ethics'* "General Introduction" concerns the *in principle* relation between the two types of ethics is the fact that Schleiermacher begins by discussing the relation between religious ethics in general and philosophical ethics. Of course, Schleiermacher's real concern is with Christian ethics; he recognizes that although one may speak of religion in general, in actuality it exists only in particularly determined expressions. At crucial points in the discussion, he shifts from the general concept of religious ethics to consider ethics that are specifically Christian.

The problem posed by the existence of both kinds of ethics is quite simple; if religious ethics and philosophical ethics are the same as regards content and the totality of their individual elements, then it seems that one is superfluous. If they are not the same, it seems that one cannot be both a philosopher and pious. Neither alternative is acceptable to Schleiermacher. He argues that philosophy cannot be jettisoned from the Christian vessel because its principles are necessary to make theology scientific. Therefore he concludes that the two forms must be compatible with each other. Schleiermacher is most concerned that the two not contradict each other; if they do, the theologian will find himself or herself trapped by a genuine dilemma—prompted at once to counsel for and against particular actions.[18] The difficulty is to determine more precisely how these two disciplines are compatible.

Schleiermacher suggests a solution to this problem that is both "eschatological" and Christian. He notes that there exists a great variety of ethical positions among the many forms of religious ethics and that similar differences are to be found among philosophical versions.

> [Given that] Christianity is the actual perfection of religious consciousness, when, on the one hand, Christianity has perfected itself such that all oppositions existing in its realm are overcome and, on the other hand, when philosophy comes to absolute and universally recognized perfection, then the result will be that every contradiction between Christian and philosophical ethics will be impossible.[19]

Still, this does not mean that either will be superfluous because each has its own distinctive source and its own form. Thus Schleiermacher is led to the formulation we have noted above: in content, Christian ethics and philosophical ethics are completely the same and in form completely different.[20]

In light of this process of thought, it becomes apparent that the assertion of identical content must be carefully interpreted. Schleiermacher's leading concern is that the two forms of ethics not contradict each other. He is worried about the moral dilemma that will result if they do. This suggests that his position is better characterized in terms of "noncontradiction" rather than "identity." And the statement about identity of content is not a statement of fact; Schleiermacher is aware of diversity within both kinds of ethics and of differences between the two kinds. This statement is prescriptive or "eschatological": it represents how matters should be or how they will be when both disciplines are perfected. Seen within the context of this movement of thought, it is clear that Schleiermacher does not affirm a simple identity of content. His actual position is perhaps better represented in a statement from his lectures of 1824–25:

> It is essential that each [form of ethics] recognize the other. Then it will be impossible that what one considers moral, the other will consider sinful. And the two forms will necessarily be congruent insofar as in both the reality and essence of that which is really essential in the one will be coestablished in the other, in spite of the fact that the one cannot reproduce the content of the other as each proceeds from a different principle.[21]

Schleiermacher seeks a relation of noncontradiction between Christian and philosophical ethics; he wants each discipline to recognize and respect the integrity and independence of the other. He certainly does not want to collapse the two disciplines into one; they remain distinct, but compatible. This is in line with Schleiermacher's characterization of the relation between faith and science as an "eternal covenant." Above all, he affirms a nonaggression pact between faith and science that includes mutual recognition and respect.[22]

FORM, METHOD, AND STRUCTURE IN PHILOSOPHICAL ETHICS AND CHRISTIAN ETHICS

As regards content, Christian ethics and philosophical ethics are to be noncontradictory. As regards form, they are "completely different." Schleiermacher's insistence that Christian ethics has a distinctive form has two different, but related, levels of meaning. Its primary meaning relates to Schleiermacher's descriptive approach. He directed his discourse to the students who heard his lectures and began with the general understanding of ethics he could presume they had. He did not presume that they were aware of his own work in philosophical ethics.[23] The most important options in Christian ethics of which the students were aware adopted an imperative approach, modeling themselves after philosophical ethics of duty or virtue. Against such approaches Schleiermacher insists on his own descriptive method. At a second level, one only hinted at in the "General

Introduction," the assertion of a distinctive form refers to the difference that obtains between Schleiermacher's own Christian ethics and his philosophical ethics. In this case both philosophical ethics and Christian ethics are descriptive, and the difference resides in philosophy's abstract and universal sweep as opposed to Christian ethics' particular and concrete focus.

Schleiermacher makes explicit the contrast between his own approach and that of other Christian ethicists. In his view, Christian thinkers have succumbed to that which is philosophically fashionable, losing sight of the characteristically Christian. As Christian ethics has followed after developments in philosophical ethics, it has become entangled in the latter's intramural battles, and its energy has been sapped. Schleiermacher claims that the result for Christian ethics has been "that the distinctive character of Christianity has become less and less apparent and that for the most part there remains nothing but philosophy clothed in Christian speech."[24] The image of the eternal covenant can be pictured as neighboring countries living by the terms of a nonaggression pact. The Christian citizen and the philosophical citizen are to live with mutual respect, but each is to maintain his or her own identity. In the case of dual citizenship, one needs to be cognizant of which land one is inhabiting at the time and operate according to its principles. But Christian ethicists appear to have given their allegiance over to philosophy and its issues. They have studied abroad so long that upon their return home, their ethics are no longer recognizably Christian. In Schleiermacher's view, they have violated the terms of the covenant and imported philosophy where it does not belong.

Schleiermacher's historical appeal in this regard begins with those who modeled their Christian ethics after the philosophical approaches of Wolff and Leibniz. He notes that after these philosophies were displaced by "popular philosophy, a mixture of rationalism and empiricism," Christian ethics was thereby reconceived with a focus on "happiness" replacing that on "perfection." More recently, Kant's "Categorical Imperative" was appropriated for theological purposes, and since then philosophical systems of duty, virtue, and the good have all been taken as models for Christian ethics.[25] Schleiermacher admits that one could argue that such transformations of Christian ethics do not affect its content—the latter remaining constant as it is expressed in different forms. But he insists that there are no grounds internal to Christianity that support the adoption of ever-changing philosophical forms. Indeed, in Schleiermacher's view, the result of chasing after philosophical form has been that the distinctively Christian element has been obscured.[26]

Schleiermacher's proposal, then, is that Christian ethics be developed in its own distinctive form, at the same time retaining the scientific strictness characteristic of philosophy. He insists that it is one thing to find in philosophy the principles of scientific discourse and quite another to appropriate from philosophical ethics the form in which Christian ethics is cast. It is at this point that Schleiermacher turns to Christian piety and the different conditions in which piety can find itself vis-à-vis impulse and action. And from these different conditions, Schleiermacher derives the form, the organizational plan for the *Christian Ethics*. It describes the actions that result from the different states in which Christian piety finds itself: religious pain gives rise to purifying action, religious pleasure or joy to broadening action, and between religious pleasure and pain a condition of relative contentment that gives rise to representational action. In this way Schleiermacher seeks to derive the form of Christian ethics from that which is distinctively Christian—the different states of Christian religious affection as these provide impulse to action. He is insistent that Christian ethics retain its independence from philosophical ethics, and he seeks to accomplish this by deriving its organizational plan from the different conditions in which piety can find itself. He describes Christian piety as it is an impulse to action. Without doubt, even while insisting on the eternal covenant's nonaggression pact, the accent is on the distinctiveness of Christian ethics.

What then of the in-fact relation between Schleiermacher's *Christian Ethics* and his *Philosophical Ethics*?[27] As Birkner has demonstrated, the key to understanding this relationship is to see where each belongs in Schleiermacher's system of all knowledge;[28] his architectonic of knowledge provides an overview of all forms of human knowledge. The different forms of knowledge are divided and subdivided, and a "family tree" is set forth showing the different branches of knowledge and where they are in relation to each other. Schleiermacher's architectonic of knowledge is set forth in his *Dialektik*,[29] and it indicates the place the two forms of ethics have in the system and thereby where they stand in relation to each other.

SCHLEIERMACHER'S ARCHITECTONIC OF KNOWLEDGE

Schleiermacher intended and accomplished a comprehensive view of all human knowledge; the goal of producing a comprehensive system of knowledge he shares with Hegel and other philosophical idealists of the day. Schleiermacher's *Dialektik* sets forth the "highest knowledge" in the sense that it brings (previously existing) knowledge to self-consciousness or transparency. For Schleiermacher, *Dialektik* has a purely formal character; it reflects on knowledge as it already exists and identifies the tasks, presuppositions, limits, and structures with which and by which it operates. These characteristics are present in the operations of knowledge: *Dialektik* makes them explicit; it brings knowledge to self-awareness.[30] Here a marked contrast with Hegel is evident. Whereas Hegel's philosophy produces the actual content of knowledge—it can describe the movement of spirit, even Absolute Spirit in history—Schleiermacher restricts philosophy to identification of the formal characteristics of knowledge.

When knowledge comes to self-awareness it becomes conscious of the different kinds of knowledge and ways of knowing that exist. *Dialektik* presents the formal theory of knowledge and identifies the two "real" sciences—Physics and Ethics. These are the two most basic realms of knowledge, and they are "real," that is, not purely formal; they deal with specified material. Physics is the science of nature and Ethics the science of reason or history (reason in history). This division of the real sciences into Physics and Ethics corresponds to the most basic opposition that is presupposed by knowledge itself—that between subject and object, between thought and being, between reason and nature. To deny this most basic opposition would be to deny knowledge itself. In addition to these two realms of knowledge, Schleiermacher sets forth two different ways of knowing. These ways of knowing he identifies as speculative and empirical. Speculative knowledge seeks to determine the essence of things, and in so doing it deals with concepts; it seeks to develop the categories necessary to a particular realm of knowledge. Empirical knowledge concerns itself with things in their existence and deals with judgments. It analyzes that which is empirically given.[31]

By crossing the Ethics/Physics distinction with the speculative/empirical distinction, Schleiermacher comes up with four basic forms of science: speculative ethics and the empirical science of history (*Geschichtskunde*), on the one hand, and speculative physics and the empirical science of nature (*Naturkunde*), on the other. This fourfold scheme represents the possibilities and limits of knowledge—the realms of knowledge and the ways of knowing. For Schleiermacher, these distinctions are completely relative; he does not advocate a separation into totally independent disciplines. Rather, each is conditioned by and dependent on the others. Each would include at least a minimum of the others within itself, and the ideal of worldly wisdom comprises a totality, a comprehensive unity of all knowledge, ethical and physical, speculative and empirical.[32]

In his *Philosophical Ethics,* Schleiermacher postulates two additional kinds of disciplines belonging to the ethical realm that combine the empirical and the speculative. These two "mixed sciences" (mixed because they combine empirical and speculative elements) are the critical disciplines and the practical disciplines. (Note the lines on the diagram of Schleiermacher's Architectonic of Knowledge. They indicate that the critical and technical disciplines are "mixed" as they combine speculative and empirical versions of ethics.) The critical disciplines such as philosophy of religion, aesthetics, grammar, and political philosophy provide a moral critique of history. This can be accomplished neither by a purely speculative, nor by a purely empirical approach. Rather, in order to assess the significance of a particular historical entity, the speculatively generated concepts must be brought to bear on empirical history. Then it is possible to assess the essence and significance of a particular historical entity by critical comparison with others and thereby to ascertain its meaning within the whole of human history. The technical disciplines such as pedagogy, hermeneutics, politics, and practical theology also combine speculative and empirical elements. That which gives a technical discipline its unity is the particular task toward which it is oriented. Technical disciplines are more art than science; they consider a particular area of human historical life and give instructions as to how its tasks are best carried out in the present.[33] In the theological realm, these critical and technical disciplines play a particularly important role in Schleiermacher's architectonic of all theological knowledge, set forth in his *Brief Outline*.[34]

At this point we can specify the relation of Schleiermacher's *Philosophical Ethics* and his *Christian Ethics* in an initial way. Both are forms of Ethics in the distinctive meaning that Schleiermacher applies to that term. That

	Schleiermacher's Architectonic of Knowledge[35]			
Formal Theory Of Science	Dialectic			
The Sciences	Physics Science of Nature		Ethics Science of Reason/History	
Kinds of Knowledge	Speculative Physics	Empirical Physics	Speculative Ethics (e.g., Philosophical Ethics)	Empirical Ethics (e.g., Christian Dogmatics & Ethics) Historical Theology
Mixed Sciences			Critical (knowledge) Philosophical Theology	Technical (action) Practical Theology

is, they deal not with nature (the realm of Physics), but with reason—with human reason in history. But although both forms of ethics belong to the realm of *Ethics*, they differ in that *Philosophical Ethics* is speculative and *Christian Ethics* is empirical. The former sets forth concepts by which the manifestation of reason in human-historical life can be understood; the latter analyzes one particular historical manifestation of reason. Thus we can see that they differ as to fundamental orientation and mode of knowing; we have here the contrast between speculative and empirical approaches to human historical life.

THE *PHILOSOPHICAL ETHICS:* SPECULATIVE PHILOSOPHY OF CULTURE

In order to define more precisely the in-fact relation between Schleiermacher's own *Philosophical Ethics* and his *Christian Ethics*, we must now characterize the former work briefly. It represents the speculative side of ethics, and as such it presents another architectonic—one that sets forth the basic structures, laws, and forms of human historical life. The *Philosophical Ethics* surveys human historical life and presents a philosophy of history, a philosophy of culture; it abstracts from historical and cultural life the general structures and categories operative therein. Schleiermacher offers a formula for the relation between speculative and empirical forms of ethical knowledge; he calls empirical ethics the "picture book" for speculative ethics, and speculative ethics the "rule book" for empirical ethics.[36] Of course, by "rules" here Schleiermacher does not mean "moral rules" that one is obliged to follow, but "scientific rules," the categories that enable understanding.

As a philosophy of history (or of culture), what Schleiermacher offers is not a longitudinal view of history that might presume to indicate where history is headed; rather, he offers a cross section of history.[37] He does view history as the progressive rule and appropriation of nature by reason: history is an ethical process, the process of the unification of reason and nature effected by human beings. The task of ethics is neither to produce the moral process by imperatives or exhortations, nor to generate a view of history's course and outcome based on an a priori approach; rather, in Schleiermacher's view, ethics presupposes that the moral process of human history is already underway and seeks to understand it. Ethics contributes to the moral process in an indirect way. It neither creates the moral process, nor commands persons to moral action; but by providing an understanding of history's structures and dynamics, it does evoke further and informed participation in that process. In this way, speculative ethics helps one discern what constitutes moral action and encourages the same.

The genius and distinctiveness of Schleiermacher's *Philosophical Ethics* is its attempt to provide a comprehensive analysis of the moral life. He recognizes that, to be complete, ethics must attend to all kinds of human activity and consider all the different viewpoints from which the moral process can be observed. This comprehensive vision of ethics grows out of Schleiermacher's 1803 work, *Grundlinien einer Kritik der bisherigen Sittenlehre (Reference Points for a Critique of Previous Ethics)* and especially his critiques of Kant and Fichte.[38] The *Grundlinien* distinguishes three forms of ethics: ethics of duty, ethics of virtue, and ethics of the highest good, and argues that a comprehensive view of ethics must include all three in an integrated fashion. An ethics of virtue focuses on the human agent and those habits or qualities of a person constitutive of moral goodness. An ethics of duty attends to moral actions and the motives that drive morally good actions. And an ethics of the highest good concentrates on the telos, the goal that moral actions seeks to accomplish. A comprehensive ethics must include and integrate all three elements; only as all three aspects are considered does one have the whole of the moral process.

In Schleiermacher's view, "Nothing which truly concerns human activity lies outside the realm of ethics."[39] Ethical systems that focus exclusively on virtue or duty result in serious omissions because they attend only to that in the individual which is identical in all persons; thus they fail to consider either the social structures and tasks inherently part of the human moral process or the individuality of persons, the ways in which the moral task is unique for each individual. The *Philosophical Ethics* provides a comprehensive vision of human moral life that overcomes the deficiencies of ethics of duty or virtue. Such a comprehensive vision is achieved particularly under the rubric of the highest good; here Schleiermacher considers important social aspects of ethical and cultural life, such as love and friendship, knowledge, art, religion, and legal and economic life. All these must be included in a comprehensive ethics.

The *Philosophical Ethics* is divided into three main sections dealing with ethics of duty, virtue, and the highest good. They are treated separately, but not equally. It is evident that Schleiermacher's main interest is in an ethics of the highest good. The lectures that comprise Braun's edition of the *Philosophical Ethics* include one series of lectures on virtue (1804/05), one series on duty (1814/16), one series on duty and virtue together (1812/13), one general introduction (1816), and three series presenting a general introduction and the highest good (1812/13, 1814/16, and 1816).[40] As these lectures are merged into one continuous analysis in Kirchmann's edition, over three hundred pages are devoted to the highest good, and less than one hundred pages each to ethics of virtue and of duty.[41] This being the case, Schleiermacher's theory of the good "provides a fair sense of his ethical theory as a whole,"[42] and we will gain insight into his philosophical ethics sufficient for our purposes by concentrating our sketch of the *Philosophical Ethics* on the ethics of the highest good.

Under the rubric of the highest good, Schleiermacher aims to fill in the gaps left open by ethics of duty and virtue. The task of an ethics of the good is to describe the products of the moral process, "everything which is and should be produced by human reason working upon earthly nature, as a totality."[43] Schleiermacher structures his analysis of the good, the products of the moral process, by considering how it is that human reason works on earthly nature. He makes two basic distinctions and, crossing these with each other, comes up with a fourfold scheme. First, he distinguishes between "organizing" and "symbolizing" activities of reason. Reason organizes nature when it forms nature into an organ through which reason can express itself, when it appropriates nature and employs it in service of its own purposes. Reason also has a symbolizing function; it appropriates nature for purposes of communication, creating systems of signs and symbols whereby reason itself can be represented. By means of these processes, nature becomes both the organ and the symbol of reason. To this first distinction between reason's organizing and symbolizing functions is added another: that between the identical and the individual, between sameness and difference. In Schleiermacher's view, human reason is defined by the polar opposition between identity and individuality. Particular aspects of reason can be either identical in all persons or stamped in each person with his or her own unique individuality. As a concrete expression of this, Schleiermacher asserts that some acts of reason must be the same for all individuals, whereas other acts of reason are stamped by an individual's uniqueness. For example, a process of mathematical computation—to be genuinely reasonable—must be the same for all persons, but an act of social relationship—equally an act of reason—partakes of the individuality of the persons involved. By crossing these two sets of opposites, Schleiermacher comes up with four distinct categories. Actions of human reason are of four kinds: the identical organizing, the individual organizing, the identical symbolizing, and the individual symbolizing. These four categories provide the structure for Schleiermacher's analysis of the good in the human moral process.

Corresponding to the actions of reason manifest in each of these four ways are what Schleiermacher considers to be the four great forms of human community. The identical organizing form represents the economic and political spheres of life; corresponding to it is the state. The individual organizing form concerns social relations and hospitality; corresponding to it is what Schleiermacher calls "free sociality" (*freie Geselligkeit*). The identical symbolizing form is the realm of knowledge; this finds expression in the school system and the academy. The individual symbolizing form concerns art and religion; its social form is the church.

An important qualification and further specification of these four kinds of moral action and the four corresponding social structures need attention. The qualification is that these four areas are distinguished in thought by Schleiermacher, but are not completely separated in reality. The distinctions among the four areas are only relative and are made for purposes of analysis. Actual human life and action, and actual social forms almost always comprise some combination of two or more of these forms of moral product.[44] This insight is further evidenced in Schleiermacher's view of the most basic human community and his philosophical understanding of the highest good. For him the family is the most basic form of human community, and it includes within itself all four kinds of activity; it represents in an original way state and "free sociality," school and church. From a philosophical point of view, the highest good is conceived as the perfection and interpenetration of all four areas and communities in and for all persons. Thus the four areas belong together, both originally (in the family) and ultimately (in the perfection of the highest good). Again Schleiermacher intends a comprehensive ethical vision, one that includes all aspects of the good in human life as a unity and totality, perfected and encompassing all persons.

Schleiermacher leaves open the possibility for a Christian ethics that can attain a comprehensiveness equivalent to that of philosophical ethics. Within his philosophical framework Schleiermacher carves out a niche in which a distinctively Christian understanding of the highest good in its totality can be established. In this way, Christian ethics need not be limited to one of four basic kinds of moral action and good; rather, it has the possibility of including in its conception of the highest good all that the philosophical conception includes. The possibility for such a Christian view is left open by the relativity of the distinctions between the four areas, the inseparability of the four such that each contains within itself the others to some degree. For Schleiermacher, this means that the highest good in its totality can be represented under any one of the four viewpoints. The essay "On the Concept of the Highest Good" affirms this most explicitly:

> According to whether we adopt one standpoint or another, the highest good appears sometimes as the golden age in the untroubled and completely satisfying communication among individuals, sometimes as eternal peace in the justly distributed rule of peoples over the earth, or as the totality and perfection of knowledge in the community of languages, or as the kingdom of heaven in the free community of piety; each of these includes the others within its individuality and represents the whole.[45]

From the Christian point of view, the highest good is actualized by Jesus in his perfect communion with God. The highest good is then also identified with the church as the community in which Christian religious consciousness—the continuation of Jesus' communion with God—is manifest. Most especially, the highest good is represented by the kingdom of God—the consummation of the church, the universal reign of God in Christ, the final and complete perfection of all humanity. The *Christian Ethics* describes the action of the church, the life of the church; and as we will see, it includes within itself a Christian appropriation and transformation of the other kinds of moral action. At this point we want to note that already within Schleiermacher's philosophical vision space is created for the representation of the highest good in its totality under one of the four basic areas; similarly, the *Philosophical Ethics* leaves open the possibility of a universal savior and thus a universal religion—again creating space for Christianity and its universal claims.

Because the *Philosophical Ethics* allows not only that the religious community, with its own vision of the good, is one of the four basic forms of human community, but also that it is capable of representing the highest good in its totality, it leaves open the possibility of a distinctively Christian ethical vision that is comprehensive in scope. This possibility is then actualized in Schleiermacher's *Christian Ethics*. In what follows we will seek to demonstrate that the *Christian Ethics* sets forth a concrete vision of the highest good that is an appropriation and transformation of the four kinds of moral activity as they are philosophically conceived. We will show how the in-fact relation between Schleiermacher's *Philosophical Ethics* and *Christian Ethics* constitutes a transformation of the former by the latter.

CHRISTIAN ETHICS ON ITS OWN TERMS

The identification of the church in the *Philosophical Ethics* as representative of the individual-symbolizing form of moral action raises the expectation that Christian ethics will focus on this form of action. Is this the case? How then does the structure of the *Christian Ethics* compare with the structure employed in the analysis of the highest good in the *Philosophical Ethics*? The structural connection between Schleiermacher's two works in ethics is not immediately evident because Schleiermacher uses different terminology in the two works. Although the language differs from one work to the other, the basic conceptuality is consistent. The *Christian Ethics'* distinction between representational (*darstellende*) activity and effectual (*wirksame*) activity corresponds to the *Philosophical Ethics'* distinction between symbolizing (*symbolisierende* or *bezeichende*) activity and organizing (*organisierende* or *bildende*) activity.[46] Organizing activity seeks to effect a change in the world, whereas symbolizing or representational activity expresses the reality of reason/spirit present in the world. So the *Philosophical Ethics'* concept of the church as community of symbolization does find resonance in the *Christian Ethics* because representational activity is the most distinctive mark of the Christian church in the latter work. In Schleiermacher's view, it is above all representational activity that maintains the church's existence through time. Representational activity sets forth the Christian spirit; it makes the Spirit come alive in the communicative interchange of believers; it nurtures and strengthens piety. Representational activity manifests the inward reality in an outward way so that it can be fixed in one's own consciousness and communicated to others. Representational activity keeps Christian piety alive. Birkner highlights very nicely Schleiermacher's view of such representation as the *sine qua non* of the church:

> The theory of the church developed in the *Christian Ethics* has its primary locus in the theory of representational activity. "Representational activity is the actual basis of religious community" (*Ethics, Beilagen*, p. 147). In representational action, which includes preaching, the inner determination of Christianly pious self-consciousness is fixed outwardly so that it can be recognized and appropriated by others. Representational action both continually re-creates the Christian community and always presupposes its existence. "The community, on the one hand, and representational activity, on the other, [are] both equally original" (*Ethics*, p. 510).[47]

Stated in more usual language, representational action is Christian worship (*Gottesdienst*). Schleiermacher does not restrict worship to the formal cultic activity of the Christian community. He insists that both worship "in the narrow sense" (*im engeren Sinn*) and worship "in the broad sense" (*im weiteren Sinn*) are equally original and cannot be separated.[48] Christian worship—the acts by which believers represent themselves as organs of the Spirit—exists both as organized cultic activity and in the everyday life of believers. This manifestation and communication recreates the church and is the most distinctive mark of its presence. Insofar then as the *Christian Ethics* understands the church above all as a community of representational activity, we have a clear correspondence with the philosophical conception of church as a community of "individual symbolization." The church, conceived both generically and in its Christian particularity, is a community of symbolization; the focus of its life is in making manifest its inward spirit, recreating itself as a community of piety as that piety becomes real in the mutual give and take of communication.

But at the same time, the Christian church is much more than this; the Christian community cannot be reduced to its representational activity. The life of the church includes also purifying and broadening activities, effectual activities that seek to bring about a restoration or expansion of the sway of the Christian spirit. In terms of the categories operative in the *Philosophical Ethics*, we have here as essential parts of the church's life that which corresponds to organizing activity. In one sense, this is unexpected; the philosophical work identifies the church with individual symbolizing activity. But in another sense it is not surprising; Schleiermacher always insists on the relativity of the distinctions made among the various kinds of action; they can be distinguished in thought, but are never separated in fact.[49]

The inclusion of the restoring action is distinctive to the *Christian Ethics*. It finds no parallel in the *Philosophical Ethics* because restoring action is based on the tension between sin and grace and is distinctively Christian. The *Christian Ethics* adopts some of the structures set forth in the *Philosophical Ethics*, but the former does not conform strictly to the expectations we would have of it, based on what the latter work says about religious community. The *Christian Ethics* appropriates the structures of the *Philosophical Ethics*, but puts them to its own use, restructuring the ethical task from its own distinctively Christian point of view, rearranging the structures of the *Philosophical Ethics* to serve its own purposes.

The *Christian Ethics'* claim to a comprehensive ethical vision can be made because it includes not only forms of action that are distinctively and properly Christian, but also a consideration of how Christians are to relate to the outer sphere, the world outside the church. The analysis of the inner sphere offers an ecclesial ethics of piety; the consideration of the outer sphere qualifies as a theology of culture. Schleiermacher employs the three forms of action (restoring, broadening, and representational) derived from Christian piety to structure his reflection on Christian participation in the outer sphere. He examines the actions in the outer sphere that are the civil analogues to the three kinds of action grounded in piety.

The result of this organizational scheme is that the outer sphere is not viewed in a truly systematic way; its organic character and its interconnections are not brought to light. This is most evident in the fact that the state is analyzed both in relation to purifying and broadening action. Under purifying action in the outer sphere Schleiermacher considers such diverse issues as criminal justice, social movements that seek to change the state (including whether there is moral justification for violent revolution), and questions of war between states; all this is comprehended under the larger rubric of the state. Under broadening action in the outer sphere, Schleiermacher offers a general consideration of the state's call to oversee the moral process by which the rule of spirit over nature is furthered through economic, educational, and scientific advance. Whereas science and education—the "identical symbolizing realm"—had occupied their own sphere in the *Philosophical Ethics*, here they are treated very briefly together with the state under the rubric of broadening action. Under representational action in the outer sphere, Schleiermacher analyzes artistic expression—both plastic arts and performing arts broadly considered (*Kunst und Spiel*)—and social relations ("free sociality"). Again here the configuration of the *Philosophical Ethics* has been rearranged. There art was considered together with religion under individual-symbolizing rubric, whereas free sociality occupied its own, individual-organizing, sphere.

The way Schleiermacher organizes his analysis of the outer sphere in the *Christian Ethics* is far from problem-free. The interconnected organic character of state and society is obscured by the way that its elements are divided up among the three kinds of action. The reader coming to this material from the *Philosophical Ethics* can be confused because of the significant differences in the conceptual structures of the two works. The point is that these difficulties arise because the organizational principle for the analysis of the outer sphere derives from his view of Christian piety. The difficulties cannot be gainsaid, but neither can Schleiermacher's commitment to a structure that is grounded in distinctively Christian religious self-consciousness. The *Christian Ethics* even alters the structures developed in the *Philosophical Ethics* to suit its own purposes.

In sum, then, the *Christian Ethics* transforms the scope and structure of what would be expected of a religious ethics, based on the perspective of the *Philosophical Ethics*. Schleiermacher does not restrict the moral activity of the Christian community to "individual symbolizing" activity, but includes also that which corresponds to "individual" and "identical" forms of "organizing" activity and "identical symbolizing" activity. In addition, he adds to the Christian analysis "restoring activity," which has no parallel in the *Philosophical Ethics*. In this sense, there is a significant correspondence between the two structures, even as the *Christian Ethics'* structure is noticeably different. The viewpoint of the *Christian Ethics* is defined by its stance within the Christian community, and the structures that organize its perception of the ethical world are distinctive, deriving from Christian piety itself and amounting to a transformation—a change in form—of the structure anticipated on the basis of the *Philosophical Ethics*.[50]

Schleiermacher's view of the in-principle relation between Christian ethics and philosophical ethics is not one of "unity," but has the character of a nonaggression pact that allows neither contradiction nor simple identity. We have also seen that the *Christian Ethics* amounts to an appropriation and transformation of the structures identified in the *Philosophical Ethics*. In addition, we have shown that the former work transcends the bounds set for it in the latter work and actually achieves a comprehensive ethical vision from its own distinctive viewpoint. Above all, Schleiermacher's *Christian Ethics* sets forth a distinctively Christian ethics, one defined by Christian piety.

Recalling the comparison between Schleiermacher and Hegel that began the chapter, we can now see, not surprisingly, that Schleiermacher the theologian gives theology a privileged place in his system. Hegel, on the other hand, gives speculative insight prominence; conceptual formulation has a kind of superiority over representation. Schleiermacher assigns philosophy a formal role in his system; it generates the concepts and categories by which thought proceeds and attains to scientific character. But where the categories are inadequate or unnecessarily limiting, they are expanded. It is the *Christian Ethics* that provides material specification of Schleiermacher's position on actual ethical issues, moving beyond merely formal considerations. Engaging material issues in this way, the *Christian Ethics* is closer to life and of more value in guiding ethical deliberation than is philosophical ethics. The *Christian Ethics*, then, may be said to culminate Schleiermacher's ethical system because it contributes more directly to the practical goal of serving an actual community, the Christian church. At the very least, the claim that the *Christian Ethics* culminates the ethical system corresponds to Schleiermacher's social location as pastor and theologian concerned that his theology—dogmatics and ethics—provide leadership for the Christian church. Once again, his life and thought mirror each other in important ways.

NOTES

1. Hajo Holborn, *A History of Modern Germany*, 3 vols. (New York: Alfred Knopf, 1959–69), vol. 2 (1648–1840), 306.
2. Richard Crouter, "Hegel and Schleiermacher at Berlin: A Many-Sided Debate," *Journal of the American Academy of Religion* 48, no. 1 (March 1980): 29–30.
3. Ibid., 19–44.
4. Ibid., 34–35.
5. Ibid., 36.
6. A translation of Hegel's Foreword is included in *G. W. F. Hegel: Theologian of the Spirit*, ed. Peter C. Hodgson (Minneapolis: Augsburg Fortress Press, 1997). See also Eric von der Luft, *Hegel, Hinrichs, and Schleiermacher on Feeling and Reason in Religion: The Texts of Their 1821–22 Debate* (Lewiston and Queenstown: Edwin Mellen Press, 1987); this work includes translations of the relevant texts by all three figures.
7. Hegel interpreter Peter Hodgson notes that Hegel's view of Schleiermacher on this point is a "caricature." Hegel does not seem to grasp Schleiermacher's view of religious feeling as immediate and prereflective awareness of absolute dependence. Hodgson also says: "However, Schleiermacher did not express himself as clearly in the first edition of *The Christian Faith* (1821–22) to which alone Hegel had access, as in the second (1830) where for the first time he introduced the adjective *schlechthinnig* [utter or absolute]." See *G. W. F. Hegel*, 278, n. 6.
8. Crouter, 37.
9. Editor's introduction in *G. W. F. Hegel*, 21.
10. Claude Welch, *Protestant Thought in the Nineteenth Century*, vol. 1, 1799–1870 (New Haven and London: Yale University Press, 1972), 105.
11. How this "subordination" of representation to concept is to be interpreted has been an ongoing debate among Hegel scholars at least since the time of his death in 1831. The issue is framed by Eric von der Luft in terms of the fate of

religious representation after it has been sublated ("*aufgehoben*") in Hegel's final philosophical synthesis. Von der Luft indicates three ways in which the final relation between religious representation and philosophical conception can be seen. He says that religious representation could be (1) replaced by philosophical concept or (2) transformed into concept or (3) included as an indispensable element within concept. Bernard Reardon is identified as a proponent of the first option, Feuerbach and many others of the second, and Quentin Laurer, S.J., of the third. The third option is also the one affirmed by von der Luft. Cf. *Hegel, Hinrichs, and Schleiermacher on Feeling and Reason in Religion*, 157–66.

12. Friedrich Schleirermacher, *The Christian Faith*, trans. H. R. MacKintosh and J. S. Stewart (Edinburgh: T. & T. Clark, 1928), 385.

13. Friedrich Schleiermacher, *Die christliche Sitte nach den Grundsätzen der evangelischen Kirche im Zusammenhange dargestellt*, ed. Ludwig Jonas in *Sämmtliche Werke*, div. 1, vol. 12 (Berlin: G. Reimer, 1843). Hereafter referred to as the *Christian Ethics*.

14. Poul Jorgensen, *Die Ethik Schleiermachers: Forschungen zur Geschichte und Lehre des Protestantismus*, ed. Ernst Wolf (Munich: Kaiser Verlag, 1959), 184.

15. James Duke, "The Christian and the Ethical in Schleiermacher's Christian Ethics," *Encounter* 46, no. 1 (Winter, 1985): 62.

16. Hans-Joachim Birkner, *Schleiermachers Christliche Sittenlehre im Zusammenhang Seines Philosophisch-Theologishen Systems*, Theologische Bibliothek Töpelmann, eds. Aland et al. (Berlin: Alfred Töpelmann, 1964), 19–20.

17. Ibid., 20.
18. *Christian Ethics*, 26–27.
19. Ibid., 27.
20. Ibid., 28.
21. Ibid., 77.

22. See Friedrich Schleiermacher, *Schleiermachers Sendschreiben über seine Glaubenslehre an Lücke*, Studien zur Geschichte des neueren Protestantismus, Quellenheft 2, ed. Hermann Mulert (Giessen: Alfred Töpelmann, 1908), 40, for the notion of the "eternal covenant." See Gerhard Spiegler agrees that the goal of the eternal covenant is "coordination, harmony, not identity." Gerhard Spiegler, *The Eternal Covenant: Schleiermacher's Experiment in Cultural Theology* (New York, Evanston, and London: Harper & Row, 1967), 24.

23. Birkner, 20.
24. Ibid., 30.

25. Schleiermacher seems to find the approach of Kant's *Critique of Practical Reason* particularly inappropriate from a Christian standpoint. See Immanuel Kant, *Critique of Practical Reason*, trans. Lewis White Beck (Indianapolis: Bobbs-Merrill Educational Publishing, 1956), esp. 128–36. Schleiermacher is willing to set aside the issue of whether it is philosophically defensible to exclude God-consciousness from a reflective system, but he insists, "religious *Ethics* always presupposes religious self-consciousness under the form of impulse." Religious ethics begins with piety and from it develops moral insight. Thus the Kantian reversal of this, which proceeds from moral awareness to the postulation of God, is wholly unsuited to Christian purposes. *Christian Ethics*, 28.

26. *Christian Ethics*, 29–30.

27. The standard edition is Otto Braun and Johannes Bauer, eds., *Friedrich Ernst Daniel Schleiermacher Werke: Auswahl in vier Bänden*, 2d ed. (Leipzig: Feliz Miner,

1927–28), vol. 2, *Entwürfe zu einem System der Sittenlehre*. Hereafter referred to as *Philosophical Ethics*.

28. The title of Birkner's work, *Schleiermachers Christliche Sittenlehre im Zusammenhang seiner Philosophisch-Theologischen Systems*, indicates its concern to place the Christian ethics in the context of the overall system. Without question, Birkner's work is the single most important interpretation of Schleiermacher's *Christian Ethics* to date. Our analysis of Schleiermacher's overall system and the place of the *Christian Ethics* within it is indebted to Birkner at many points.

29. Friedrich Schleiermacher, *Friedrich Schleiermachers Dialektik*, ed. Rudolf Odebrecht (Leipzig: J. C. Hinrichs Verlag, 1942). Schleiermacher's *Dialektik* exists in three different versions. In addition to the one edited by Odebrecht, there are two earlier versions. The first was edited by Ludwig Jonas and published as part of the *Sämmtliche Werke*, div. 3, vol. 4, and the second was edited by Isidor Halpern (Berlin: Mayer and Mueller, 1903). At his death, Schleiermacher left behind lecture notes for his courses on *Dialektik* from the years 1811, 1814, 1818, 1822, 1828, and 1831. In addition, Jonas had available student notebooks. Jonas based his edition on the outline from the 1814 notes, with insertions from other years and from student notes. Halpern draws instead on the form from 1831 and fills it out with materials from other years. Odebrecht uses the version from 1822 as his basis and fills it out with student materials from the same year. Although there are dangers inherent in Odebrecht's mixing of primary and secondary sources in creating his edition, his version does provide the most integrated and whole version of the *Dialektik* and therefore is a good general orientation to Schleiermacher's system. Our references are to the Odebrecht edition. An English translation of the notes to Schleiermacher's 1811 lectures is Friedrich Schleiermacher, *Dialectic, or The Art of Doing Philosophy*, trans. Terrence N. Tice (Atlanta: Scholars Press, 1996). A significant study of Schleiermacher's *Dialektik* is Thandeka, *The Embodied Self: Friedrich Schleiermacher's Solution to Kant's Problem of the Empirical Self* (Albany: State University of New York Press, 1995).

30. Introduction to the *Dialektik*, esp. 12–28 and 42–44; and Birkner, 31–33.

31. *Dialektik*, 174–83, 187–208; *Philosophical Ethics*, 531–40; Birkner, 33. See also Walter E. Wyman, Jr., *The Concept of Glaubenslehre: Ernst Troeltsch and the Theological Heritage of Schleiermacher* (Chico, Calif.: Scholars Press, 1983), esp. 181–14.

32. *Philosophical Ethics*, 536–37, and Birkner, 33–34.

33. *Philosophical Ethics*, 252, 365–67, 549–56; and Birkner, 34–36.

34. Friedrich Schleiermacher, *Brief Outline on the Study of Theology*, trans. Terrence N. Tice (Richmond: John Knox Press, 1970), esp. 25–27. Here Schleiermacher presents his understanding of theology comprising historical theology (an empirical ethical discipline), philosophical theology (a critical discipline), and practical theology (a technical discipline). Historical theology (including *The Christian Faith* and *Christian Ethics* as well as biblical theology and church history) is at the center of theology; it is "the foundation of practical theology . . . [and] the verification of philosophical theology." *Brief Outline*, 26.

35. This chart is a slightly modified version of one produced by B. A. Gerrish, "Theology and the Organization of Science," distributed in a graduate seminar in the University of Chicago Divinity School, Spring 1982.

36. *Philosophical Ethics*, 549.

37. Birkner, 38

38. Ibid., 37–38.

39. Friedrich Schleiermacher, *Grundlinien einer Kritik der bisherigan Sittenlehre*, in *Sämmtliche Werke* 1, 3: 261 (Berlin: G. Reimer, 1846).
40. *Philosophical Ethics*, xvi–xvii.
41. Friedrich Schleiermacher, F. *Schleiermachers philosophische Sittenlehre*, ed. and intro. J. H. v. Kirchmann, Philosophische Bibliothek 85 (Berlin: Heimann, 1870).
42. Duke, 54.
43. Birkner, 39.
44. *Philosophical Ethics*, 567–68.
45. Friedrich Schleiermacher, "Über den Begriff des höchsten Gutes," in *Sämmtliche Werke*, div. 3, vol. 2, ed. Ludwig Jonas (Berlin: G. Reimer, 1843), 466.
46. Birkner, 109.
47. Ibid., 115–16.
48. *Christian Ethics*, 536.
49. *Philosophical Ethics*, 567. Cf. also *Christian Ethics, Beilagen*, 21.
50. That the differences between philosophical and Christian analyses of similar material can be characterized in terms of different viewpoints corresponds to Schleiermacher's own position as expressed, for example, in the *Brief Outline*, 29–30. Schleiermacher characterizes the viewpoint of philosophical theology as one "'above' Christianity, in the logical sense of the term, i.e., in the general concept of a religious community or fellowship of faith." Whereas philosophy looks from outside Christianity, viewing it in comparison with other religious communities, distinctly Christian theology looks out from within Christianity. Our notion that different categories then structure the comprehension of similar material in different ways is also consistent with this. Different viewpoints arise because of what is viewed and from where it is viewed. Thus we have the basic formal, structural difference between the two kinds of *Ethics*. James Duke offers a similar analysis of the relation between philosophical ethics and Christian ethics in Schleiermacher; he speaks of the structure of the former being modified by the latter. Cf., Duke, 64.

5
PASTOR SCHLEIERMACHER AND HIS ECCLESIAL ETHICS OF PIETY

"Being a preacher was for Schleiermacher at least as important as being a professor, for it was the basis for everything else. As a result of his educational experience he could have been nothing but a preacher, and it was precisely this that he wanted to be with his whole heart." This is the conclusion of Andreas Reich, who has contributed a massive study[1] of Schleiermacher's years (1808–34) as pastor and preacher at Berlin's Trinity Church (*Dreifaltigkeitskirche*). Before everything else, Schleiermacher was a pastor. His work and experience as a pastoral leader gave him, literally and figuratively, a place to stand, a pulpit from which to preach. And the focus of his work, as pastor of a particular congregation, as leader in the Berlin synod, and as theologian, was on building up the church as a community of faith.

Schleiermacher had already served in pastoral ministry for some twelve years when he came to Berlin from Halle in 1807. He had served as pastor in Landsberg, 1794–96; his first period in Berlin as chaplain at the Charité hospital, 1796–1802; an "exile" to Stolp on the Baltic Sea 1802–04; and then two years in Halle as preacher and professor. In the end, Schleiermacher served in pastoral ministry for forty years, and during that time he preached almost weekly and had leadership roles in all areas of church life. At Trinity Church, Schleiermacher preached and led worship, taught confirmation classes, dealt with a gamut of administrative issues involved in congregational life, offered pastoral care to the sick and bereaved, and officiated at countless baptisms, weddings, and funerals. "That he regularly preached in his congregation along with his academic, literary, and societal activities, is imaginable, but that he was so intensively active in congregational work is astonishing."[2]

Although he was only officially installed as pastor of Trinity Church in June of 1809 and was not paid a salary until then, Schleiermacher began his ministerial work already in spring 1808. His predecessor, Karl Friedrich Thiele had served at Trinity from 1787 until his death in May 1808. Thiele's widow was then supported for a "grace year" with his salary, so there was no money for Schleiermacher. Nonetheless, in light of the congregation's need, he began his work. At that time, Trinity Church was a *Simultankirche*, a home for both Lutheran and Reformed congregations. The much larger Lutheran congregation was part of the parish system with its boundaries, whereas the Reformed congregation served by Schleiermacher knew no boundaries; persons could affiliate with it by choice. Trinity Church's Lutheran parish was located in Friedrichstadt, one of the eleven "quarters" that comprised Berlin at the time. The parish covered the western third of Friedrichstadt, and it included within its boundaries a great diversity of socioeconomic situations. Wilhelmstrasse, where Schleiermacher came to live in 1817 in the house of his friend and publisher Georg Reimer, was home to government ministers and professionals. Other parts of Friedrichstrasse were home to many "working class" folk and, below them, the poor and destitute, suffering under difficult, overcrowded conditions.

In 1822, with the creation of the Church of the Prussian Union, the two congregations of Trinity Church merged to form one union congregation. This new situation had a profound effect on Schleiermacher's ministry. Before the merger he had been the pastor of a relatively small Reformed congregation; after 1822 he is copastor of a huge, 12,000-member parish. The change is clearly reflected in the dramatic increase in the number of occasional services (baptisms, funerals, and weddings) for which he officiates. The Reformed congregation had, on average, nine weddings and forty-four baptisms per year, and Schleiermacher did not officiate at all of these; in some years his pastoral assistant officiated at more than half. For the twelve years of his ministry after the Union, Schleiermacher averaged about 121 baptisms and thirty-five weddings per year.[3] Clearly, the Union had a profound practical effect on Schleiermacher's life and ministry.

Based on his careful study of the congregational records, Reich concludes that in his years as pastor of the Reformed congregation, Schleiermacher drew to that community many professionals and leaders in the state and military—both nobles and commoners—who were committed to Reformist politics. Many were nominally Lutheran, but associated with the Reformed congregation because of Schleiermacher. After the Union, as parish pastor Schleiermacher's responsibilities expanded in scope, and he functioned no longer as chaplain to a community drawn to his charisma and united in Reformist convictions, but as one of senior pastor in a huge, parish-based congregation.[4]

Trinity Church had been established by Friedrich Wilhelm I in 1737 and was under royal patronage, so Schleiermacher was called to his position by King Friedrich Wilhelm III, who was in 1808 exiled in Königsberg. The congregation had veto power over the king's choice of pastor, but the call came from the king himself. In the same year in which Schleiermacher received the call from the king, he wrote an essay on church government, not published during his lifetime, in which he called for the church's independence from the state, proposed a synodal-presbyterial gathering of clergy to provide oversight over congregations, and rejected the rights of patrons, like the king, over the church.[5] This tension, even contradiction between being called to his position by the king and rejecting the practice of ecclesial patronage, is representative of Schleiermacher's situation. He was at once a royal appointee (in his position as pastor and later as a member of the Ministry of Education and as university professor) and at the same time a critic of governmental policies. Schleiermacher's thinking about church government develops over the years; one constant, from the *Speeches* through his important 1817 essay on church government to the second edition of *The Christian Faith*, is his insistence that the church be independent of and separated from the state, with its own constitution.[6] In all this, Schleiermacher plays the role of loyal opposition; he voices vehement criticism of the state's control of the church in a time when that control is tightening, and he does so from his position as a minister in the church. In all this he is driven by his focus on the church as an independent community where piety is nurtured and cultivated.

Schleiermacher's personality, the particular gifts he brought to ministry, were not incidental to his pastoral work. Schleiermacher was a charismatic leader. Evidence of this includes the way the Reformed congregation in the *Simultankirche* period of Trinity Church comprised cultured folk who were drawn to Schleiermacher's person and political orientation. We gain a similar sense from his understanding of himself as one occupying a spiritual office and from what was distinctive in his preaching. Reich argues that Schleiermacher's view of himself as a minister included an element characteristic of Moravian pietism. Schleiermacher had a deep inner sense of himself as one called to ministry; it was a crucial aspect of who he was, and his ministry then can be understood as giving expression in all of one's life and relationships to this inner religious self-consciousness. This is the art of ministry, the artistic self-expression of piety in all the arenas of life. Who one is in the depths of one's being and one's ability to give expression to that inwardness in an effective way constitute the art of ministry.[7] So one's person and one's personal gifts are crucial to the office and functioning of ministry. At the same time, this is not sheer individualistic subjectivity, for piety is grounded in the community, and one's ministerial art is representative of the community's piety, refracted through the particularity of one's own person and gifts. Martin Redeker comes to a similar insight in his reflection on Schleiermacher's preaching. He argues that an original element in Schleiermacher's homiletical practice is the way the sermon becomes the "confession and witness of the Christian community which enjoys a living relationship with Christ, and which, through the preacher, brings this relationship to expression in 'representative communication.'"[8] There is a drive to authenticity in Schleiermacher's understanding and practice of ministry; who one is in the depths of one's religious feeling and the particularity of one's gifts and graces for ministry are vital to authentic pastoral practice.

Consistent with Schleiermacher's emphasis on the particular giftedness of persons in ministry is the way he seeks to relativize distinctions of position and rank within the Christian community. For Schleiermacher, the accent is on personal gifts as opposed to positional power. Certainly he does not reject the office of ministry nor the distinction between ordained folk and lay folk in the church; but his emphasis is on mutuality, equality, the priesthood of all believers. This, he argues, is a distinctive mark of the Protestant Church and sets it in contrast to the hierarchical character of the Roman Catholic Church. A distinction between "productive" people and "receptive" people is not characteristic of the Protestant idea of the church; the ideal is the equality of all church members. In the actual church such inequality does exist, so there is a need for leadership, but part of the task of leaders is to work to overcome inequality between clergy and laity.[9]

In a similar vein, Schleiermacher reflects on the dynamics of a pastoral staff that includes persons in a variety of roles. He recognizes that the greater the number of persons involved in the ministry of a particular congregation, the more diversity of interpretation and practice will obtain. The pastoral staff must "strive after such unity, that the administration appears as one."[10] Also noteworthy in this regard is Schleiermacher's relation with August Pischon, who was his pastoral assistant at Trinity Church, 1810–15, and later preacher at the Nicolaikirche, 1827–58. In making his request for a pastoral assistant to the ecclesiastical office of the Prussian state, Schleiermacher asked that the assistant be allowed to do a variety of tasks including regular preaching, officiating at baptisms and weddings, pastoral calling on the sick, teaching of catechism classes, and chairing meetings of the church staff. This was well beyond what assistants were usually allowed to do, and Schleiermacher did not get all that he had requested. Still, Schleiermacher's attempt indicates the sense of shared ministry and collegiality with which he operated. His relationship with Pischon was one of mutual respect and friendship; for twenty years Pischon was an almost daily guest for the midday meal at the Schleiermacher home. Pischon also delivered one of the three speeches at Schleiermacher's funeral.[11]

Schleiermacher's long years of ministry at Trinity Church involved him in all areas of pastoral practice. He preached and led worship, he officiated for hundreds of occasional services, he provided pastoral care, he worked to serve the needs of the poor and offered prophetic critique of the society around him, and he functioned administratively, overseeing a church building and large staff and ever struggling with financial difficulties. This congregational ministry, as well as his work with the Berlin synod and his struggles with the king, was a practical expression of Schleiermacher's vision of the church. The question that confronts us now is how this glimpse of the church and its ministry glimpsed in Schleiermacher's life compares with the understanding in his theological work, both *The*

Christian Faith and the *Christian Ethics*. Schleiermacher conceives of the church as a living organism; the *Christian Ethics* develops a view of the church's life in terms of the kinds of actions expressive of its being.

THE NATURE OF THE CHURCH IN SCHLEIERMACHER'S THEOLOGY

Given the focus on piety in Schleiermacher's theological system and the irreducible character he ascribes to individuality, it is not surprising that there are those who find his position "subjectivistic" and "individualistic."[12] Against this, we will argue that Schleiermacher's theology, both dogmatics and ethics, "rests not so much on 'psychologism' (Brunner) as on a 'sociology of religious consciousness' (Troeltsch)."[13] Schleiermacher's is a theology of consciousness in which the social character of Christian existence and awareness is always presupposed. As we argued in Chapter 3, this is an ethics of piety: the ground and goal of Christian action is piety, and the very structure of the *Christian Ethics* is determined by the different conditions in which piety can find itself. At the same time, this is an ecclesial ethics. It is also true that the ground and goal of Christian action is the church—the community in which piety lives. Finally, community and piety are inseparable for Schleiermacher. Thus it is that Troeltsch's characterization of his theology as a "sociology of religious consciousness" is so apt. The focus on Christian piety that always and only exists within the context of community is one of the distinctive features of Schleiermacher's theological program. We will argue that although a balance between the individual and the community does obtain in Schleiermacher's dogmatics and ethics, there is a clear predominance given the community as compared with the individual.[14] We will demonstrate that neither *The Christian Faith* nor the *Ethics* can be adequately understood unless the ground of both in the social character of Christianity is recognized.

THE STATUS OF THE CHURCH IN *THE CHRISTIAN FAITH*

An important question to pose regarding *The Christian Faith*'s view of the church concerns its status in the dogmatic system. This is so because at first glance the church appears to be on the periphery, at best. The main discussion of the church in *The Christian Faith* is located under the third of the three forms of dogmatic propositions—those dealing with the constitution of the world. Schleiermacher considered the first form, that describing human states, "to be the fundamental dogmatic form."[15] He even entertains the idea of omitting the second and third forms from *The Christian Faith* altogether. Such an omission Schleiermacher rejects for practical, historical, and ecclesial reasons.[16] Still, that the omission is considered puts the burden of proof on those who would affirm the importance of the church in his dogmatic scheme.

However, the concept of the church surfaces not just within the third form of dogmatic proposition. In fact, it is present from the start, making its first appearance in *The Christian Faith* in paragraph 2, where Schleiermacher identifies dogmatics as a discipline pertaining solely to the Christian church. In paragraphs 3–6, Schleiermacher develops his conception of piety as that which is the basis of the church, concluding in paragraph 6 that "religious self-consciousness, like every essential element in human nature, leads necessarily in its development to fellowship or communion."[17] Not only is there a natural pious instinct to form or participate in community; existing communities also play a major role in awakening the feeling of absolute dependence.[18] From the very first, Schleiermacher's is not an atomistic theology of religious self-consciousness. Although "inwardness" plays a key role, this is not Kierkegaardian individualism. Schleiermacher's theology is from the first solidaristic.

Nowhere is this more apparent than in his explication of the most distinctive feature of Christian self-consciousness—the consciousness of grace. Here Schleiermacher develops his Christology. And Christology and ecclesiology are complementary and interdependent. These topics, intertwined as one, are treated initially under the first dogmatic form—the Christian religious self-consciousness. Thus, far from being altogether banished to the nether regions of the third form of dogmatic proposition, the concept of the church actually functions importantly at the very heart of Schleiermacher's theology. Schleiermacher's basic conception of the church is woven into paragraphs 87–105, which deal with the person and work of Christ under the first dogmatic form. Thus stands the church at the very center of things.[19]

In paragraph 87 Schleiermacher affirms that Christian consciousness includes within itself the awareness that all blessedness is "grounded in the new divinely-effected corporate life."[20] This means that the claim for the union of the divine and human in Christ and in the church are corollaries one of the other. Schleiermacher says, "[T]o regard our corporate life as divinely-created, and to derive it from Christ as a divinely-given One, are the same thing."[21] Again, Schleiermacher can assert that the true "manifestation of [Christ's] dignity" is "identical with His activity in the founding of a community."[22] The church as corporate life is the fellowship of believers in Christ such that "Christ is to be the soul also in the individual fellowship, and each individual the organism through which the soul works."[23] Thus, for the contemporary Christian, indeed for all Christians since the first generation who have not had immediate personal access to Jesus, the church is the exclusive means of communion with Christ. In Jesus initially, and then in the church enlivened by his spirit, the God-consciousness inherent in human beings finds perfect expression; thus Jesus and the church are two moments in one divine "act." Although the perfection and blessedness of no one Christian is identical with that of Jesus, individual believers do appropriate his perfection and blessedness by faith and then produce a life "akin to His perfection and blessedness."[24] The perfection of the church as a whole is on a par with that of Jesus. Jesus and the church are for Schleiermacher but two temporally distinct aspects of one reality.

That Jesus and the church together comprise the very heart of the Schleiermacherian credo is evidenced in his discussion of the Trinity. Although this doctrine as traditionally understood is for Schleiermacher inherently problematic and consists of an admixture of dogmatics and speculation, he does seek to transform and rehabilitate it. Rightly understood, the Trinity is "the copingstone of Christian doctrine."[25] The Trinity is rightly understood when it is seen to express "that in Christ there was present nothing less than the Divine Essence, which also indwells the Christian Church as its common spirit."[26] If the copingstone of Christian doctrine gives such place to Christ and the church, this must reflect their status also for piety. Far from being an element of the dogmatic system that can be consigned a secondary status, the church belongs very near the heart of piety's matter.

THE CHARACTER OF THE CHURCH
IN *THE CHRISTIAN FAITH*

How then does *The Christian Faith* conceive of the character of the church? Holger Samson notes that Schleiermacher refers to the church as a "common life" nearly forty times in paragraphs 87–90.[27] This metaphor expresses Schleiermacher's most basic conception of the church, combining as it does sociological and biological connotations. For Schleiermacher the church is, above all else, a community of persons, a genuine historical society; its life is held in common—thus the sociological side. But this church has also a life of its own; it is not merely the sum of its component parts—the individuals who comprise it. Rather, it is an organic, living whole, itself an individual life—thus the biological side. Of course, the church as a mediator of the communion with God bears a theological meaning, but these sociological and biological notions express well the character of the church as a living community.

This interpretation is borne out by a consideration of paragraphs 115–25, which deal with the origin of the church. Although it would seem that the origin of the church would be inaccessible to us, hidden as it is in the recesses of history, Schleiermacher asserts that the church originates repeatedly as persons pass over from the "outer circle" into the common Christian life. Thus, to understand the beginnings of the church is actually to have "a right grasp of the distinction between the converted and all the rest."[28] For Schleiermacher, this means that if we want to grasp the essence of the church, we should attend to this demythologized discussion of its "origin," for there we can see its distinctiveness.

Schleiermacher discusses the origin of the church under two rubrics: election (paragraphs 117–20) and the communication of the Holy Spirit (paragraphs 121–25). In his discussion of election, Schleiermacher emphasizes the church's "natural" operation; election occurs in history as persons are drawn into the church. Election is not, from this point of view, something hidden from human sight in the mystery of God's decree, formulated from eternity and inaccessible to mortals. Schleiermacher identifies a single divine decree (the goal of which is complete communion of humans with God), made known in Christ, and gradually working itself out in human history. Thus Schleiermacher emphasizes the natural means by which divine election is effected: "What proceeds from a single point spreads only gradually over the whole area."[29] Growth, or expansion, is characteristic of the church as the meaning of election is manifest in history. In his discussion of the communication of the Spirit to the church, Schleiermacher emphasizes the Spirit as "the vital unity of the Christian fellowship as a moral personality."[30] The church is the moral agent willing a particular end; the goal that directs the church is "the will for the Kingdom of God."[31]

The Christian Faith understands the church as a living organism that grows naturally, spreading its life and influence gradually as any human community might. For Schleiermacher, the church is distinct from other human communities in that it is the vine that has its origin in Jesus, who manifests God's purpose for the world. In Jesus the single divine decree for the world begins its fulfillment. Of course, all human communities are grounded in the divine causality, but the Christian confession is that Jesus manifests God's purpose for the world; thus Schleiermacher can also claim that the church is the common life into which all other human communities are destined to pass.[32] As a "moral person" the church is analogous to "an earthly system of government" in which individuals are welded together in quest of a common goal.[33] But again the church is distinct from other such communities because of its relation to God's purpose: the church is founded by Jesus, who manifests the divine decree; it has as its own goal the kingdom of God. The church is like other human communities comprising individuals united for a common goal, but it is distinctive in its source and goal—Jesus and the kingdom of God.

For Schleiermacher, the task of dogmatics is to answer the question, "What must *be*, given the reality of Christian self-consciousness?"[34] This analysis of the church in Schleiermacher's dogmatics indicates that Christian self-consciousness or piety includes an immediate sense of the corporate nature of Christian existence; the church is among the most basic themes of dogmatics for Schleiermacher. It is by being drawn into the living fellowship of the church that an individual can attain to what is distinctively Christian—communion with God through Christ and participation in the ongoing manifestation of God's purpose for the world. The task of dogmatics is the didactic description of the Christian reality; an indispensable element of that description is the presentation of the church as an organic, living, purposive whole that stands in unique relation to God and God's goal for the world.

THE LIFE AND ACTIVITY OF THE CHURCH IN THE *CHRISTIAN ETHICS*

Given the complementarity of dogmatics and ethics, we would expect that the conception of the church set forth in the former would be picked up by the latter. Indeed this is the case. Ethics addresses the question, "What must *become* given the reality of Christian self-consciousness?"[35] So, whereas dogmatics seeks to describe the church, identifying its essence or nature, ethics seeks to describe what must develop through the church or, we might say, how it is that this organism lives out its life. For Schleiermacher the church is a life process, and the *Christian Ethics* describes that process. The *Christian Ethics* receives its structure from the three kinds of action that together comprise the life process of the church: restoring action, broadening action, and representational action. This focus on what must become corresponds to the teleological character of Christianity. The church is a moral agent acting in order to realize a purpose. This life, this process, this purpose, the *Christian Ethics* seeks to describe.

Modifying slightly the claim that piety is the ground and goal of the *Christian Ethics*, we can say more precisely that it is the church, as the community of piety, that is the ground and goal of Christian ethical reflection. The *Christian Ethics* is an ecclesial ethics of piety. The very first sentence of the *Christian Ethics* defines Christian ethics as "an ordered system of rules, according to which a member of the Christian church should structure his life."[36] Subsequently, Schleiermacher develops the relation of Christian ethics to the church with more precision. Echoing the dogmatics, the *Christian Ethics* asserts, "Every representation of Christian teaching can only be an exposition of what is valid as teaching in the Christian church."[37] The church is then the ground of ethics as all Christian ethical teaching derives from that which is valid in the community. And the church is the goal of Christian ethics; that is, ethics like all other Christian teaching serves a practical interest, "the expansion of Christianity."[38] So it is that ethics exists in a circular relationship with the church, or we might say that in Schleiermacher's view ethics is a part of the ever-widening spiral that is the church in its history. Christian ethics derives from the church as it seeks to describe action that has its locus in the church, and this description seeks to contribute to the growth and increase of the very reality from which it originated—the church as a community of piety.

As in *The Christian Faith* the church represents the ongoing presence of Christ in the world, so in the *Christian Ethics* the actions of the church are identified as the actions of Christ. Schleiermacher claims that all Christian actions are

> either completions of the church-forming action of Christ . . . or continuations of the same; in either case therefore continuations of the relationship between Christ as the Redeemer and the human race, as the redeemed.[39]

Christ's activity as Redeemer is for Schleiermacher above all the establishment of the church as a community in which the new God-relation he brings binds persons together. The *Christian Ethics* describes the actions of the church, the ongoing actions of Christ. Without question, this is an ecclesial ethics: an ethics of, for, and by the church. The action of the church in the present is the ongoing redemptive action of Christ.

The three types of action that spring forth from Christian piety structure the *Christian Ethics'* reflection on life in the "inner sphere," the life of the church. As the *Christian Ethics* develops its understanding of purifying, broadening, and representational actions, we come to the heart of the ethical matter. To this point, so much of our analysis of the *Christian Ethics*, following its own penchant, has been at a formal and abstract level—attention to the grounding of ethical reflection in Christian piety and to the place of Christian ethics within Schleiermacher's larger philosophical and theological system. Now we move to a less abstract level of reflection and consider the material content of the *Christian Ethics*. In what remains of this chapter we examine the *Christian Ethics'* view of life in the church and how it is to be ordered. In doing so we can give only the broad outlines of Schleiermacher's thought, lifting up ideas that are characteristic of his position. The depth and breadth of his reflections as we have them in the Jonas edition of the *Christian Ethics* are staggering; some 138 pages are devoted to restoring action in the church, 149 pages to the broadening action in the church, and 118 pages to representational action in the church.

RESTORING ACTION IN THE CHURCH: DISCIPLINE AND REFORM

The impulse to a restoring or purifying action arises in Christian consciousness from moments in which flesh gains ascendancy over spirit. This is felt as pain, and the spirit or higher self-consciousness responds with an impulse to reverse this dominance of the flesh and restore the rule of the spirit. Schleiermacher structures his analysis of restoring action using a series of polar opposites, the most important of which is the "individual" and the "whole" (or "community"). The individual person may be in need of restoration; here Schleiermacher deals with church discipline or education. The church as a whole or the larger ecclesial community may also come under the rule of the flesh; the need then is for betterment of the church, its reform.

Schleiermacher asserts the continued existence of sin in individuals and in the church as a whole in unequivocal fashion: Christianity "presupposes that everything which belongs to the natural person, reason not excluded, is infected with sinfulness and as contaminated with sin stands in opposition to the Holy Spirit. If we would not accept that, were reason without sinfulness, then it could produce complete purification by itself, and the original presupposition of Christianity would be negated."[40] Restoring action has a distinctively Christian character as it is grounded in the reality of sin and grace; the continued presence of sin among Christians creates the need for the grace of restoration. Schleiermacher can even identify restoring activity with salvation; he does so by appeal to the Gospel of John.[41] John's understanding of salvation can be understood in terms of three claims: (1) to know the truth is to have salvation, (2) whoever denies truth and the call to repentance excludes himself or herself from the community; (3) restoring activity proceeds from the community to which Christ communicated his spirit. Restoring activity has an important role in the Christian life; it represents the heart and center of Christianity—redemption in Christ.

The distinction between the individual believer and the community as a whole qualifies as a polar opposite for Schleiermacher because both retain significance. Neither can be dissolved into the other for purposes of theological-ethical reflection; some balance between the two is required. More specifically, there is an oscillation, a movement from one polar opposite to the other, as the logic of Schleiermacher's thought unfolds.[42] As he works with this polarity, Schleiermacher seeks to protect the individual from coercive pressure. He asserts, "An influence of the whole upon the single person in his individuality must always be willed by the latter. This is the rule which cannot be overlooked: here there can be no use of force."[43]

Even as the individual is to be protected from coercion, the role of the community is clearly asserted. Schleiermacher rejects the notion that there could be restoration of an individual in which the whole has no influence. "That would mean to set oneself totally outside the community, and this contradicts our most basic presupposition, that every Christian must always see himself as a member of the Christian church."[44] He argues that in instances of conflict or question about the proper course of action, the morality of a particular deed is measured against a proper grasp of the *community* spirit. He also insists that in certain instances the individual can have a clearer grasp of the community's actual spirit than does the community itself. This grounds the possibility for reformation of the church as a whole by the individual. In such a case it is an individual who takes the lead by comprehending the need for reformation of the current state of the church, but he or she does so by appeal to a deeper apprehension of the common spirit of the church. In this way, the community's spirit remains normative.

Schleiermacher develops his notion of church discipline or education, that is, the restoration of the individual, by way of contrast with Roman Catholic practice and understanding. He is critical of Roman Catholic practice, even while acknowledging that it contains "inner truth."[45] Schleiermacher is particularly critical of ascetic practices. He rejects flagellation, saying Christians are called to bear suffering but not seek it; he rejects fasting, saying that as a privation it does not create anything positive; and he says that if formalized prayer is to be used it must be relevant to the particularity of a given individual.[46] In a similar fashion, Schleiermacher rejects Roman Catholic practices of penance for what he sees as heterogeneous domination—the use of compulsion to command adherence and obedience. By means of its hierarchical organization, the Roman Catholic Church rules from above; the officials of the church impose restorative action upon the laity in the forms of prescribed penance and, in the extreme case, excommunication. Schleiermacher rejects the latter as a form of purifying action; it does nothing to effect restoration.

In contrast to the Roman Catholic view, with its asceticism and failure to protect the individual from coercion, Schleiermacher seeks to set forth a distinctively Protestant approach in which the integrity of both individual and community is preserved. Instead of ascetic practices of self-privation, Schleiermacher proposes a spiritual "gymnastic"[47] of works of mercy, particularly care of and service to those who are sick and poor. Schleiermacher affirms such practices because they are productive of something positive and because they can work genuine purification of spirit in those doing the service. It seems he has cultured folk in mind here as he argues that the need for restoration arises from a "one-sidedness" in vocation where one is limited to one's own social sphere and afforded no opportunity to be in service of the basic needs of others. In service of this sort, the church takes a small step toward fulfilling its call to remove inequality from society.[48]

This gymnastic of the spirit is a means of working on flesh; restoration can also occur by working directly on the spirit. Here Schleiermacher calls for individuals to "sink themselves in the common life, allowing it to work on them in a life-giving way."[49] Above all, he points to participation in the worship life of the community, mentioning especially the sermon, the sacraments, and singing. Worship, of course, belongs under the rubric of representational action, but, Schleiermacher argues, it includes within itself an element of restoration. What is represented, set forth in worship, is the church as a whole. In worship the visible, limited, and imperfect church points beyond itself to the invisible, unlimited (by space and time), and perfect church. In this way the visible church transcends itself and participates in the reality of the church in its ideality. The church is established by Christ in absolute perfection, with the qualification that this perfection exists in "an eternal way" and "never in appearance."[50] Still, the church participates in perfection, and perfection mediated to individuals through worship practices becomes a vehicle for restoration.

Yet Schleiermacher remains unhappy with the means for restoration of the individual in the church of his day. He complains that much of the Protestant Church exercises no discipline at all and blames this, at least in part, on the fact that the church is dissolved in civil society with no distinctive disciplinary process of its own. He also complains that exclusion of unrepentant sinners rarely occurs, asking, "What can [exclusion] mean when the relation between the individual and the community is almost non-existent?"[51] Schleiermacher calls for some institution in the church that can offer care for and discipline of individuals in the community; this is an essential aspect of the "brotherly love" that characterizes the Christian church. Lacking an institution of this sort, he calls on individuals to call each other to account, appealing to the instructions in Matthew 18.[52]

On the other hand, Schleiermacher notes that most Christian ethics focus on the individual and neglect the community.[53] This means that attention must be given to restoration of the whole by the individual. Schleiermacher provides a lengthy analysis of this type of restoration, including an examination of the Protestant Reformation, in his view the prime example of such an effort to purify the church. Schleiermacher carefully defines the "limits and actual nature of this restoring action"[54] because it is so important. In doing so he does not elevate the individual above the church, nor does he abrogate his earlier position and make the individual independent of the church. Rather, he sees the reformer as a servant of the ecclesia, calling for the church to return to itself.

Schleiermacher again defines his Protestant position over against Roman Catholicism. He claims that the Roman Catholic Church denies the legitimacy of such restoring action because it understands the church to be established by Christ in absolute perfection. For Schleiermacher the church's perfection exists in "an eternal way" and "never in appearance."[55] The appearance of the church is never perfect and is therefore in need of constant betterment, an ongoing reformation. The task for the church is to realize the perfection that was, in fact, established in Christ. In particular, it is the task of the official representatives of the church to effect restoration of the whole when necessary and to make superfluous a special restoration of the whole by an individual. This connects nicely with Schleiermacher's view of the presbyterian system of the early church in which the elders were true representatives of the community. In such a system the official representatives could effect restoration. The need for special restoration by an individual comes when the officials are no longer true representatives; this was the case, Schleiermacher asserts, at the time of the Reformation.

In Schleiermacher's view, the morality of particular attempts at restoration of the community hinges on the state of the church's organization and the intent of the reformer. The church needs to be so organized that it can live out its call to realize perfection as manifest in Christ. In particular, such organization must allow for restoration of the community when such is needed. Thus Schleiermacher can conceive of two cases in which the individual is justified in working restoratively upon the whole: (1) when the church exists without any form of organization and (2) when the form of organization in the church is incommensurate with the church's essence. In the first case, the reformer must seek to establish such an organization, at which time his or her function as reformer is complete and further work can be turned over to the organization. In so functioning, the individual acts as a representative of the community. In the latter case, the individual reformer is called to effect restoration by means of "self-presentation," manifesting the true common spirit of the church so that its sickness is revealed. In Schleiermacher's view, the common spirit of the church remains the decisive norm, even in cases where an individual seeks to reform the church.

Schleiermacher's appropriation of his Protestant heritage, more particularly his Reformed heritage, is evident in his understanding of restoration of the church. His argument for presbyterian polity dovetails nicely with his call for an institutionalized means of church reform, for he sees elders as representatives of congregations and thus accountable to those they represent. He brings these claims to bear on the situation of the Prussian church of his day. Whereas the base deficiency at the time of the Reformation was people's inadequate understanding of scripture, the current problem is deficiency of organization. This problem could be solved were the church allowed its own constitution and independence from the state, along with a synodal-presbyterial organization so that a representative form of church government could replace a hierarchical one.

BROADENING ACTION: CHRISTIAN EDUCATION AND MISSIONS

In Schleiermacher's reflection on the church's broadening action, themes and concepts central to his view of ecclesial life come to expression. Broadening action connotes growth, a theme that resonates profoundly with Schleiermacher's view of the church as a living organism. The growth brought here into focus is growth of the Christian disposition, aiming at nothing less than the kingdom of God. The broadening action encapsulates key themes in Schleiermacher's theology—the (relatively) supernatural in Christ becomes natural in the church and grows toward the inclusion of all in redemption. Schleiermacher says, "The whole saving action of Christ can be seen under the type of the broadening action."[56] This action is bounded by two limiting points: "The individual personality of Christ as the point of origin of the process and the perfection of all human beings in Christ as the endpoint."[57] The focus is at once inward on disposition or piety and outward on the universal goal of the process.

Schleiermacher's analysis of broadening action is structured by several pairs of polar opposites. Three sets of polarities—individual and community, the natural and the supernatural, and disposition and talent—receive significant treatment in relation to the threefold distinction among *sarx* (flesh), *nous* (human spirit), and *pneuma* (Christian spirit). By means of these distinctions, Schleiermacher is able to articulate the christological and ecclesiological commitments that come to expression in his view of broadening action. A further opposition, that between intensive broadening (education or formation) and extensive broadening (missions), shapes the view of the practices of this action.

In introducing the conception of the broadening action, Schleiermacher distinguishes between spirit, which is the agent of action, and flesh, which is its organ. Then he examines the issue of the relation between the individual and the community in broadening action. In general, he asserts that all broadening action both presupposes the existence of community and establishes it.[58] This is obvious enough in the case of the ongoing church: the already existing community is the source of broadening action, and the church is established by broadening action when, as a result, community is created. But, Schleiermacher asks, what about Christ? Certainly he established a community, but was community also a precondition of his action? On the one hand, in Schleiermacher's view, Christ's God-consciousness is supernatural in the sense that it cannot be explained as an effect of that which went before; a sinful community cannot produce the sinless Redeemer. But, on the other hand, there must have been some form of community around Christ, or the analogy between his action and that of the church is completely negated.

Schleiermacher resolves this question by positing a community of desire for *pneuma*, which preexisted Christ. In Schleiermacher's view, this desire for *pneuma* corresponds to the Apostle Paul's notion of the "fullness of time"; the world was ready for Christ because there existed a sense of dissatisfaction with the Law and the expectation of something more. So he concludes that even for Christ there existed a community around him, a community of desire and expectation. In Christ these find fulfillment, and the pneumatic community becomes a reality; *pneuma* is no longer simply the object of inchoate desire, but is now the vital spirit of the community. Schleiermacher insists that the transition from desire to fulfillment could not be achieved by human effort, but only by means of the new reality in Christ.

Christ then introduces something new—*pneuma*. This term indicates the way individual and community are balanced even while it represents what is unique in Christ. The argument for this community of desire reveals Schleiermacher's insistence that the Christian spirit exists only among people, that is, as it indwells a community. Even in the otherwise unique case of Christ, a community of desire preexisted his advent. At the same time the uniqueness of Christ is protected by the insistence that in him there is something genuinely new—it remains inexplicable on the basis of what has gone before. So there exists an analogy between the situation of Christ in relation to community and the community of the church. A corresponding analogy exists between the broadening action of Christ and that of the *ecclesia*. The church and its activity mediate the reality of redemption. This also indicates the resolution of the paradox that broadening activity both presupposes and creates community. Finally, the church is inseparable from its activity; the church exists as it acts. "The church retains its reality only through that which establishes it—namely, through continuous activity."[59] Broadening activity is necessary for the very existence of the church.

Schleiermacher's addition of *pneuma* to the *nous/sarx* distinction also enables him to clarify the relation of the "natural" and "supernatural" in Christ and mediate between "rationalistic" and strictly "supernatural" views of Christianity. On the one hand, *pneuma* is seen to be a higher development of *nous*, and on the other hand, *nous* is seen as incapable of becoming *pneuma* by itself. The "community of desire" that preexisted Christ indicates the aspiration of *nous* for *pneuma*. So the relation between spirit in a general human sense and spirit in a Christian sense combines continuity and discontinuity. On the other hand, from a Christian point of view, *nous* is to be classed with *sarx* rather than *pneuma*. This being so, Schleiermacher identifies non-Christian virtues as Augustine's "magnificent vices" because they relate only to a limited area of human life—for example, the nation. If, however, *nous/sarx* is appropriated by *pneuma*, the former becomes an agent/organ of the divine spirit. Then one might act to expand the absolute community of all in Christ, that is, the kingdom of God. The broadening action of the church has a transcendent significance because of its source and goal. It derives from Christ, the "Second Adam" who achieves God's original intention for humanity, and it is in service of the highest good, the kingdom of God, the inclusion of all in Christ's perfection.

The distinction between *nous* and *sarx* corresponds to that between inward disposition and talent. Schleiermacher defines talent in terms of the development of skills and disposition as unity in the direction of the will. He asserts that both disposition and talent can be agents of *pneuma*. The distinction between the two is only relative, and a development in disposition will mean a corresponding gain in talent, and vice versa. Still, it is disposition that is the focus in the church. This corresponds to the centrality of piety in Schleiermacher's theology and view of church life. So Schleiermacher says that the church develops the Christian disposition and talent only for the sake of the disposition.[60] Ecclesial broadening action has the goal of "the broadening of the Christian disposition and the broadening of all actual gifts of the Spirit for the sake of the disposition."[61] Schleiermacher defines Christian disposition as love, "including love of Christ and of neighbor—these two cannot be separated."[62] Increase of the inward disposition of love, then, is the prime goal of broadening action.

Schleiermacher speaks of both "intensive" broadening—education or formation, and "extensive" broadening—mission work. Whereas the latter aims at making more people Christian, the former has as its goal making the rule of the Spirit more complete in folk already Christian. In relation to intensive broadening, Schleiermacher says that we must postulate continual progress in the church because of the Holy Spirit, the principle of the common life of the church. Still, he argues that such increase is not automatic; in order for it to occur, the church must exist in a public, open way where there is free exchange of views among all members. Open exchange of this sort enables the church to discern what is genuine progress and what is an unhealthy deviation. This is the birthright of the Protestant church, and it is only this ongoing openness to critical reflection that preserves the church from relapsing into a false estimate of its perfection.[63]

In connection with its educational mission, Schleiermacher can speak of the church as a school with a twofold task. On the one hand is the practical task of moral formation of members of the community, and on the other hand is the theoretical, "linguistic" task of formation of the understanding. Moral formation occurs by means of the common spirit of the community communicating itself to its members. This happens particularly by means of the "good example" that is not an action specifically intended to be exemplary, but simply good actions that emerge as part of the church's ongoing life. The church "should be an institution which supports itself by always newly arousing its principle in each of its members and building itself permanently in them and through them."[64] Schleiermacher recognizes that participation in the community's ethos and common feeling leads individuals to internalize its moral values: this is precisely what the church as school is called to do.

A similar kind of transformation occurs in terms of an individual's understanding. Schleiermacher says, "[T]he entry of the Christian spirit in a human life effects a complete change in the formation of thought."[65] Exclusive focus on what is merely sensual and material is transformed into spiritual, pious understanding. This new understanding cannot exist without "an altered process of speech."[66] For Schleiermacher the education process of the church is a process of formation through which the church's values and understandings are internalized. "When the Christian spirit enters a person, it must first become personal in him before he can stop being purely receptive in the church and begin to himself be productive in it. In this becoming personal exists the true living appropriation of the Christian way of thought."[67] In its educational mission we see then the organic, naturalistic character of the church: Christian piety reproduces itself out of its very life; it deepens and spreads by means of persons' participation in the community's life.

Schleiermacher's analysis of missionary work is much less developed than his reflection on education or formation. Jonas notes that Schleiermacher's approach to missions varied considerably over the years during which the material of the *Christian Ethics* was presented in lecture form.[68] Schleiermacher does say that the distinction between the intensive and extensive aspects of broadening action are only relative, and, "The expansion of Christianity is such a general task that no Christian can exclude himself from it."[69] He goes on to say that it would seem that all Christians should participate in both aspects of broadening, but he then concludes that mission work requires a special calling.[70] Missionary work is necessary and appropriate where there are geographic regions that do not share a border with Christian people or where people are nominally Christian but lack sufficient interest in the faith.[71] Based on the diffusion of Christian people in the world, one could conclude that missions are now unnecessary, but Schleiermacher argues that because many nominally Christian folk have gone to foreign lands out of economic interest, with insufficient interest in the faith, persons with a specific call to missionary work are needed.[72]

Schleiermacher notes ways in which missionary work or evangelism requires a catholic and pastoral spirit to be genuinely faithful. He reflects on the division between Protestant and Roman Catholic churches and argues that in mission work Protestants will convert others to Christianity in general and Protestantism in particular. But this must be done in such a way as to leave open the possibility that the division between the two churches may be overcome; in other words, demonizing the Roman Catholic Church as unchristian is not appropriate.[73] Similarly on an individual level, when one is witnessing to another, one ought not seek to destroy a conviction in the other unless one has reason to believe that one can also help construct something positive to replace it.[74] In these ways Schleiermacher recognizes that excess in evangelistic witness needs to be reined in for the sake of an open and broad vision of the church and pastoral concern for the well-being of persons.

Schleiermacher's basic view of the church as a living organism and his understanding of broadening action cohere nicely together and reinforce each other. Although unique in its origin, the church grows by natural means, expanding its sway as persons are drawn to deeper participation in its life. The kingdom of God is shorn of apocalyptic connotations and seen as the goal to be attained by steady growth. The church is an earthen vessel, containing the transcendent good within itself. Aligned with the purposes of God in a unique way, it grows by the most ordinary and natural of means—people sharing common life together.

REPRESENTATIONAL ACTION: PUBLIC AND HOUSEHOLD WORSHIP AND CHRISTIAN VIRTUE IN DAILY LIFE

The third member in Schleiermacher's trinity of Christian actions is perhaps the most important. Representational action derives from a "higher" form of Christian self-consciousness, beyond the feelings of pain and pleasure that ground restoring and broadening actions. Representational action is grounded in a sense of "blessedness." This is a relative blessedness, to be sure, but it points to "the perfected rule of the spirit in all to whom there is given any recognition of the union of spirit with the flesh."[75] This concept of blessedness, with its connotation of wholeness and perfection, is "the ground of the concept of eternal life."[76] There is, then, a sense of completion to this blessedness. This means that the only kind of action that can issue from this state is one that seeks no result "because no further result is to be expected, only an indication and expression of the completed process and of the achieved result."[77] Representational action then seeks only to express an inner state in an outward way; Christian worship is approached by means of this concept—representational action.

The importance, even centrality, of representational activity is evident in its grounding in Christology and ecclesiology. The focus on activity that communicates an inner state to others matches precisely Schleiermacher's view of Christ. The Redeemer is unique in the power of his God-consciousness, and the outward manifestation of this piety is "the absolute beginning of the Christian church.... It is always and everywhere the first ground of the community to recognize Jesus as the Son of God, which is nothing but an inference from his outward expression to his inner being, accomplished through representational action."[78]

The church, then, continues what was begun in Christ. Schleiermacher says that representational action and community are "equally original."[79] By this he means that representational action manifests community and proceeds from it, presupposing it. He argues that the very concept of a representational action as action, which seeks only to communicate an inward condition in an outward manner, makes sense only in the context of community, in relationship to an "other" with whom one can communicate. Schleiermacher notes that this is true even in the case of an individual considered in isolation from all other persons. In such a case representational action would be intended only for oneself; but even this presupposes a kind of community among the different moments in which the individual exists. This reflects the character of self-consciousness in which previous moments become the object of consciousness. The point of such solitary communication is to express and fix one's inner state so that it can be made manifest and thereby remembered and retained. Even in the case of the individual, there is a kind of community at work. In terms of the church a real community of persons is presupposed by and made manifest in representational action.

> The outward expression of an inner determination of self-consciousness, representational action, rests upon community and produces community. We have expressed this in the formula, which says that both [community and representational action] are equally original. This is a formula which we transform into an actual conception when we say, "Representational action is the manifestation [*in die Erscheinung treten*] of community itself, therefore also that through which community can become an object of consciousness."[80]

In Schleiermacher's view, then, representational action and community together constitute Christian reality in its most basic form. Grounded directly in his Christology, representational action is essential to the church as a community of piety.

Of course, the distinctions among the various forms of action are only relative, and Schleiermacher says that all effectual action includes within it an element of representational action. Representational action or worship is defined as "the totality of all actions through which we are able to represent ourselves as organs of God by means of the divine spirit."[81] Worship, then, is the expression of piety, the expression of the living spirit of

Christ. To act for the glory of God is then defined in similar terms. Schleiermacher appeals to 1 Corinthians 10:31 and says: "To act for the glory of God is nothing other than to act such that one represents oneself to be an organ of God. The apostle wants the character of representational action to stamp itself absolutely on all actions."[82] In developing his analysis of worship or representational action, Schleiermacher distinguishes between worship in the narrow sense—public, cultic worship—and worship in the broad sense—the manifestation of the Christian spirit in daily life. Both are necessary. Without worship in the broad sense, public worship becomes *opus operatum*; it is reduced to a superstitious work without connection to life. Public worship is also necessary, for it is the perfection of effectual action. This is so "because effectual action can only cease being practice, can only be increased to pure performance, if the self-consciousness is given room to develop itself into actual representational action."[83] Representational action has a crucial significance, for it transcends the striving of effectual activity and gives expression to the sense of completion and wholeness that is of the essence of Christian piety.

The analysis of public worship, worship "in the narrow sense," begins with the recognition that Christian representational action does not begin *ex nihilo*. That is, it does not seek to produce its own means of representation, but makes use of given art forms. But because "intelligence," with its faculties of representation and desire, is "the first organ of the Holy Spirit," artistic forms that privilege language over corporeal expression will take precedence in Christian worship. Schleiermacher claims that the worship of the earliest Christian communities included no pomp or sensuality; he argues that Protestant worship, unlike Roman Catholic forms, distances itself from the plastic arts, with their Jewish and heathen overtones. Instead, the focus is on language—the spoken word and sung word (especially congregational singing) come to the fore. In all this Schleiermacher's Protestant and Reformed sensibilities are evident.[84]

In terms of what he calls the "form" of worship, Schleiermacher gives attention to the special role of the clergy in the cult. He argues that representational action "rests upon the principle of brotherly love, upon the principle of the equality of Christians" as partaking of the same Spirit and as equally dependent on Christ.[85] He then asks if public worship is to correspond exactly to this fundamental equality. He argues that this is the case in Quaker worship. At the opposite end of the spectrum he places Roman Catholic worship, with the dominance of the priest and the passivity of lay folk. Schleiermacher opts for a form of worship between these two extremes, arguing that worship must be a living art form. As living, it is in need of active participation by all members of the community, and as an art form there is the need for those who shape the form and content of worship, who fill a leadership role. All have been given the same Spirit, so leadership in worship is a matter of "talent formation"—those who have developed their gifts for public expression are placed in leadership roles. Schleiermacher asserts that the inequality caused by some being given responsibility to lead must not obscure the fundamental equality of all. And so he points again to congregational singing as a form of worship that involves the "productivity of all."[86]

Among the other issues that Schleiermacher addresses in relation to public worship are the size of the congregation and the catholicity of the church in light of division along confessional lines. He asserts that the size of the congregation is an important matter. If the congregation is too large, all living connection among members is lost; if it is too small, it devolves to become a loose form of private worship. For Schleiermacher, the morality of worship is at stake in the matter of numbers of people. He also asserts that although the church should preserve "natural relationships," it should not create divisions along cultural or linguistic lines, and he explicitly rejects church splits based on social class.[87] On the other hand, Schleiermacher allows that splits in the church along confessional lines can be moral if they are based on legitimate differences related to worship. He argues that although the differences between Lutheran and Reformed churches are disappearing, those between Protestantism and Roman Catholicism are not. He asserts that efforts at reunification with Rome can occur only when the Roman Catholic church "overcomes the abuses that existed at the time of the Reformation."[88] Still, the catholicity of the church must be kept in view; "the absolute community of all Christians is nothing other than the ethical side of the dogma of the unity of the church."[89] One ought not be indifferent toward one's own "partial church," but one must recognize its temporality. It is not the universal church and must not absolutize itself or its forms of worship.[90]

Worship in the broad sense concerns Christian witness in daily life. Schleiermacher thinks of this in terms of the representation of the rule of the Christian spirit over the flesh by means of the expression of four Christian virtues. The key to the expression of the virtues as worship is that they are internalized and set forth with an "ease of performance." No internal struggle is involved; at the point of its being actual worship, virtuous action is no longer a matter of training or of self-control, but of natural performance and good judgment. The virtues come to expression without exertion; they are morally "beautiful or graceful."[91] Schleiermacher develops a structure for thinking about these virtues by crossing two sets of polar opposites related to determinations of the sensual self-consciousness: pain and pleasure, and personal and communal self-consciousness. When the self-consciousness is determined as pleasure of a personal sort, the virtue is chastity or purity. Where purity exists, there may be attraction, but not desire. Sensual pleasure is not lacking, but it does not provide the impulse on which one acts. When the self-consciousness is determined as pain in a personal way, the corresponding virtue is patience. This is the ability to endure unpleasant impressions without a sensual reaction. There is a tone of serenity here that can be "truly moving."[92]

Forbearance is the third virtue Schleiermacher identifies; it arises in response to pain in communal feeling. The virtue involves the "undisturbed continuation of brotherly love in spite of the moral imperfection of the object."[93] Schleiermacher insists that this is not a matter of apathy; pain is felt, but love rather than pain is the impulse behind the action. Finally, the virtue of humility corresponds to self-consciousness determined as pleasure in communal feeling. Moral pleasure rests upon an awareness of a surplus of power, and humility recognizes the pleasure and that credit for this surplus of power does not belong to it. This occurs when we see ourselves in comparison to Christ and recognize that in light of this contrast, all other comparisons are meaningless.[94] The four virtues are variations on a common theme: God is worshiped in daily life as individuals, acting as organic parts of the whole, take and represent the being and moral essence of the whole in an individual action. The Christian principle is brotherly love grounded in a sense of the joy of redemption that overflows in love for others. As this comes to expression, there is worship of God in the mundane tasks of daily life.

The themes and concerns that animate Schleiermacher's pastoral work are also evident in the *Christian Ethics'* reflection on the way the church is to live out its life. In his practice of ministry and in his reflection, Schleiermacher conceives of the church as a living organism characterized by the mutuality and equality of its members. This leads to his call for the church's independence from the state and for a presbyterian polity that Schleiermacher interpreted in democratic, representative terms. He affirms the priority of the community, even as he would protect the individual from all coercion in matters of faith. Above all, the church is a community of Christian piety, and the task of ministry is the nurture and development of that piety. "Finally, all church government and service have one goal: the strengthening of the Christian disposition, building it up."[95]

In the first place, the *Christian Ethics* attends to the life of the church. Schleiermacher promotes a vision of the church as a living organism that exists by virtue of acting, moving, and growing. This is especially evident in its broadening action; the accent is on growth, expansion in intensive and extensive ways. Under this rubric, as under that of representational action, the church continues to exist as it acts. This theme also finds important expression in Schleiermacher's definition of worship: the community as a whole and individual members as organic parts of the same represent themselves as organs of God. Worship needs to be a living representation;

therefore, all members of the community must participate. For the *Christian Ethics*, the church is the living body of Christ that is constituted by its actions.

The themes of equality and mutuality are sounded repeatedly in the *Christian Ethics*. In reflecting on church discipline, Schleiermacher insists that the individual be protected against coercion on the part of the larger community. Similarly, under the topic of intensive broadening where the church functions for the formation of individuals, Schleiermacher calls for open, public exchange, rejecting authoritarian imposition on persons. In terms of representational action, the call is for the reality of the priesthood of all believers to be apparent; the fundamental equality of all must be evident in public worship. Concern for equality and mutuality also informs Schleiermacher's reflections on the size of a congregation. His call for the church's independence from the state and for a representative, presbyterian structure within also echoes values of equality and mutuality.

Above all, the church is a community united in its piety. This theme is evident in the notion of broadening activity, with its focus on the growth of the Christian disposition. Talent formation is decidedly secondary. Schleiermacher calls for persons to be shaped morally and in terms of their understanding in a Christian way. The goal of these practices is that Christian disposition be internalized in persons. Similarly, under representational action the focus is on piety; worship is grounded in blessedness and seeks to manifest the same in an outward way. Worship in daily life, with its virtues of purity, patience, forbearance, and humility, also speaks to visible evidence of a particular inward disposition. Community life springs from piety, and the actions of the community, through which it lives, seek the restoration, expansion, and representation of piety in all of life. The prime task of the *Christian Ethics* is to set forth with clarity the actions of the church as a living community of piety. To that task Schleiermacher devotes considerable energy, as we have seen. The second task of the *Christian Ethics* is to analyze the relation of the Christian community and individual to the larger society and culture. That is the topic of the next chapter.

NOTES

1. Andreas Reich, *Friedrich Schleiermacher als Pfarrer an der Berliner Dreifaltigkeitskirche 1809–1834* (Berlin and New York: Walter de Gruyter, 1992), 41.
2. Ibid., 36.
3. Ibid., 411, 426, 427–28.
4. Ibid., 430–31. Reich takes pains to indicate that Schleiermacher was not exclusively a pastor to the cultured, but "was loved by many laborers, sales people, and citizens" and that Schleiermacher wanted to be pastor to the poor. "While Schleiermacher cannot be called a 'people's preacher,' he never lost sight of the simple and

often impoverished members of the community" (431).

5. Cf., ibid., 24. Schleiermacher's essay was "Vorschlag zu einer neuen Verfassung der protestantischen Kirche in preussischen Staate," *Kleine Schriften und Predigten*, ed. H. Gerdes and E. Hirsch (Berlin: Walter de Gruyter, 1969–70), 113ff.

6. Reich sums up his helpful analysis of the development of Schleiermacher's thinking about church order, indicating "the steps he takes from his early ideal of a free religious community to a constitutional church with a synodical organization. In the *Speeches* he understands the contemporary church as a link between those with true religious sentiments and seekers, then in 1804 he wants to strengthen spiritual life through various practical measures. In 1808 he raises the issue of a church constitution for the first time. Next he wants to unite all ministers with a simultaneous self-determination of the individual congregations. On this theme he lifts up again the notion of a synod of pastors in 1812, before he calls for congregations having representation in the synod in 1817. From the immediate community of the Spirit comes a plan for church order. And as a theme running through all of this is the most wide-reaching independence of the church from the state" (26).

7. Ibid., 32–33.

8. Martin Redeker, *Schleiermacher: Life and Thought*, trans. John Wallhausser (Philadelphia: Fortress Press, 1973), 206.

9. Reich, 33–34.

10. Friedrich Schleiermacher, *Die Praktische Theologie nach den Grundsätzen der evangelischen Kirche im Zusammenhange dargestellt.* In *Sämmtliche Werke*, div. 1, vol. 13, ed. Jacob Frerichs (Berlin: G. Reimer, 1850; Reprint, Berlin: Walter de Gruyter, 1983), 485, as quoted in Reich, 35.

11. Reich, 43–45.

12. Not least Emil Brunner. Cf. his *The Divine Imperative*, trans. Olive Wyon, (Philadelphia: The Westminster Press, 1947). He speaks of Schleiermacher's ethics as "psychologically subjective" (573).

13. B. A. Gerrish, *Tradition and the Modern World: Reformed Theology in the Nineteenth Century* (Chicago: University of Chicago Press, 1978), 41.

14. We will demonstrate in what follows the predominance assigned the community; there are of course places where Schleiermacher reverses this, and individuals are understood to precede the community and come together to form a society. See the fourth speech in Friedrich Schleiermacher, *On Religion: Speeches to Its Cultured Despisers*, trans. Richard Crouter (Cambridge: Cambridge University Press, 1988); see also Friedrich Schleiermacher, *The Christian Faith*, trans. H. R. Mackintosh and J. S. Stewart (Edinburgh: T. & T. Clark, 1928), 26. These instances cannot be explained away; they remain a significant counterpoint to Schleiermacher's usual understanding. It is noteworthy that in both of these instances Schleiermacher is talking about religion in a general, abstracted sense. When talking specifically about the Christian way of being religious, there is always a precedence ascribed to the community over the individual.

15. *The Christian Faith*, 126.

16. Ibid., 128.

17. Ibid., 26.

18. Ibid.

19. Holger Samson, *Die Kirche als Grundbegriff der theologischen Ethik Schleiermachers*, (Zollikon-Zürich: Evangelische Verlag, 1958), 43, argues that Schleiermacher's Christology in *The Christian Faith* contains his ecclesiology "in nuce." In our

analysis of the church that follows, we are in line with Samson at several points.
20. *The Christian Faith*, 358.
21. Ibid., 360.
22. Ibid., 377.
23. Ibid., 428.
24. Ibid., 505; on faith as the appropriation of blessedness and perfection, see p. 481.
25. Ibid., 739.
26. Ibid., 738.
27. Samson, 59.
28. *The Christian Faith*, 529.
29. Ibid., 536.
30. Ibid., 535.
31. Ibid.
32. Cf. ibid., 536.
33. Ibid., 562.
34. Friedrich Schleiermacher, *Die christliche Sitte nach den Grundsätzen der evangelischen Kirche im Zusammenhange dargestellt*, ed. Ludwig Jonas in *Sämmtliche Werke*, div. 1, vol. 12 (Berlin: G. Reimer, 1843), 23. Hereafter referred to as *Christian Ethics*.
35. Ibid.
36. Ibid., 1.
37. Ibid., 10.
38. Ibid., 16.
39. Ibid., 74–75.
40. Ibid., 112–13.
41. He cites specifically John 5:24; 8:31–36; 18:37; 10:24–30; 12:47–48; 16:7; and 20:22. Ibid., 177.
42. Cf. Albert L. Blackwell, *Schleiermacher's Early Philosophy of Life: Determinism, Freedom, and Phantasy* (Chico, Calif.: Scholars Press, 1982), 163, 298, for the importance of oscillation in Schleiermacher's early thought. Blackwell speaks of "unending oscillation in . . . between the ever enlarging spheres of philosophical understanding and mystical intuition" (163) and "oscillation between idealism and realism. . . . [T]he romantic poet looks with and sees the world reflected in himself; he looks without and finds himself reflected in the world" (298).
43. *Christian Ethics*, 117.
44. Ibid., 118.
45. Ibid., 150–51.
46. Cf., ibid., 142–50.
47. This is clearly an allusion to Schleiermacher's contemporary, Ludwig Jahn, the father of German gymnastics. Jahn advocated physical exercise as a way to attain fitness and health.
48. *Christian Ethics*, 154–57.
49. Ibid., 158.
50. Ibid., 122.
51. Ibid., 167.
52. Ibid., 171–73.
53. Ibid., 173.
54. Ibid., 122.

55. Ibid.
56. Ibid., 292.
57. Ibid., 330.
58. Cf. ibid., 300–04.
59. Ibid., 322.
60. Ibid., 327. Schleiermacher argues that the task of the state is the opposite of this—the development of talent and of disposition for the sake of talent.
61. Ibid., 330.
62. Ibid., 310.
63. Ibid., 384–85.
64. Ibid., 389.
65. Ibid., 392.
66. Ibid., 393.
67. Ibid., 394.
68. Ibid., n. 380.
69. Ibid., 379.
70. Ibid. Cf. also 422, where Schleiermacher appeals to a divine call as the basis for Paul's missionary work. He also argues that it is "perseverance," not results, that justifies a sense of call to missionary work.
71. Ibid., 433.
72. Ibid., 380–81.
73. Ibid., 411–12.
74. Ibid., 410–11.
75. Ibid., 502–03.
76. Ibid., 508.
77. Ibid.
78. Ibid., 511–12.
79. Ibid., 510. The discussion of the relation between representational action and community occurs on 509–14.
80. Ibid., 512–13.
81. Ibid., 525–26.
82. Ibid., 530.
83. Ibid., 536.
84. Ibid., 537–41.
85. Ibid., 542.
86. Ibid., 556.
87. Cf. ibid., 566–69.
88. Ibid., 579.
89. Ibid., 574.
90. Ibid., 580.
91. Ibid., 599–604.
92. Ibid., 612.
93. Ibid., 614.
94. Ibid., 615–16.
95. Reich, 35.

6
SCHLEIERMACHER AS REFORMER AND TRANSFORMATION IN THE *CHRISTIAN ETHICS*

Schleiermacher held three appointed positions during his long second stay in Berlin; he was pastor of Trinity Church, professor at the Humboldt University, and for six years he held a post in the Ministry of the Interior's Department of Instruction. All three positions he held, ultimately, at the behest of the Prussian king. This would seem to support the claims of some interpreters that Schleiermacher's theological program was one of "cultural accommodation." In the mid–twentieth century, H. Richard Niebuhr classified Schleiermacher, notably his Christian ethics, as belonging to the "Christ of culture" type; that is to say, an ethics that surrenders a distinctive Christian identity in order to accommodate itself to its cultural context.[1] This line of argument is furthered by others who add a Marxist angle to the charge of accommodationism.[2] Schleiermacher surrendered prophetic criticism of his social world, so the argument goes, captive to the privilege and comfort of his official positions.

The task of this chapter is to examine the social-political orientation of Schleiermacher's life and his *Christian Ethics*. Was Schleiermacher primarily one who accommodated himself to the world that surrounded him, or are there elements of social criticism in his life and thought? Is there a transformative impulse at work here? That is, is there an impulse to identify ways in which the social order is in need of greater justice and equality and a contribution to change along those lines?

SCHLEIERMACHER AS SOCIAL-POLITICAL ACTOR

To begin, we must take account of Schleiermacher's actual involvement in the social-political arena. He was, for most of his career, a thorn in the king's side. He was a champion of Stein's reforms during the Prussian springtime (1806–19) and was under continual suspicion in the reactionary period following the Karlsbad Decrees of 1819. Finally, no fewer than four times, Schleiermacher was on the verge of losing his position or even being banished from Prussia altogether because of his political orientation and activity.

It is true that German intellectuals of Schleiermacher's day, like generations before them, focused on religious and philosophical issues to the exclusion of explicitly political concerns. In contrast to their French and English counterparts for whom political action and reflection were central, the thinkers of the German Enlightenment maintained their distinctive focus. This may be in part because of the fertility of German soil for religion—the strong tradition of German mysticism, the Reformation, and Pietism being noteworthy examples. Even more, it was because of the tight control that German princes exercised over intellectuals. Having little opportunity to wield influence in the political arena, they continued to plow in the fields of religion and philosophy.[3]

Although remaining in these traditional fields, Schleiermacher transcends the political restrictions that inhibited his forebears and many of his contemporaries. He moves to a new level of political consciousness and activism. Robert Biglar goes so far as to argue that Schleiermacher is the key player in the politicization of the Prussian church in this period. "As both a stimulator and a prototype, Schleiermacher was primarily responsible for the emergence of the most politically oriented elements of the clergy in the period 1815–1848."[4] That the members of the clergy should be politically active was against the desires and designs of the king, who wanted to continue the tradition of political quietism on the part of the clergy. Schleiermacher's political consciousness was awakened by Napoleon and the humiliation of his country at the hands of the French dictator. After Napoleon, Schleiermacher's activity and thought, not least his theology, has a political edge to it. By the very act of political engagement, Schleiermacher sets himself in opposition to the king.

As it so often does, war and its aftermath created an opportunity for social and political change. Napoleon's defeat of Prussia made for a triangulated relationship among three parties: Napoleon, Friedrich Wilhelm III, and the Prussian Reformers, led by Baron Karl Freiherr vom Stein, whom Napoleon appointed as the prime minister in Prussia. The goals of the three parties were diverse, with Napoleon and Friedrich Wilhelm at opposite poles and Stein in the middle. Where Napoleon wanted to maintain control over Prussia and instigate internal reform along republican lines, Friedrich Wilhelm wanted liberation from the French and restoration of the monarchy's power, and Stein, in the middle, shared desire for liberation with the king and for reform with the emperor. In his short fourteen months as minister, Stein "left an indelible mark on modern German history."[5] Stein believed in balancing power among different groups, and he sought to achieve such balance in the reorganization of rural and urban governments. Schleiermacher was a passionate supporter of Stein's reforms.

Stein's work for the liberation of the peasants bore much fruit, but ironically much of it turned out to be bitter. Friedrich Wilhelm III had already freed his own serfs beginning in 1799. His serfs were freed of obligatory work and of their lord's rule in matters of marriage and inheritance. This was a reform of enormous proportions as some fifty thousand freehold farms were established. But with Friedrich Wilhelm's weak political will and the strength of the Junker nobility, the latter's peasants were freed only on the basis of Stein's edict, signed in 1807. Because of his short time in office, Stein's accomplishments in regard to the peasants were limited, but he did begin a process that would lead after many years to true liberation. More immediately, these changes bore bitter fruit; although Junker peasants were freed of the worst of their servitude, they were totally lacking in economic and political power. Stein's plans for the reorganization of rural government would have given the peasants some voice, but the plans were shelved when Stein was forced from office. Thus, in the agrarian crises of the 1820s, former serfs and small landowners were rendered destitute. Unable to secure the needed capital, some fifty thousand peasant farms and seventy thousand small family farms were claimed by the nobility.

The now landless peasants flocked to the cities, and their situation was difficult, often desperate. This resulted in a significant increase in Berlin's population, especially during the 1820s, and a corresponding increase in urban manifestations of poverty. The population of Berlin rose from 206,309 in 1822 to 265,122 in 1834. Shortages in work and in housing created great difficulties for people. In the period 1700–1800, real wages for workers had shrunk. Many workers did not have a subsistence wage, so women and children entered the workforce in order to survive. Housing was overcrowded; often there were seven families in one dwelling. Shortages in nutrition and health problems resulting from overcrowding and the beginnings of industrialization led to significant growth in begging and prostitution.[6]

Schleiermacher had firsthand experience of Berlin's new urban poor. The distribution of relief monies for the poor was an important aspect of the church's ministry, and "the Trinity Church community, especially Schleiermacher, took this task very seriously, doing as much as their resources made possible."[7] Schleiermacher also served on Berlin's "Poverty Directorate" (*Armendirektion*) for the last five years of his life. The Directorate was headed by the city's mayor and included other officials and clergy; it oversaw the distribution of funds to hospitals, poor houses, and other relief agencies.[8] In his role as pastor, Schleiermacher's main approach to the poor was to stress the organic character of the Christian community and urge those better off to assist those in need. But he also preached a sermon in spring of 1832 that dealt with poverty. Schleiermacher rejects notions of "worthiness" regarding the poor—relief is to be given solely on the basis of need—and he calls for "social insurance" to provide for the poor, anticipating by fifty years such a program in the Prussian state.[9] Certainly then, Schleiermacher was not indifferent to the poor; he was involved with relief efforts throughout his ministry and gave them particular attention during the final years of his life and ministry. Still, with Schleiermacher our expectations are always high, and one cannot but share Reich's sense of disappointment; perhaps Schleiermacher could have been more proactive in moving beyond charitable relief.[10]

Stein also began significant reform in education. At his suggestion as he was leaving office (having been forced out by Napoleon, who had discovered his anti-French activities), Wilhelm von Humboldt was appointed minister of education. Prior to this time, education, especially in the form of military training schools, had been controlled by the nobility and extended only to their children. Humboldt opposed this exclusion of the majority of children from schools, and he succeeded in advancing the principle that general education be available to all children. Over a period of years, *Volksschule* ("people's schools") were established and elementary education provided for all children. Schleiermacher served under Humboldt in the Ministry of the Interior from 1808–14 and contributed to the reformation of the educational system.

If Humboldt's work in reforming the universities was the crowning achievement of his career, the greatest single gem in the crown was the University of Berlin, and Schleiermacher was Humboldt's chief collaborator in making the university a reality. Balance between the philosophical vision of a universal and coherent system of human knowledge and attention to historical particularity is the hallmark of Schleiermacher's view, and it becomes incarnate in the new university. The philosophical vision of the interconnection of all knowledge was to pervade all departments of the university; at the same time, Schleiermacher championed such practical and particular fields as theology, medicine, and law against critics such as Fichte, who saw no room for them in a true university. Schleiermacher also insisted on the interconnection between research and teaching and on the university's freedom in both fields from state censorship. Schleiermacher also had a role in the ongoing leadership of the university: he helped select the original theology faculty, was dean of theology four separate times, and taught an impressive array of courses in philosophy and theology.

The tension between the king and the nobility, on the one hand, and the leaders of the reform movement, on the other, came especially to the fore in the struggle against Napoleon. Although both groups shared the objective of throwing off the French yoke, they differed markedly in their visions of a restored Prussia. The Reformers' window of opportunity remained open from Stein's short tenure as prime minister through the first nine years (1810–1819), when Prince Karl August von Hardenberg filled the role. The Reformers blamed Prussia's defeat by Napoleon on the autocratic absolutism of Friedrich II and wanted in its place a state based on broad, popular assent and guided by the ideals of *Aufklärung* ("enlightenment"), idealism, and neohumanism. Thus they believed that the overthrow of the French required the broad support of the people. Movement toward such a populist revolution took different forms: one was the formation of conspiratorial cells (an underground, revolutionary movement in which Schleiermacher took part); another was the establishment of a national guard (*Landswehr*, created in February 1813) and provincial militias (*Landsturm*, created in April 1813) peopled and led by ordinary citizens (burgher and peasant alike). As could be expected, the king was ambivalent toward these armies of the people; he desired their support, but was concerned lest the democratic spirit of these institutions spread and contaminate the state as a whole. Schleiermacher was ardent in his advocacy of the *Landswehr* and the *Landsturm*; he volunteered to serve in the former and drilled with the latter.

Friedrich Wilhelm had good cause for concern. The Reformers' patriotism, which for many, not least Schleiermacher, spilled over to become German nationalism, was melded with their reformist convictions. There were spirits at work in all this that the king feared and knew he could not easily control. The Reformers had been at work in the period 1807–13, drumming up the patriotic spirit of the people. They "had rightly judged that great moral forces were slumbering in the people which could be activated for the state."[11] The result was that the morale of the people was high, and this high morale was not an insignificant factor of the defeats of Napoleon in 1813 and 1815. In this same period, Schleiermacher was identified by some in the government as an enemy, and pressure arose that he be let go from his positions and sent into exile. In 1813–14 he worked as editor of the *Preussische Zeitung*, a reform-minded newspaper that was regularly critical of the government, particularly of any compromise with Napoleon. Schleiermacher's criticism of the government was such that the Royal Cabinet accused him of high treason and ordered his resignation as editor and his exile from Prussia. The order was never carried out, likely because of Schleiermacher's popularity with the people.

The presence and influence of reform-minded people within the ministries and bureaucracy of the Prussian government was drained away in the period 1815–19. The spirit of reform did not die, however, but arose in other places. Most prominent of these were the student associations (*Burschenschaften*); the first was established at the University of Jena in 1815, and by 1818 there was a union of *Burschenschaften* that brought together student organizations from universities across the German states. Many students had participated in the War of Liberation and returned with a spirit of patriotism and a sense of personal and political responsibility. The *Burschenschaften* were open to commoner and nobility alike, and with their commitment to reform in the direction of liberal and democratic ideas, they amounted to a transformation of earlier student associations that had been exclusive clubs where students could play at being nobility.

Schleiermacher was a strong supporter of the *Burschenschaften*; he saw them as a way in which students responsibly participate in the moral life of the community and state.

An event that quickened the move of the Prussian government in the direction of monarchical conservatism and brought about repression of dissent arose out of the student associations. Karl Follen was the radical leader of one student group; he advocated the union of the German states in a republican form of government and was disdainful of conventional morality to the point of allowing for the murder of unjust rulers. Inspired by Follen, the student Karl Ludwig Sand stabbed to death the reactionary poet August von Kotzebue in March 1819. Sand's ignominious deed brought about a strong reaction. Friedrich Wilhelm III was frightened and ordered that reform-minded leaders be spied upon and investigated. This work was concentrated on the universities, and a period of persecution and witch-hunts ensued known as the *Demagogenverfolgung*.

In reaction to Kotzebue's assassination and the general agitation of the *Burschenschaften*, the Karlsbad Decrees of September 1819, passed by the Congress of the Germanic Confederation, called for the suppression of all "subversive" expression in the press, universities, and Diets of the states. The Decrees were enforced throughout the German territories: freedom of the press was overturned (it had been affirmed in the Federal Act of the Confederation); censors were positioned in the universities; spies were sent to hear lectures and sermons (for most of the 1820s Schleiermacher could count on his sermons and lectures being reported to the political authorities); and the *Burschenschaften* were banned.

The political reaction that gathered momentum in responding to Kotzebue's assassination and dominated the political scene in the 1820s and '30s was supported by a growing tide of religious conservatism. The religious movement is dubbed the "Awakening," an expression of Neo-Pietism. The Awakening united religious and theological conservatism with social-political conservatism and created the "throne and altar" movement—the backbone of popular support for the reactionary policies of Friedrich Wilhelm in this period. The leaders of this movement have been defined as antithetical to the thought and action of Schleiermacher. Whereas the Neo-Pietists called for obedience to the king and the church and conformity to the status quo,

> in an entirely different response, Schleiermacher and some lesser-known clergymen from the ranks seemed to develop and take pride in a feeling of responsibility as representatives and leaders of the public generally and of liberal forces aiming at political and social change in particular.[12]

In 1810, Ludwig Nicolovius became minister of the ecclesiastical section of the Ministry of the Interior. He stressed the experience of regeneration to the point that it became for him the mark of an authentic theologian, but he also believed that the church could exist only in connection with the state. In this he typifies Neo-Pietism—at once holding deep pietist convictions and pledging unwavering allegiance to the state.

The Neo-Pietist/Orthodox coalition succeeded in having Schleiermacher's colleague on the theology faculty, Leberecht De Wette, dismissed from the university.[13] He was accused of inflaming students with liberal passions. The key evidence against De Wette was a letter of condolence he wrote to Sand's mother, in which he affirmed the student movement. When Schleiermacher protested De Wette's dismissal, the conservatives turned their anger on him. It seemed that he too might lose his position, but for him the storm passed. De Wette's firing and Schleiermacher's escape from the same fate were a portent of the future. Again in 1823 Schleiermacher came close to losing his position when letters critical of the king were found in the possession of his brother-in-law, Ernst Moritz Arndt. This controversy led to a complete severing of Schleiermacher's relation with the king that lasted until 1831. Neo-Pietism, with its commitment to "throne and altar," was on the ascendancy, and Schleiermacher was to spend most of the rest of his political life resisting its ideology and actions.

After the crisis period of Prussia's humiliation by Napoleon had passed and the German state had regained its feet as a military and political power, Friedrich Wilhelm III turned his attention to controlling all areas of Prussian life. Not least, he fixed on the church, for with the military, the government bureaucracy, and the monarchy, the established Protestant Church was one of the pillars of Prussian society. Under the ministry of Hardenberg, after 1810, state control over the church was increased as church properties were secularized, making the church financially dependent on the state. Then, in 1815, in order to gain control and religious unity in the expanded Prussian state, local ecclesial governing bodies were replaced by new Consistories that were directly controlled by the state. In 1816, the state, through its newly established general superintendencies, claimed the right to ordain and appoint pastors.

In 1817, the Church of the Prussian Union was created, bringing together Lutheran and Reformed. On October 31, 1817, on the three hundredth anniversary of the Reformation, a joint communion service was celebrated in Berlin; the language of its liturgy was framed in such a way that communion could be understood in either a Lutheran or Reformed way.

Whereas other union churches were created with the consent of church leaders (e.g., in Baden, Naussau, and the Palatinate), the Church of the Prussian Union was imposed from above by Friedrich Wilhelm. In 1817 Schleiermacher was the presiding officer of the Synod of Berlin. He favored the union and considered himself a theologian of the united Protestant Church, but he resisted the imposition of the union by royal fiat. He defended the union in print against conservative Lutheran critics, even as he affirmed the church's independence from state interference. Conflict with the Prussian government came to a head with the liturgical dispute that lasted from 1822 until 1829. Friedrich Wilhelm III wanted liturgical uniformity in the Prussian churches; when the liturgy he proposed was not accepted voluntarily, he imposed it on the basis of his authority as head of state and *ipso facto* head of the church. Schleiermacher led the opposition; he was one of the "twelve apostles," Berlin pastors who held out against the king. Schleiermacher found the liturgy "too Catholic," in his view more Catholic than Luther would have approved. He particularly opposed making the sign of the cross, saying the Apostles' Creed, and praying with his back to the congregation. The dispute raged on for seven years, finally ending when the king made an ultimatum: conform or lose your pastorate. So for a fourth time, Schleiermacher came close to losing his position. Having won only small concessions that allowed for continuing some local practices that were not part of the king's liturgy, Schleiermacher and the other "apostles" gave in. Although he ultimately lost the battle, in this ecclesiastical realm as in the political realm, Schleiermacher resisted the king's drive for increased control over Prussian life. He exercised his pastoral role in accordance with his convictions and was able to hold out against royal pressure for seven years.

Schleiermacher died in 1834. He had been a player in the political crises of 1806 and 1819. He inspired the church and the people to political activism in the causes of the liberation of Prussia and then its reform. And when the change in the social-political climate came in the 1820s, he resisted the new direction. How, then, does this correspond with the *Christian Ethics* and its orientation to social and political issues? To that we now turn.

TRANSFORMATION OF CULTURE IN THE *CHRISTIAN ETHICS*

The *Christian Ethics* takes up the issue of the relation between Christian faith and the larger society under the rubric of Christian action in the outer sphere. Schleiermacher recognizes in the social and cultural world outside the church civil parallels to the Christian actions of purification, expansion, and representation. This recognition then leads to the sixfold structure of the *Christian Ethics* as the three forms of action are crossed by the two spheres. The question addressed in Schleiermacher's analysis of the outer sphere is how the Christian individual and community are to relate to and interact with the larger social and cultural world.

Our reflection on Schleiermacher's conception of the inner/outer relation will show that, in its basic orientation to the issue of Christ and culture, the *Christian Ethics* has strong affinities with H. Richard Niebuhr's "Christ transforming culture" type.[14] In some places he uses the language of transformation, and even where he does not, the idea of transformation is present. Schleiermacher most typically speaks of cultural action appropriated by the Christian spirit and thereby given a new ground and goal. In the service of the Christian spirit, its impulse and ultimate aim are changed.

It is in his analysis of the broadening action in the outer sphere that Schleiermacher employs the language of "transformation." He speaks of the outer sphere being transformed by Christ. He notes that the outer sphere preexists Christianity; it does not need Christ or the church for its establishment. So, for a Christian consideration of the outer sphere, "the actual question will not be, 'How is the whole [broadening] process to be construed on the basis of the Christian principle?' but rather 'How does it transform itself by means of the Christian principle?'"[15] In a footnote,[16] the editor of the *Christian Ethics*, Ludwig Jonas, argues against the term "transformation" (*umbilden*) as it is not Schleiermacher's favored term in this connection. Jonas claims that the usual term is "appropriation," which indicates more clearly that the actual content of the moral action itself is not changed, but that moral activity is appropriated by the Christian spirit. But, as *pneuma* now provides the impulse to moral action and brings the action into the service of a new and higher goal, the form of the action is changed, even if its "matter" is unchanged. The action itself appears the same, but its impulse and goal, one might say its "form," has changed. Thus, in spite of Jonas' argument, the appropriation of moral action in the outer sphere by the Christian spirit does constitute a particular kind of "transformation."

The *Christian Ethics'* general orientation to the question of Christian relation to the wider society, then, includes strong overtones of transformation. As we have seen, the term "transformation" is used in relation to broadening action. Even where the language of transformation is not used, in relation to restoring and representational actions, the concept is present. The outer sphere is seen as that which exists prior to and independent of the Christian faith; it is to be taken up and transformed by the Christian spirit.[17]

The *Christian Ethics* also envisions transformation in concrete, particular ways as it analyzes the three different types of action. Each kind of action evidences a version of transformation appropriate to its sphere of activity. Under the rubric of restoring activity, Schleiermacher attends to issues related to punishment and war. Transformation in this connection is manifest primarily as a prophetic critique of social immorality; in some cases Schleiermacher includes a positive vision of a way in which a moral alternative can be put in place, but the emphasis is on critique. Transformation in regard to broadening action takes the form of transvaluation whereby cultural goods come to be seen in their relation to the highest good—the kingdom of God. Here the role and status of cultural goods is transformed as they are subordinated to and taken up into service of the kingdom of God. In regard to representational action, the distinctive image is that of the Christian spirit's permeation and modification of the cultural world. As the Christian spirit comes to inspire cultural communities of social and/or artistic expression, they are transformed from within. In what follows, then, we will demonstrate in some detail how these three manifestations of transformation are evident in the three different kinds of action.

RESTORING ACTION AND TRANSFORMATION AS PROPHETIC CRITIQUE

Prophetic critique is the way in which transformation is manifest under the rubric of restoring action, because it is in this realm that the opposition between civil and Christian moral vision is most acute. Opposition arises here because the civil exercise of restoring action typically includes the use of corporeal punishment within the state and the waging of war between states. The *Christian Ethics* does allow that punishment and war can be morally justified, but only within carefully prescribed limits, and only in the service of purposes that are ultimately constructive (rehabilitation or self-defense). In principle, Christian faith is opposed to violence.

This is evident in the "Introduction to Restoring Action," where Schleiermacher briefly attends to theories of criminal justice and distinguishes three different views of the nature and purpose of punishment. He argues that the Christian need not choose among these three views "because for us there is no punishment needed for betterment and no retribution for freedom from guilt because we have both of these only through our relationship to the Redeemer.... [T]he Christian as such finds no peace in [these views] and makes no use of them."[18] This does not resolve the issue of punishment altogether, for Schleiermacher admits that it can have a place in the civil realm. The issue comes to a head in regard to the family or household, for it belongs equally to the Christian and civil spheres. The issue of punishment comes into focus as Schleiermacher considers the discipline of children. He argues that reward and punishment have no place in Christian restoration because they work on a sensual level and provide no gauge of what a child has actually internalized. From a Christian point of view, punishment has no place because it cannot effect spiritual restoration; it only causes bitterness. He does allow that punishment may be used in a household, but only for the purpose of maintaining order, that is, to protect the weaker members of the household. This is analogous to the state's use of punishment: to protect the health and welfare of individuals from harm by others.[19] Schleiermacher concludes, "punishment and Christian discipline are opposites."[20]

Schleiermacher's consideration of war follows a parallel line of thought. He sees defensive wars as morally justifiable, when waged in order to protect or restore the rights or freedom of persons. But underlying his consideration is a fundamental opposition to war. He asserts that war, in and of itself, has no place in the moral task and that "all wars of aggression are absolutely immoral."[21] Schleiermacher does allow for wars of self-defense, but at the most basic level there is a clear opposition between violence (punishment and war), on the one hand, and Christian morality, on the other. This opposition is the ground for Christian critique of civil restoration and for efforts to transform civil practice.

The opposition between Christian and civil morality is, then, the reason that prophetic critique looms prominently in the Christian response to restoring action. The theme that runs throughout is the rejection of violence as immoral (except for self-defense); Schleiermacher identifies the death penalty, violent revolution, wars of aggression, and forceful colonization as immoral ways in which states or social-political movements attempt to work out "restoration." All of these actions are of a violent and coercive nature, and Schleiermacher, arguing from a "just war" stance, rejects them as immoral.

The *Christian Ethics'* opposition to the death penalty is a prime example of the transformative impulse expressed as prophetic critique. Schleiermacher identifies the death penalty as immoral from a Christian point of view, asserts that Christians must strive resolutely to abolish it, and urges Christian rulers to move toward such abolition.[22] He argues that the death penalty is immoral because it is a form of suicide that violates the social contract. By choosing to remain as a citizen of a state, the individual is implicitly assenting to the state's laws, including the punishments it prescribes. Actually, then, when the state punishes an individual in accord with its laws, it imposes a punishment that the individual is willing to have imposed upon her or him. But suicide is contrary to Christian morality; no one can assent to his or her own death. This applies also to the state itself; the exercise of the death penalty is suicide, a "partial self-murder,"[23] as the state kills part of itself.

Schleiermacher concludes that the death penalty is a barbaric practice that the Christian must oppose. He asserts that as the state is taken up by Christianity, the identification of capital punishment as superfluous, unnecessary, and immoral must grow. Schleiermacher's argumentation becomes specifically Christian at another point as he counters the assertion that there are persons who should be put to death because they are irredeemable. Such a claim is unchristian, for it denies the power of grace.

Schleiermacher not only critiques the practice of capital punishment; he also offers the ruler suggestions as to how change might be made. He calls for the suspension of executions. This is to be a test period, and he is confident that experience will show that crime does not worsen without a death penalty. Convinced of this, the law can be changed, the death penalty abolished. In this way, Schleiermacher offers not only a critique, but also a constructive alternative. He specifies a way in which transformation might occur.

The consideration of punishment, discussed above, has its locus in the *Christian Ethics* under the restoration of the individual, effected by society as a whole. Schleiermacher also takes up the reverse question—restoration that the individual might work on society. Here the issue of social change is addressed, and Schleiermacher emerges as an advocate of attempts to better society and state, even as his prophetic critique is directed against those who would call for violent revolution. The arguments of this section move on two different fronts. The main front is the issue of force. Schleiermacher identifies the use of force (*Gewalt*) in effecting change as immoral, and asserts that one must remain content with the results of nonviolent efforts at change, even when its pace is slow. He claims that "it would always be against the spirit of Christianity to seek to restore a better condition through force,"[24] and says that because the Christian tendency is to overcome coercion as the basis of political rule, it can never be Christian to replace one tyrant with another.[25] Here the prophetic critique is directed against those who call for violent revolution.

On the other front, Schleiermacher affirms Christian responsibility to advocate change and provide a check on the power of the rulers. He calls for each individual to act according to his or her political position and for each to contribute his or her "best insight" (*höchste Berathung*) to reforming tendencies.[26] Schleiermacher calls for Christian engagement in the political process, for involvement in movements that would seek to improve the social order. As Birkner notes, the key presupposition to Schleiermacher's position is that there be freedom of public communication and a relation of mutual influence between society as a whole and its individual members.[27] This notion of reciprocity between the individual and society and the call for openness in society (and church) is explicit in Schleiermacher's consideration of the relation between the individual and the whole, and is presupposed in the analysis of the state's betterment.[28] The question left unanswered in this analysis is whether violence could be justified in a situation where there is no (or severely limited) freedom of public communication. It is possible that Schleiermacher would allow for revolution under circumstances of extreme repression. Birkner suggests as much when he says that it is only on the presupposition of such open communication, including the rejection of censorship, that revolutionary action in state or church is ruled out.[29] Still it is evident that the argument leans heavily against violent revolution. Schleiermacher's affirmation of societal openness is, in itself, a prophetic critique of the order in Prussia after 1819, when an atmosphere of repression prevailed.

Under the rubric of restoring activity, Schleiermacher takes up the issue of war. War is considered in this locus because the only kind of war that can be morally justified is one in which an "injured" (*verlezt*) state seeks reparation from an aggressor state. Schleiermacher here presupposes the sovereignty of individual states; one state cannot seek to restore another unless it has been the victim of the other state's aggression. He affirms relations of mutual influence between peoples and states, but limits war to this one case.[30] The purpose of war can be only restoration—the righting of a previous wrong. Schleiermacher insists that the relation among states is moral in character and must be recognized to be such. The rights of other states must be recognized, even as the rights of one's own state may be protected. Thus wars of aggression are rejected as immoral, as are wars that purport to be defensive but are in fact based on the state's own self-interest.[31] At the same time, Schleiermacher limits even defensive, restorative wars; they are morally justifiable only when all other avenues have been exhausted: direct negotiations, the influence of other states, and submission to a third state's arbitration must be tried first.[32] Here, then, is a significant expression of critique: Schleiermacher, standing in the just war tradition, rejects all wars of aggression as immoral. He does not advocate pacifism,[33] but he does critique violence by carefully limiting the conditions under which war can be morally justified.

Schleiermacher's rejection of coercion finds explicit expression in his consideration of the state's relation to those who are citizens of another state or of no state. He argues that the same rights and protection must be accorded those who are not citizens as are accorded citizens. It is unchristian not to extend such rights to all persons.[34] He then addresses the issue of colonization, the spread of "civilization" to those who are "uncivilized." Although he asserts Christian responsibility to spread civilization, "to help those outside of the state into a state,"[35] he rejects all use of force in such efforts. To force persons into civilization is a contradiction in terms; coercion cannot create civilization. Of even more importance, from Schleiermacher's point of view, coercion is and must be opposed by Christianity. It is the use of force that has undermined attempts to spread Christian faith in "new" lands. Schleiermacher concludes this argument with a rhetorical flourish. He recognizes that his analysis has come "somewhat late" (force has already been employed in colonization and evangelization); he notes that "theory always comes somewhat late. Unfortunately it never comes too late because the use of force has always not yet stopped."[36] In this way, the urgency of his critique comes to expression: the use of force is an ongoing issue, and its use must be challenged. Here prophetic critique can be a first step toward transformation.

PROPHETIC CRITIQUE IN RELATION TO BROADENING AND REPRESENTATIONAL ACTIONS

Prophetic critique can also be found under the rubrics of broadening and representational action, although it is not the dominant form of transformation manifest there, because in these areas violence and coercion play little or no explicit role. Where violence and coercion are explicit, the *Christian Ethics'* transformative impulse takes the form of critique—that which is opposed to the Christian spirit of love and respect for all persons is rejected as immoral and opposed. Included in the analysis of broadening action in the outer sphere is rejection of divorce, slavery, and dehumanization in labor as immoral. Under the rubric of representational action, prophetic critique is directed against dueling, competitiveness, and games of chance. Schleiermacher makes it clear that such activities are immoral from the point of view of Christian ethics, and he opposes them.

Schleiermacher's rejection of divorce occurs as he considers the family under the rubric of broadening action.[37] He sees the family as the most basic human community and one that occupies a unique position because it belongs equally to civil and ecclesial society. When the family is Christianized, it is "modified in a distinctive way."[38] This is so especially as propagation and formation come together and are imprinted with the Christian spirit. The family becomes the basic unit of the church and the key vehicle for the expansion of Christianity as children are raised and nurtured in the faith. The marriage relation that is the basis of the family is seen by Schleiermacher as necessarily monogamous because Christianity asserts the equality of men and women. In this context, he claims that "the true ideal of Christian marriage is that both parties feel themselves bound in a wholly individual and indissoluble way"; this means then that "in the Christian church, marriage is absolutely indissoluble."[39] Even while making this claim, Schleiermacher recognizes that it is at odds with the practice of the Prussian church. This he attributes to the fact that marriage is both a civil and ecclesial institution. He reasons that if the state allows divorce, the church should not hinder it. Nor does he want the church to insist in a legalistic fashion that all marriages must be maintained even when both partners desire dissolution. The solution he proposes is that the church gain more influence over the establishment of marriage so that it might nurture it and move closer to the ideal of marriage as a unique and spiritual union. Here then we have expression of a clear critique of culture from a Christian point of view, and a suggestion as to how the church might transform cultural practice and move toward the Christian ideal.[40]

The other important critique set out under the rubric of broadening action is that directed against the dehumanization of workers in the industrial revolution that Schleiermacher saw in its very early stages. This includes a vehement rejection of slavery. Overall, Schleiermacher's ethical vision—in both its philosophical and Christian forms—can be seen as undergirding the technological and industrial developments of the nineteenth century in that an important goal is for humans to rule and shape the natural world. Along with this goes a kind of ethical optimism—faith in progress as human knowledge and control grows.[41] But Schleiermacher is not unaware of the underside of such technological and industrial development. He is particularly concerned that contemporary forms of production are dehumanizing, because the human person becomes just another cog in the wheel. Such a complete domination of "nature formation" over "talent formation" Schleiermacher calls "mechanism." This is promoted by the division of labor and results in dehumanization because the spirit of the worker is destroyed. Schleiermacher rejects such dehumanization of individuals and also rejects the domination of any one social-economic class over the others. Both of these—dehumanization of individuals and domination by a ruling class—are, in essence, forms of slavery.[42]

Schleiermacher rejects slavery on explicitly Christian grounds, arguing for a real divergence between philosophical ethics and Christian ethics at this point. Whereas philosophical ethics—Schleiermacher cites Aristotle—tacitly approves of the differences between slaves and free persons, Christian ethics cannot.

> From a Christian standpoint such a difference [between slave and free] has never been capable of validation; one must always insist on its being overcome. This is so because one who is capable of community with Christ—and according to the Christian view, this is all persons—must be a free being and participate in a spiritual life, not be a human machine.[43]

Here one might well question Schleiermacher's seemingly selective interpretation of Christian history. Much more could be said about these issues; certainly, Christian opposition to slavery has not been universal. Still, Schleiermacher's own opposition to dehumanization and slavery is clear, as are the Christian grounds he claims for it.[44]

Under the rubric of representational action in the outer sphere we also find moments of critique in which Schleiermacher speaks out against immorality. Under this rubric, Schleiermacher deals with the social and artistic life of society, from friendship to "high" cultural art forms. Here he is explicit about the need to identify those forms of expression that are immoral. He calls for open communication within the church so that together persons might identify those forms of social and artistic expression that give rise to "a purely sensual tendency in social pleasure and [are] lacking in every higher impulse."[45] To be moral, all social representation must proceed from the spirit, not merely from sensual impulses. Social and artistic expression that merely excites pleasure or pain without calling persons to genuine subjectivity and intersubjectivity fails to be truly spiritual. Thus dueling is rejected, as are competition and gambling.[46] These critiques are consistent with Schleiermacher's emphasis on spirit, understood as the affirmation of human subjectivity and mutuality. The distortion inherent in dueling, competition, and gambling is the denial of personhood or interpersonal relation in one way or another. Dueling denies personhood by risking life—both one's own and that of one's opponent. Competition denies equality in intersubjective relations as it affirms the superiority of "winners" over "losers." Gambling is frivolous because its outcome is determined by the luck of the draw and its prize is sensual. Schleiermacher rejects these forms of social life as immoral and dehumanizing.

BROADENING ACTION AND TRANSFORMATION AS THE TRANSVALUATION OF CULTURAL GOODS

Under the rubric of broadening action, the distinctive form of transformation is a transvaluation of cultural goods. Cultural goods are seen in a new way in light of Christian faith. In Schleiermacher's view, Christian ethics has most affinity with an ethics of the highest good; from the Christian point of view the highest good is the kingdom of God. For the Christian, the valuation of cultural goods is altered, relativized as they are seen in relation to the kingdom. Cultural goods remain good, but they are subordinated to the highest good and taken up into its service; they are transvalued in light of God's reign.

Broadening action is action by means of which the rule of human spirit over nature is expanded.[47] Such action is based on the original identity of spirit and nature, and is manifest as spirit taking possession of nature; nature thereby becomes the organ of spirit. Schleiermacher envisions the broadening process in terms of the complementary aspects of "talent formation" and "nature formation." The former concerns the development of human skills and abilities by means of which the human person is able to form the natural world. The latter concerns that formation of the external, natural world by humans. Thus, broadening action comprises educational and economic activity, both broadly construed. The rule of spirit over nature is accomplished as persons grow in knowledge and ability and as this knowledge and ability is employed in their cultivation and formation of the natural world.

The custodian of this broadening process is the state. In Schleiermacher's view, the state's real task is to oversee the economic and educational development that together comprise broadening action.[48] This is indicative of the importance of the state as a human community; it is the custodian of the most basic form of moral activity. Schleiermacher also comes to identify the state as the crucial human community in this regard, because it is the determinate form of community with concrete relation to the broadening process. He sees the state as existing between two extremes: at one end there is the individual and at the other end the absolute community of all persons together. In Schleiermacher's view, no individual is alone in the process of broadening, so the individual cannot be its locus. The absolute community is not yet realized in any concrete way; thus he appeals to the state as the determinate community existing between these two extremes.[49] The state, in Schleiermacher's view, is the "form of a people,"[50] and Schleiermacher cites scripture as affirming the significance of state and people as expressions of human community and morality.

The state preexists the advent of Christianity, and in Schleiermacher's view Christianity presupposes the existence of the state as a crucial bearer of civilization, so the issue for Christian ethics becomes that of the relation between the Christian community and the state as custodian of the broadening process. Schleiermacher rejects the notion that the state is only a necessary evil from a Christian point of view, and he stands against those who see the negation of national differences inherent in the perfection of the kingdom of God. Instead, he appeals to the scriptural notion of the state as a divine institution and insists on a careful analysis of the Christian relation to the state.

Asking whether Christian ethics is to sanction or transform the state, Schleiermacher calls to mind his view of the relation between Christian ethics and philosophical ethics—identical as to matter, different as to form. Here he works out this relation, appealing to Romans 13:5, where Paul calls for his readers to subject themselves to the authorities both for the sake of avoiding punishment and for the sake of conscience. The difference between the citizen and the Christian is a difference of conscience. Whereas the citizen's conscience subordinates itself to the nation as a whole as its norm and goal, Christian conscience is governed by the divine will, which aims at the absolute community of all persons. The action of the Christian citizen and the non-Christian citizen may appear to be the same, but there is an important difference in motivation and in the goal for which each strives. Schleiermacher identifies this change as quite literally a "transformation," a change in form. It is the form of the action that is different—the motivation and ultimate goal that shape the action.

One of the clear implications of this view is that Christianity opposes any form of "selfish nationalism."[51] From the Christian point of view, the nation is not the highest good, and when it is treated as such the result is idolatrous distortion. Nationalism provides a concrete example of the way in which Schleiermacher interprets and appropriates the Augustinian notion of non-Christian virtues as magnificent vices. Rather than being oriented toward and aiming at the highest good, these virtuous vices aim only at a limited good. The prime example of a magnificent vice is a nationalism that elevates the nation (a limited good) to the status of the highest good.[52] This is idolatrous perversion. In another context, Schleiermacher claims that moments when the Christian spirit transforms nationalism—bringing the nation into the service of the kingdom of God—represent the "greatest triumph of the Christian spirit." This is the case because the self-interest of the state is the most powerful force that can oppose Christianity.[53] This "transvaluation" of cultural goods includes within it an element of prophetic critique. Schleiermacher is vehement in his rejection of a nationalism that sees the nation as the final goal of the moral process.[54]

Positively, Schleiermacher's view is that the work of the state in the broadening process is to be appropriated by the Christian disposition and brought into its service. Not only does Christianity oppose selfish nationalism and anything in the state that might hinder the expansion of the kingdom of God; it also "intends the whole sphere of nature and talent formation for the broadening of the Kingdom of God according to the Christian idea."[55] Schleiermacher argues that a people acts morally when it pursues its formation process only for the sake of the whole human race. So the broadening process, manifest as it is in and with the particularity of people and state, is to be taken up into the service of the kingdom of God and the universal goal that it seeks. In this way the value of a particular cultural good is reordered in light of the kingdom of God. The good that the state represents is subordinated to the kingdom of God and taken up in its service. Schleiermacher affirms that the Christian principle seeks to overcome all conflictual national differences without negating a nation's individual character. Here we have transformation by means of transvaluation. The state and its participation in the moral process are transformed; its distortions are named and its appropriation as a vehicle for the highest good affirmed. This happens as the state's value is reassessed, transvalued by being seen in light of the kingdom of God.

In the context of this analysis of the relation between the state and the Christian vision of the kingdom of God, Schleiermacher suggests that the moral life and ethical understanding receive a particular, material specification from Christianity. Schleiermacher says that we cannot know for certain whether rational ethics would have grasped the notion of the absolute community as the goal of the moral process without Christianity. He says, "Now, rational ethics must also set forth this [idea]. But we cannot know if it would have come to this [comprehension] without Christianity, for that

[case] is not given to us."[56] Thus, in this instance Schleiermacher says that perhaps Christianity contributes not only a new form but also a particular and crucial idea to moral reflection—that of the highest good as the absolute community of all persons.

Under the rubric of broadening action we have a second, distinctive kind of transformation at work. Although what we have identified as transvaluation includes within it an element of prophetic critique, it is distinctive in its focus on the Christian view of the reign of God as the highest good. The status and value of cultural goods is transformed for Christian ethics in light of the kingdom. Cultural life is changed, for it is no longer an independent realm; its ultimate value is self-contained, self-defined. Rather, cultural goods are appropriated for and by the Christian spirit and community and made to serve the Christian goal, which is universal in its scope. Schleiermacher suggests that this is a distinctively religious, and perhaps even a particularly Christian, contribution to ethical vision. The cultural drive to develop persons and have dominion over the earth is transformed by the Christian vision as it is brought into service of the latter's teleological drive for God's reign.

REPRESENTATIONAL ACTION AND TRANSFORMATION AS CHRISTIAN PERMEATION OF CULTURE

Transformation as the Christian spirit's infiltration and permeation of cultural communities finds expression in Schleiermacher's consideration of representational action in the outer sphere.[57] The distinctiveness of this version of transformation resides in its vision of the Christian moving out into the world of social and artistic expression and transforming it from within by the infusion of Christian spirit. Representational action in the outer sphere is action that seeks to express the inner feeling of a particular human community in an outward and visible way. Schleiermacher understands social and artistic actions, from informal gatherings of friends to the most sophisticated art forms, as representational actions of this sort. The feeling or immediate self-consciousness that representational activity in the outer sphere expresses is particularly human self-consciousness of its own nature as embodied spirit, its distinctive role as overseer of the natural world, and its sense that this consciousness and activity is thoroughly corporate. The issue to be sorted out in this section of the *Christian Ethics* is how the Christian community is to relate to the social and artistic activity that goes on outside of it.

Early on in his discussion of representational action in the outer sphere, Schleiermacher takes up the issue of conflict between Christian morality and civil morality.[58] He notes that such conflict was particularly common for the earliest Christians, and that often individuals were faced with a difficult choice—either to "give up the stringency of the Christian principle or be excluded from society."[59] Neither of these options is desirable from a Christian point of view, because it is important both that persons be true to Christian conviction and that they remain within society and attempt to influence it. Schleiermacher also claims that the reason for such conflict is the fact that society "is not yet rightly permeated by the Christian principle."[60] It is not surprising then that he concludes that given the choice between surrender of the Christian principle and exclusion from society, a Christian must remain faithful and suffer such exclusion. But even while he recognizes that, given an extreme case, accepting such exclusion is the proper response, Schleiermacher cautions that such a conclusion needs to be properly understood. In general, he warns that withdrawal from society and its temptations does not produce true virtues but only apathy.[61] Except in such extreme cases where Christian morality will be compromised,[62] the Christian is not to withdraw from social and artistic life.

Positively stated, the Christian moral task in this regard is to "seek in all his social relations to manifest the Christian virtues, but at the same time always to work so that the common feeling in each totality to which he belongs is ever more in agreement with the demands of the Christian principle."[63] Here Schleiermacher notes that most individuals will belong to several such communities and that each will contradict the Christian principle in some way. So the task for the individual in each community to which he or she belongs is to express the Christian virtues, identify the community's imperfections, and manifest the Christian principle so that the common feeling of the community will be altered by it. This is transformation by infiltration so that communities of the outer sphere can be permeated by the Christian spirit and changed from within. Appealing to Jesus' participation in weddings and banquets and Paul's rules about Christian participation in heathen banquets, Schleiermacher argues that this is also the view of scripture. Social and artistic representation is not to be avoided, but is to be preserved and ever more Christianized.[64]

At this point we might well ask what this part of the Christian life, seeking to transform cultural communities from within, looks like. The material we have from this section of the *Ethics* is not itself very concrete on this point. But there is reference to the "Christian virtues" and the "Christian principle" being manifest, so if we examine the understanding of these concepts, which he develops in other contexts, we will have some clues as to how he might envision this aspect of the Christian life in more concrete terms.

In Chapter 5 we noted that Schleiermacher identifies the Christian virtues as purity, patience, forbearance, and humility. These virtues express the individual's moral and spiritual character. They bespeak the "serenity" that is the overall tone of the Christian life, they express its "moral grace," and they enable one to avoid the moral dangers inherent in the four different determinations of self-consciousness. So the virtue of purity represents a serenity that experiences pleasure without its becoming desire. The virtue of patience enables one to experience pain without responding in a sensual way (e.g., angrily). Forbearance represents the "undisturbed continuation of love, in spite of the moral imperfection of its object"[65] (e.g., one who has offended the Christian community). And humility is indicative of resistance to pride in regard to the Christian community, (e.g., the recognition that all are equally dependent on Christ, so there is no basis for boasting or a sense of superiority). Schleiermacher insists that the virtuous Christian experiences real pain and pleasure, but his or her response is not determined by these feelings. Instead, the Christian spirit directs one's response, and its serenity issues in purity, patience, forbearance, and humility. These are the Christian virtues that are to characterize all Christian action, including participation in communities of social and artistic representation.

The other concept that can help concretize Schleiermacher's vision of Christian transformation in this context is that of the "Christian principle." Consistently in this section of the *Christian Ethics* (pp. 623–31) there is reference to the "Christian principle"; often it is identified as the principle of "brotherly love."[66] Of even more importance for our purposes, "brotherly love" is seen as the principle of Christian representational action.[67] Previously we have seen that community and representational action are "equally original."[68] Now we can say that representational action has a similar relationship with love: it both presupposes and creates love. The essence of such love, which is also the essence of representational action, is the "continual joining together of self-consciousness which is separated by personality."[69] Such expression of self-consciousness, which manifests and makes real union and community, must be mutual; all persons must give and take; each must be spontaneous and receptive. Without such mutuality, the true equality of all Christians—an equality of the Spirit and under Christ—becomes a facade. As Schleiermacher develops his view of "brotherly love" and representational action, it becomes clear that they are, above all, characterized by the equality and mutuality of all persons in Christ.[70] We may suggest, then, that it is this mutuality and equality in Christ that is a crucial goal in the Christian transformation of communities of representational action in the outer sphere.

Again in this chapter the close correspondence between Schleiermacher's life and ministry, on the one hand, and the ethical vision set forth in the *Christian Ethics*, on the other, is evident. From his positions at Trinity Church, the University of Berlin, and the Interior Ministry, Schleiermacher was consistently an activist promoting reform. He was ardent in his advocacy of the reform movement initiated by Stein, contributing to changes in the educational system. In the wars of liberation against Napoleon and in his support for the student *Burschenschaften*, Schleiermacher encouraged popular movements of the people aimed at reform. And in the reactionary period after 1819 he opposed the "throne and altar" movement and resisted the king's efforts to wield control over the church. Over the years there were at least four times when Schleiermacher was on the verge of losing his position as a result of his orientation and actions in the social-political realm.

The transformative impulse of the *Ethics* can be seen as a theoretical reflection of Schleiermacher's reformist actions. It was also a practical action itself. During Schleiermacher's life, the *Christian Ethics* existed only as the twelve semester–long lecture series on Christian ethics. As Schleiermacher enunciated his positions—rejecting wars of aggression and the death penalty, slavery and the dehumanization of workers, selfish nationalism, dueling and gambling, and calling for openness in society, mutuality and equality in relationships among persons, and commitment to the reign of God as the absolute community of all with all—he was acting. The *Christian Ethics* existed originally as a speech act, one permeated with a reformist orientation to the social and political issues of the day.

So as we have it today, the *Christian Ethics* is not only an ecclesial ethics of piety, but also a theology of culture.[71] The transformative character of this theology of culture is now evident. The *Christian Ethics* promotes its vision of culture transformed by Christ by means of particular manifestations for each of the three kinds of action in the outer sphere: prophetic critique for restoring action; transvaluation of cultural goods for broadening action; and infiltration and permeation by the Christian spirit for representational action. Schleiermacher, and particularly his *Christian Ethics*, have marked affinity with Niebuhr's "Christ transforming culture" type. This places Schleiermacher in a tradition that, according to Niebuhr, includes the Gospel of John, Augustine, Calvin, and F. D. Maurice—all envisioning culture transformed by Christ.

The connection with Calvin anticipates an important theme for the seventh and final chapter of this book. How might we assess where Schleiermacher stands in relation to the Reformed tradition, particularly in terms of his *Christian Ethics*? The final chapter asks the question of the Reformed character of the *Christian Ethics*, even as it seeks to draw the lines of our analysis together.

NOTES

1. H. Richard Niebuhr, *Christ and Culture* (New York: Harper & Row, 1951), 93–94.

2. Yorick Spiegel, *Theologie der bürgerlichen Gesellschaft: Sozialphilosophie und Glaubenslehre bei Friedrich Schleiermacher* (Munich: Kaiser Verlag, 1968); Dieter

Schellong, *Bürgertum und christliche Religion: Anpassungsprobleme der Theologie seit Schleiermacher* (Munich: Kaiser Verlag, 1975); and Frederick Herzog, *Justice Church: The New Function of the Church in North American Christianity* (Maryknoll, N. Y.: Orbis Books, 1980). Cf. Richard Crouter, "Schleiermacher and the Theology of Bourgeois Society: A Critique of the Critics," *Journal of Religion* 66, no. 3 (July 1986): 302–23. Crouter argues that the above-cited interpretations "illustrate the intellectual bankruptcy of the sociology of knowledge when its insight is taken in lieu of judicious historical reflection as a means of understanding the past" (303).

3. Hajo Holborn, *A History of Modern Germany*, 3 vols. (New York: Alfred Knopf, 1959–69), vol. 2 (1648–1840), 308.

4. Robert M. Bigler, *The Politics of German Protestantism: The Rise of the Protestant Church Elite in Prussia, 1815–1848* (Berkeley: University of California Press, 1972), 32.

5. Ibid., 396.

6. Andreas Reich, *Friedrich Schleiermacher als Pfarrer an der Berliner Dreifaltigkeitskirche 1809–1834* (Berlin and New York: Walter de Gruyter, 1992), 1–4.

7. Ibid., 289.

8. Ibid., 266.

9. Ibid., 282–84. The sermon was preached on the Eleventh Sunday after Trinity and is found in *Sämmtliche Werke*, div. 2, vol. 3, ed. Ludwig Jonas (Berlin: G. Reimer, 1843), 364ff.

10. Having identified Schleiermacher's positive work in providing relief to the poor and his proposal of "social insurance," Reich still wonders if Schleiermacher "didn't underestimate the social phenomenon of poverty. To all appearances, he perceived it only in a limited way; this is painful in view of his usual way of thinking" (ibid., 37).

11. Ibid., 425.

12. Ibid., 33.

13. On de Wette, see John W. Rogerson, *W. M. L. de Wette, Founder of Modern Biblical Criticism: An Intellectual Biography* (Sheffield, Eng.: JSOT Press, an Imprint of Sheffield Academic Press, 1992), esp. 146–59.

14. Cf. below for a further development of the particular kind of transformation that Schleiermacher envisions in regard to representational action; his primary image is of the permeation of the outer sphere by the Christian spirit.

15. Friedrich Schleiermacher, *Die christliche Sitte nach den Grundsätzen der evangelischen Kirche im Zusammenhange dargestellt*, ed. Ludwig Jonas in *Sämmtliche Werke*, div. 1, vol. 12 (Berlin: G. Reimer, 1843), 441. Hereafter referred to as the *Christian Ethics*.

16. Ibid.

17. Cf. Niebuhr, 190–229.

18. Ibid., 98.

19. Ibid., 234–37.

20. Ibid., 236.

21. Ibid., 454, 484. Cf. Hans-Joachim Birkner, *Schleiermachers Christliche Sittenlehre im Zusammenhang seines Philosophisch-Theologischen Systems*, Theologische Bibliothek Töpelmann, edited by Kurt Aland et al. (Berlin: Alfred Töpelmann, 1964), 134.

22. See *Christian Ethics*, 247–50.

23. Ibid., 249.

24. Ibid., 267.

25. Ibid., 269. This corresponds to Schleiermacher's attitude toward the French Revolution of 1789 and the execution of King Louis XVI in 1793. Richard Crouter quotes Schleiermacher's letter of February 14, 1793, in which he says he is "not afraid of confessing that upon the whole [he] heartily sympathize[s] with the French Revolution," even as he says that "no policy in the world can justify men in committing murder, and that it is infamous to condemn a man who is convicted of no guilt." See *The Life of Schleiermacher as Unfolded in His Autobiography and Letters*, trans. Frederica Rowan (London: Smith, Elder and Co., 1860) 1: 109; as quoted in Richard Crouter, "Schleiermacher and the Theology of Bourgeois Society: A Critique of the Critics," *Journal of Religion* 66, no. 2 (July 1986): 310. Here we see a position similar to that articulated in the *Christian Ethics*—at once affirming social change and rejecting violence. This seems also to correspond with Schleiermacher's position in 1808, when there was Prussian agitation against French domination under Napoleon. In these circumstances, "Schleiermacher went the way of agitation, but not the way of conspiracy." See Martin Redeker, *Schleiermacher: Life and Thought*, trans. John Wallhausser (Philadelphia: Fortress Press, 1973), 131–32.

26. *Christian Ethics*, 265–66.

27. Birkner, 96–97.

28. On the "principle of openness," see *Christian Ethics*, 189, 216, 272.

29. Birkner, 96–97.

30. *Christian Ethics*, 273–85, provides this analysis of war.

31. Schleiermacher recognizes that it may be impossible to discern with certainty whether a particular war is just or not, whether it is based on self-interest or the legitimate rights of a people. Still he insists that the principle is right, even if difficult to apply in some cases. Ibid., 277–78.

32. Ibid., 279.

33. At this point we can also recognize the "limits to transformation" that are part of Schleiermacher's analysis of war. There are three that are of particular note. The first is the rejection of pacifism. He argues that pacifism ought not be an option for individual persons, unless the state itself declares that it will never go to war. In the second place, his optimism regarding the technological "improvements" in the weaponry of war leads him to conclude that modern means of waging war (muskets, cannon) are more moral than traditional means. Third, he asserts that, because the individual citizen cannot discern whether a war waged by his or her state is just or not, the citizen's duty is to obey orders in carrying out the war, even while making known his or her reservations through appropriate channels. (See *Christian Ethics*, 280–85.) Birkner (134–35) notes that the rejection of individual pacifism makes sense only if we bear in mind Schleiermacher's view of the goal of war—not to shed blood, but only to occupy the enemy's territory. We would suggest that the same applies to optimism regarding modern weaponry. He seems to see warfare transformed from hand-to-hand combat into strategic maneuvering in which actual combat will be minimized. Seen within the context of his view of the goal of war, his "optimism" about modern warfare may not be as laughable as it first appears.

34. *Christian Ethics*, 286–87.

35. Ibid., 288.

36. Ibid., 290.

37. Ibid., 336–64. Cf. also the sermon on divorce in *Sämmtliche Werke* 2, 1: 585ff.

38. *Christian Ethics*, 337.
39. Ibid., 352, 340.
40. Other readings of Schleiermacher's rejection of divorce are, of course, possible. As one would expect, Karl Barth thunders against what he perceives to be duplicity—Schleiermacher first rejecting divorce and then finding "loopholes" that allow it. See Karl Barth, *The Theology of Schleiermacher*, ed. Dietrich Ritschl, trans. Geoffrey W. Bromiley (Grand Rapids: Eerdmans, 1982), 113–19. Barth's interpretation must be noted, but Schleiermacher's opposition to divorce and attempt to overcome it cannot be gainsaid.
41. Birkner, 138.
42. *Christian Ethics*, 464–66, 489.
43. Ibid., 466.
44. Barth's commendation of Schleiermacher's social-political vision is relevant to this point. In a chapter on Schleiermacher's "Sunday Sermons from the Last Years," Barth lauds their social awareness. Schleiermacher is aware of and opposed to the poverty and oppression of the lower classes; he "discharged with openness of vision and a powerful voice a watchman's office" in regard to issues of social inequality. See Barth, 39.
45. *Christian Ethics*, 636. Even while he calls for such communal discernment, he recognizes the difficulty in achieving consensus about such issues. This is the case because no action is sinful in and of itself (he offers dancing as an example). Sin and temptation have crucial subjective elements: what is temptation for one is not for another. Appeal to the scriptural notion that one ought not offend the weaker brother or sister might lead one to conclude that Christians should avoid all social representation, but Schleiermacher argues that this is not the orientation of the New Testament. Jesus participated in social life (e.g., wedding festivals), and Paul presupposes such participation by Christians. The message of scripture is that social representation not be shunned, but Christianized. In this way Schleiermacher affirms Christian participation in social life, even while he acknowledges the need for communal discernment of the immoral elements in this realm. See *Christian Ethics*, 632–42.
46. On dueling, see *Ethics*, 625–26; on competition and games of chance, 693–96.
47. The introductory analysis of broadening action in the outer sphere is found in *Christian Ethics*, 440–69.
48. Birkner, 136.
49. *Christian Ethics*, 449–51.
50. "Materially State and people are the same; the State is the form which a people gives itself in order to bring its common consciousness into appearance" (ibid., 455).
51. Schleiermacher says that not only Christianity, but any religious standpoint supports "no patriotism which makes the fatherland into a selfish moral person" (ibid., 461).
52. Ibid., 306.
53. Ibid., 491.
54. This is an important counterpoint to the argument of Jerry F. Dawson, *Friedrich Schleiermacher: The Evolution of a Nationalist* (Austin and London: University of Texas Press, 1966). Dawson concludes that nationalism was "the single most important factor in [Schleiermacher's] life" and that he elevated "nationalism to a level equal to religion" (161 and 163). Clearly, Dawson's conclusions do not jibe with the critique of nationalism set forth in the *Christian Ethics*.

55. *Christian Ethics*, 461.

56. Ibid., 476. He makes a similar claim regarding monogamy, asserting that although monogamy did preexist Christianity, it "finds its true moral ground and its essential posture first in Christianity" (ibid., 342). This is important for Schleiermacher because he sees the congregation as most perfectly organized when it comprises families that are bound together; it is only as the family is Christianized that propagation and education/cultivation are united, thus providing monogamy with its "true moral ground."

57. Ibid., 620-31.
58. Ibid., 623ff.
59. Ibid., 625.
60. Ibid., 626.

61. Schleiermacher cites as an example here the Moravian practice of separating boys and girls in order to avoid sexual temptation. Such a practice "rests upon a misunderstanding, and thus the virtue of purity does not arise, rather it is hindered . . . because . . . purity has no opportunity to indicate its presence; sense is uprooted and natural apathy is produced" (ibid., 627-8).

62. It is in this context that Schleiermacher argues against dueling. Such a practice is a clear contradiction of Christian morality. No Christian ought to participate in a duel. Ibid., 625.

63. Ibid., 631. Schleiermacher identifies purity, patience, forbearance, and humility as the Christian virtues. See ibid., 607-16.

64. Ibid., 641-42.
65. Ibid., 614.
66. Ibid., 619, 693.

67. Ibid., 514. Schleiermacher can also speak of love as the absolute principle of community. Ibid., 614, 651.

68. See Chapter 5 above.

69. *Christian Ethics*, 517-18.

70. Ibid., 517-19, 542. It is noteworthy in this regard that Schleiermacher sees Jesus' relation to social and artistic representation in terms of a marked tendency at overcoming social differences. Cf. 703-04.

71. Birkner, 113, citing W. Trillhaas, *Ethik* (n.p., 1959), argues that the *Christian Ethics* includes within it the first great Protestant theology of culture (192).

7

A CALVINIST OF A HIGHER ORDER: THE *CHRISTIAN ETHICS* IN SCHLEIERMACHER'S REVISIONIST REFORMED THEOLOGY

The task of this concluding chapter is to draw the lines of our argument together. The correspondence between Schleiermacher's own life and experience, on the one hand, and the vision set forth in the *Christian Ethics*, on the other, is striking. We reviewed Schleiermacher's experience among the Moravian pietists and saw the *Ethics* as an ethics of and for piety, with Christian piety as its ground and goal. We considered Schleiermacher's relationship with his philosophical colleague Hegel and the different ways the two leading lights of the University of Berlin conceive of the relationship between philosophy and theology. For Schleiermacher, philosophy's crucial role is to provide a conceptual map of the territory of knowledge. Theology then appropriates these concepts for its own use and, at points, expands or even transforms the framework generated for it by philosophy. Theology stands as the crown of Schleiermacher's intellectual system, and his *Christian Ethics* fulfills a crucial role in providing vision for the life of the church. As we saw in reflecting on Schleiermacher's pastoral experience, the church is the community to which Schleiermacher was unalterably committed. In spite of his dazzling accomplishments in other public and intellectual arenas and in spite of the deficiencies of the church—particularly as it was dominated by the Prussian state—he was, first and foremost, a pastor and theologian of the church. Corresponding to this, the *Christian Ethics* gives fully half of its attention to Christian community. It sketches out under the rubrics of restoring, broadening, and representational action the inner life of the community. Finally, as Schleiermacher was an activist on the side of social and political reform in Prussia, the *Ethics* adopts a transformational orientation toward the cultural world.

The summary above indicates how we have explored Schleiermacher's life together with the *Christian Ethics* and observed how the two mutually illumine each other. There is an additional aspect of Schleiermacher's identity—undeveloped to this point—that can function in a similar way in relation to the *Christian Ethics*. Dilthey sees in Schleiermacher's ethics the clearest indication of Schleiermacher's Reformed identity.[1] This chapter will conclude our examination of the *Christian Ethics* by considering it in relation to important characteristics of ethics in a Reformed key.

The issue of Schleiermacher's Reformed identity is complex. For some interpreters who doubt whether Schleiermacher's theology is even

Christian, the question of his being Reformed could seem wholly inappropriate.[2] As always, Schleiermacher's context is crucial to an assessment of the orientation of his theology. He lived out his Reformed identity in a particular context and in a particular way because of his own sense of that context. To be Reformed in Prussia involved two distinct but related moments—"moments" in the temporal sense of the word. The first moment involves the fact that the people of Prussia were predominantly Lutheran, so to be Reformed was to be part of the "royal minority." To be Reformed was to be simultaneously at the center and on the margin, ecclesiastically aligned with the king and out of step with the majority population. The danger of Reformed triumphalism was not present in this context. This was Schleiermacher's heritage, for there were generations of Reformed clergy on both sides of his family. The second moment involves the fact that in Schleiermacher's day the union of Lutheran and Reformed churches was declared by Friedrich Wilhelm III. Schleiermacher understood himself as a theologian and pastor of the Union Church, and both his *Christian Faith* and *Christian Ethics* are meant to serve that church.

Yet, alongside of his commitment to the Union, Schleiermacher continues to wear his Reformed identity, loosely but comfortably. Schleiermacher was not at all a Reformed counterpoint to the narrow Lutheran confessionalists who rejected the union as a degradation of their heritage. Rather, as B. A. Gerrish indicates in his masterful study of the Reformed character of Schleiermacher's theology, it was at once "unionizing and unabashedly Reformed."[3] Schleiermacher supported the Union because he believed that the theological differences between the Lutheran and Reformed confessions though real were not essential. Nor did he desire a new confession for the Union church; he was afraid this would only add a third party that was neither Lutheran nor Reformed. At the same time, as Gerrish demonstrates, Schleiermacher was "in his own intention ... an evangelical theologian who at least took his Reformed origins seriously."[4] In terms of theological issues, this is perhaps most evident in the way Schleiermacher wrestles with the concept of election, but we have also noted his strong preference for a presbyterian form of church government. Schleiermacher develops his view on election both in *The Christian Faith* and in his 1819 essay, "On the Doctrine of Election, with Special Reference to the Aphorisms of Dr. Bretschneider."[5] In both writings, Schleiermacher stands with Calvin, affirming that election is unconditional. To compromise on election is to surrender the gratuity of grace and thereby undermine what is most basic to the Christian faith. His views on election are the clearest example of Schleiermacher's identification with the theology of the Reformed tradition.

Still, assessment of the Reformed character of Schleiermacher's theological-ethical program is difficult because he claims the freedom to reinterpret the tradition as he appropriates it. Schleiermacher's program is revisionist in orientation. He seeks to interpret the Christian faith in a way that is at once faithful to the tradition and relevant in a changed and changing social-historical location. For Schleiermacher, it is never the question of a simple repristination of Reformed orthodoxy. Instead, he develops a much more complex understanding of tradition that involves both continuity and change. He claims that traditions as living organisms necessarily develop and change. This is most evident in his appropriation of the doctrine of election. He departs from Calvin and orthodox divines in asserting that the divine decree underlying election is single, not double. This means that the whole human race is ultimately elected to salvation. He argues that election is worked out in and through history, particularly through the work of the church as a living organism. Through an entirely natural process (save for its origin in Christ), the church will expand its sway until all are drawn into the saving knowledge of God in Christ. "The defense of Calvin's doctrine thus leads beyond the doctrine defended; and we may wonder if a resurrected Calvin would have embraced his unpredictable advocate."[6] Schleiermacher's tree is deeply rooted in the Reformed tradition, and it may well be appropriate to identify it as Reformed, but it grows in some surprising directions. Perhaps Schleiermacher is also a "Calvinist of a higher order."

Given the complexity of Schleiermacher's appropriation of the tradition, our argument here is more modest than trying to demonstrate that the *Christian Ethics* is Reformed in some simple and straightforward way. Rather, I will seek to show that the Reformed spirit lives on in the *Christian Ethics*; there is a clear affinity with a theological-ethical trajectory rooted in Zwingli and Calvin. This chapter will consider the *Christian Ethics* in relation to five characteristics of the Reformed tradition in ethics. The comparison will illumine both the *Christian Ethics* and the tradition in which it is rooted more clearly, and it will contribute another angle of vision on the *Christian Ethics*.

Christian ethics in a Reformed key exhibits certain family resemblances. Without attempting anything like a final definition, we can offer a characterization that seeks to set down the typical contours and orientation of Reformed ethics. The place of ethics within Reformed theology as a whole will be identified, as will some characteristic emphases. The first four of the traits identified are related directly to Reformed ethics; the last trait concerns the tradition as a whole and has important consequences for ethics. Our characterization identifies five important traits.

Reformed ethics is

1. An ethics of response;
2. Comprehensive, including in its scope all areas of human life;

3. Open to and willing to appropriate for its own purposes insights from nontheological sources of knowledge;
4. Aimed at the transformation of society; and
5. Part of an ongoing, developing tradition.[7]

1. Reformed ethics is, perhaps above all else, an ethics of response. At the very heart of the Reformed piety is a sense of awe and gratitude for the grace of God manifest in creation and redemption. The Christian life, then, on which ethics reflects, is a matter of human response to what God has done and is doing. Reformed ethics as an ethics of response was given classic formulation in H. Richard Niebuhr's *The Responsible Self*.[8] One begins with divine activity; then comes human responsiveness to what God is doing. In this way the character of Reformed ethics is given not only definition, but also its place in the theological system. Ethics does not come first. If one conceives of theology as comprising dogmatic and ethical moments (as Schleiermacher does), it is clear that the dogmatic moment precedes the ethical moment. In this sense Reformed ethics is theocentric or theological ethics;[9] it does not occupy the first place. The ethical moment reflects on the human response, flowing out of the sense of wonder and gratitude toward God.

Reformed ethics as an ethics of response finds clear resonance in Schleiermacher's *Christian Ethics*. This is most evident in the centrality of Christian piety as the ground and goal of the *Christian Ethics*. Christian ethics is grounded in pious apprehension of the divine activities of creation and redemption. Christian piety is the immediate self-consciousness of absolute dependence (God's creating and sustaining activity) and redemption in Christ. Together this apprehension in feeling of God as creator and redeemer is the *sine qua non* of Christianity for Schleiermacher. The Christian life is not the self-generated work of the autonomous individual; it is a response to the living reality of divine grace as encountered in and through the Christian community, where piety is birthed and nurtured. The *Christian Ethics* describes "what must become" on the basis of piety; it describes the actions that flow from persons who have been recipients of grace. Piety gives rise immediately to knowledge and action, and at the level of reflection, to dogmatics and ethics. Schleiermacher's ethics of piety is the way he gives voice to the Reformed notion of ethics as response; ethical action flows out of, and is a response to, the pious apprehension of divine activity.

In the second place, the *Christian Ethics* must be characterized as an ethics of piety because its primary concern is with the Christian religious consciousness of persons within the ecclesial community. Not only does the very structure of the *Christian Ethics* derive from the different determinations of Christian feeling that Schleiermacher identifies, but the objective of the analysis developed under those rubrics is a clear understanding of the purification, expansion, and expression of the Christian consciousness.

Such understanding can then provide direction for the church in its actual purification, expansion, and expression of piety. In an age that Schleiermacher perceives to be oblivious to the distinctively religious and particularly Christian, the first task of ethics is to help the church be the church. The analysis of action within the inner sphere of the church contributes reflection on the church's mission with its consideration of discipline, nurture, education, missions, and worship. Piety, then, is not only the ground of Schleiermacher's ethics; it is also the goal. In the analysis of life within the church, the issue taken up is how Christian piety can be restored, expressed, and expanded. This activity takes up the work of Christ and is in that sense a continuation of and response to what God has already done.

The descriptive method of the *Christian Ethics* reinforces its character as an ethics of response. The descriptive approach arises from the polar opposition between faith and theology. Methodologically, faith is the given upon which theology reflects. Theology does not seek to prove its first principles; rather, its task is to analyze and describe Christian faith as it is already given. Theology seeks to bring faith to self-awareness; it is a second-order, descriptive enterprise. Ethics, as a constitutive element of theology as a whole, describes the actions that flow from faith. Not only is faith a given from a methodological standpoint; it is also a given from a theological standpoint. That is to say, faith is a gift, a result of God's grace. Christian action is grounded in grace and faith; these are givens to be described by Christian ethics. Here we see Schleiermacher distancing himself from moralistic tendencies. Christian ethics is not, in the first place, imperative; rather, it describes the results of God's grace. So neither Christian action itself nor the ethical description of that action is self-generated. Instead, it is a matter of human response to what God has given out of God's mercy and grace.

2. A second trait of Reformed ethics is its comprehensive scope. As God's activity calls for a response, and as the living God is at work in all the world, so all of human activity is to have the character of response to God. God's activity is cosmic; God is creator and redeemer of the world. Thus, God's claim is universal; in the Reformed view, all of life is to be lived in grateful response to God. Here a distinctively Protestant theme is sounded, and the opportunity to respond to God by love of the neighbor wherever one may find oneself is affirmed. Because salvation is a free gift, there is nothing one can or need do to earn God's favor. Still, one does good works; one seeks to live a life of goodness, but out of a changed motivation. Where the non-Christian might seek to be good out of fear, to placate a demanding God, the evangelical Christian's goodness springs from a sense of liberation, joy, and gratitude. Related to this, the Reformers formulated a changed concept of "vocation." Whereas in medieval Roman Catholicism, vocation was understood to refer to those who followed a specifically

"religious" call (those in the priesthood or monastery), the Reformers see all Christians as called by God to service in whatever vocations they find themselves. Reformed ethics affirm faithfulness in all of one's life as the appropriate response to the gift of salvation, thus its comprehensive scope.

The *Christian Ethics* takes up the Protestant sense that all life is to be lived out of gratitude to God and brings it to a new level by being the first comprehensive Protestant theology of culture. The *Christian Ethics* not only claims that all arenas of life belong to God; it also produces an analysis of cultural life inclusive of everything from criminal justice and warfare to friendship and artistic expression. That ethics must be comprehensive of all aspects of human life is a conviction that Schleiermacher grounds both philosophically and theologically. As we saw in Chapter 4 above, both the *Philosophical Ethics* and *Christian Ethics* include comprehensive ethical visions. They accomplish this through their organization around the highest good and human actions that are productive of the good. Whereas an ethics of duty or virtue focuses on the individual's agency and character, an ethics of the good has an intrinsic drive to include all areas of social and cultural life in its scope. Schleiermacher's claim is that "Nothing which truly concerns human activity lies outside the realm of ethics."[10] One of the clear strengths of Schleiermacher's ethical vision, in both philosophy and theology, is the drive to be inclusive, comprehensive.

The *Christian Ethics* does provide a comprehensive analysis of the various aspects of cultural life (in the "outer sphere"), but because of the way Schleiermacher organizes this material, its character and scope is easily obscured. The way the various social-cultural areas are structured in the *Christian Ethics* varies considerably from that of the *Philosophical Ethics*.[11] Birkner complains that the structure of the *Christian Ethics* is problematic. This, he claims, is true in spite of its originality and in spite of the fact that this structure derives from Christian piety and therefore does express its distinctiveness as compared with philosophical ethics. The structure is problematic because the categories Schleiermacher employs conceal the issues to be dealt with under each rubric. The *Christian Ethics*' structure "results in an arrangement which, on the one hand, separates material which, thematically, belongs together, and, on the other hand, brings with it many curious connections."[12] This is particularly true in the outer sphere, where the work of the state is divided up and considered in two different places and where the academy, the arts, and free sociality are thrown together in ways that make them difficult to locate. The organization of the *Christian Ethics* conceals the scope of its ethical vision. Still, careful analysis makes clear its character as a comprehensive theology of culture.

Not only does the *Christian Ethics* provide an analysis of cultural life that is comprehensive in scope, it also explicitly affirms that Christians are called to live out their faith in all arenas of life. This is most evident in terms of the notion that all of life is to permeate with the Christian spirit. Christians are to "seek in all [their] social relations to manifest the Christian virtues, but at the same time always to work so that the common feeling in each totality to which they belong is ever more in agreement with the demands of the Christian principle."[13] As was noted in Chapter 6, the *Christian Ethics* calls on Christians to participate in all cultural life (unless such participation requires that the Christian principle be compromised), witness to the faith by virtuous action, and work to Christianize cultural communities from within. The claim of Christ on all of life is evident here. Christian faith leaves no aspect of cultural life untouched, but includes every relation and community in its promise to make all things new.

3. The third trait of Reformed ethics, its openness to insights from nontheological sources of knowledge, connects with its comprehensive character. If one is to witness to one's faith in all spheres of life, one needs knowledge of all cultural arenas. Knowledge from nontheological sources is important in the Reformed tradition, at least in part, because the earliest Reformers, particularly Zwingli and Calvin, gained significant insights from Renaissance humanism. Emphasis on and openness to learning was undergirded by theological concerns that all be able to understand scripture and live out their faith in the diverse vocations to which the faithful are called. Secular knowledge then gains significance as it informs the life of faith; it becomes a means by which God is glorified in daily life. Thus there is in the Reformed tradition an attitude at once open and expansionistic. Sources of insight from the world are welcome; they will be appropriated by the tradition, perhaps being transformed in the process, then incorporated into a theological vision where they can contribute to the final goal of the Christian life—giving glory to God.

For Schleiermacher, philosophy is an important resource for theological and ethical reflection, particularly as it generates concepts helpful in expressing theological and ethical ideas. This is evident already in the *Brief Outline*, where the task of philosophical theology is to identify concepts that can be used to develop the claims of historical theology (and be tested for their appropriateness in the process). This relationship also obtains in the ethical arena, as is clear from the analysis of the relation between philosophical and Christian ethics in Chapter 4.

One of the several polar oppositions that structures Schleiermacher's system of thought is the opposition between philosophy and theology. Careful attention to the theoretical and practical way in which Schleiermacher works out the relation between philosophical and theological versions of ethics reveals that it is more than a simple polar opposition in which the two poles balance each other. Despite the way in which

Schleiermacher sometimes characterizes this relation, these two ethical visions are not reducible to simple unity. The way Schleiermacher works out this relation, in principle and in fact, allows the distinctively Christian character of the *Christian Ethics* to stand forth.

The *Christian Ethics* explodes the boundaries set for it by the *Philosophical Ethics* and sets forth a comprehensive ethics of its own, addressing itself to all areas of human life. In doing so, the work in the *Christian Ethics* takes up and alters the categories identified in the *Philosophical Ethics*, rearranging them and adding the rubric of restoring action that is based on the Christian antithesis between sin and grace. Christian ethics transforms the moral vision of philosophical ethics. The categories that structure moral life are seen differently when looked at from the point of view of Christian faith, and the content that is developed is stamped in a characteristically Christian way. The way Schleiermacher works out the relation between philosophical and theological ethics is a prime example of the Reformed trait regarding nontheological knowledge. Schleiermacher stands with many in the Reformed tradition, appropriating knowledge from a secular source to serve a theological purpose and transforming it in the process.

4. The scriptural claim cited above that Christ makes "all things new" (Rev. 21:5) suggests the comprehensive scope, openness to secular knowledge, and transformative character of Christian faith, all of which find emphasis in Reformed ethics. Transformation of human life, at individual and corporate levels, develops out of the Reformed emphasis on sin and grace. A radical conception of human sin in which all of humanity in all its expressions is tainted by sin establishes the *need* for transformation. An equally radical accent on divine grace as the free gift that justifies persons and leads them toward sanctification creates the *possibility* of transformation. This dialectic between sin and grace, then, is the theological ground for persons, institutions, and societies being reformed. The Reformed tradition understands itself as called to participate in the ongoing reform of church and society and as the bearer of an egalitarian impulse that seeks to level all hierarchy. There is a profound sense of hope that social and cultural transformation can be realized. By the grace of God, society can be changed from its dehumanizing, hierarchical state to become life-giving and egalitarian and thereby more reflective of God's intentions for the world.

The polar opposition between the inner and outer spheres provides the structure by means of which Schleiermacher addresses the issue of Christ and culture. This opposition is an important structural principle in the *Christian Ethics*; together with the three kinds of action that Schleiermacher identifies, it provides the sixfold structure of the work. The issue posed in his analysis of life in the outer sphere is how the Christian community and individual are to relate to it. As we have seen, inner and outer spheres do not constitute a simple polar opposition, two sides of one coin. Rather, as in the case of the philosophy-theology opposition, one pole transforms the other. In this case, the outer sphere is transformed by the inner sphere. In Chapter 6 we showed the affinity of Schleiermacher's *Ethics* with the "Christ transforming culture" type as described by Niebuhr. The transformative character of the *Ethics* is manifest in three different ways: as prophetic critique, transvaluation of cultural goods, and the permeation of cultural communities by the spirit of Christ. Schleiermacher's profession is that Christ transforms the human spirit, raising it to a new level. By means of the theology of culture developed through his analysis of the outer sphere, Schleiermacher articulates the Reformed impetus to the transformation of culture by Christ. Once again his ethics resonates with a characteristic of the Reformed tradition that he claimed as his own.

5. The final trait of Reformed ethics shared by the larger tradition and evident in Schleiermacher's work is awareness of the changing, developmental character of the tradition itself. The tradition is a living organism, and it develops and changes over time. This is not only descriptively true; it is also an aspect of the prescription for the tradition to remain healthy. The paradox is that the tradition must change if it is to remain faithful to the intention embedded in its origin. Faithfulness to the Reformed tradition necessitates reformulation as historical and social context changes. This is a common contention in the many significant Reformed thinkers in the modern era; there is a self-conscious embrace of the dynamic, developmental character of the Reformed tradition. This is for practical, ecclesial reasons. This is not change for change's sake; rather, it is change that the tradition might find expression in a way relevant to a particular people in a particular time and place.

The Reformed sense of its own development and change can, perhaps, be traced back to Calvin. He was a second-generation leader of the Reformation, following in the footsteps of Zwingli and Luther. Though he comes after Zwingli chronologically, it is Calvin who gives decisive shape and inspiration to the Reformed tradition. Calvin is not the initiator of reform; rather, he stands in a tradition, appropriates that tradition, and gives it his own distinctive stamp. Although Calvin did not have the consciousness of change and development in history that becomes prominent in the nineteenth century, his historical location as a second-generation Reformer and his attitude toward his predecessors incline him to live out a developmental view of tradition. As B. A. Gerrish points out, Calvin recognized that Luther had initiated a new movement, and believed that those who would follow were to carry it further. When Calvin was pressed to follow Luther more closely, he insisted on the distinction between an ape and a disciple.[14] The clear implication is that a disciple follows the master's lead, but does so in freedom, adapting to a changing situation. Thus it may be that Calvin is the ultimate source of the Reformed tradition's developmental self-understanding. What is clear is that by the nineteenth and twentieth centuries, theologians and ethicists in the Reformed tradition self-consciously affirm the changing character of the tradition, seeing it as a positive value. In fact, Schleiermacher is one of the first to articulate a view of tradition as adapting itself to new and changing contexts in order that the faith might remain vital.

Gerrish goes so far as to claim that one of Schleiermacher's "enduring contributions to the Reformed tradition was a profound grasp of the meaning of 'tradition' itself."[15] Proving connections of historical causation is difficult in the extreme, so we are not claiming that Schleiermacher's work is directly or indirectly the source of the awareness of the dynamic, developmental character of tradition, shared by our nineteenth and twentieth-century Reformed ethicists. We note simply that Schleiermacher is one of the first to integrate a dynamic concept of tradition into his thinking about church and theology and that many subsequent Reformed thinkers share this conviction.

As we noted in chapter 2, it is in the *Brief Outline* that Schleiermacher first articulates the centrality of historical consciousness to the theological enterprise. The body of theology, including the disciplines of dogmatics and ethics, consists of historical work; the tradition in which one stands must be mined for its treasure so that contemporary works of art can be fashioned out of its resources. These vessels are fired in the kiln of the contemporary world to make tempered and serviceable vessels in service of the work of the church. Or in terms of the more familiar organic metaphor, church and theology are alive and as such growing and changing.

Not surprisingly, the *Christian Ethics*, too, expresses this historical consciousness. Christian ethics is historical in the sense that, as Christian teaching, it "includes only what is valid in the church" at a particular time. The key point is that there is no universal Christian teaching that is valid everywhere and for all time.[16] *Christian Ethics'* historical character is crucial because "a presentation that remains the same for all time is completely impossible," as evidenced, for example, by the fact that translation into different languages amounts to change.[17] Still, Schleiermacher argues that ethics is not nakedly historical, if this means only an aggregate collection of ethical stands the church has taken at various times and places. Schleiermacher's conception of historical ethics includes its ability to set forth what is valid in the present as a systematic whole. This is based on the "power of movement" of a living tradition embodied in community.[18] So ethics has the task of presenting an ethical vision for the contemporary church based on the historical work of taking up for the present the way the tradition has been lived out in the past.

Schleiermacher argues that demonstrating historical continuity is more difficult for ethics than for dogmatics. He makes this assertion as he considers how one shows the distinctively Protestant character of the *Christian Ethics*. This is accomplished by indicating continuity with scripture and with the Protestant confessional writings. "In regard to the Christian faith, there is hardly a point that is not warranted by being grounded in Scripture or in the symbolic books," but ethics is not in the same favorable position.[19] Schleiermacher asserts that the confessions' focus is on dogmatic issues, and ethical concerns receive little attention (though they are equally important); so it is difficult to show the Protestant character of the *Ethics* by appeal to confessional documents. As regards scripture, the difficulty arises because the social world of the New Testament is so different from nineteenth-century Prussia. In the New Testament much attention is given to the issue of how Christians are to relate to non-Christians, not much of a question in Schleiermacher's day. Similarly, slavery had been taken for granted in the scriptural world, but was abolished in nineteenth-century Prussia. The relation between authorities and subjects had changed from New Testament time to Schleiermacher's day, based on the fact that rulers were then Christian. Schleiermacher suggests ways to overcome the difficulties in demonstrating the Protestant character of ethics. He proposes a calculus for translating the social ethics of scripture into a contemporary context and identifies the "moral ethos" of the Protestant church as a significant criterion in ethical deliberation. He calls for a Protestant version of probabalism that assesses the weight to be given to particular ethical claims and finds a way between severe and relaxed views on ethical issues.

Clearly, Schleiermacher does not take the work of historical appropriation lightly. He recognizes particular challenges inherent in the task of ethical construction that seeks to remain deeply grounded in tradition. He has a keen awareness of changes in the organization of society and the bearing this has on ethics. Schleiermacher envisions the ethical task as being at once historical and constructive. Christian ethics is called to deep engagement with the tradition; one begins by listening carefully to its witness. One also listens attentively to the current context in order to develop an ethical vision faithful to the tradition and relevant to the present. The result will combine elements of continuity and change.

Schleiermacher's vision of the church as a living organism, and particularly the corresponding view of tradition as dynamic and developmental, is perhaps his signal contribution as a theologian. This insight is crucial in allowing Schleiermacher to transcend the Rationalism, Orthodoxy, and Pietism that had preceded him. He develops an attitude of critical appropriation of tradition that provides a new way beyond the iconoclasm of much Enlightenment thought about tradition, on the one hand, and the simple standing firm with tradition of most folk of orthodox or pietist ilk. Viewed from another perspective, Schleiermacher's contribution to the theological enterprise is his "Christian naturalism," his sense that the new and higher life of Christian faith is primarily a "mode of being in the world" that lives and grows in and through the social and cultural medium of the church and is therefore open to investigation like any other human historical phenomenon. Together, Schleiermacher's organic view of the church, dynamic view of tradition, and naturalistic view of the faith provide the key to his revision of a Calvinistic understanding of election. His focus is on God's election of the human race to salvation and the historical life of the church as the means by which election is effected. This provides a concrete, this-worldly locus for election even as it affirms the transcendent and salvific significance to the life and mission of the church. Schleiermacher's theological revisionism is brought to bear most fruitfully on the doctrine of election, at once the genius and *bête noire* of the Reformed tradition.

As Schleiermacher weds the doctrine of election to ecclesial life and activity, the significance of the church in the divine economy of salvation is underscored. Schleiermacher understands the church as the agent of God's decree, although to protect the sovereignty of God and the gratuity of grace, the church is seen only as the instrument or organ of God, infused with life and led by the Spirit. The church is not at all an autonomous agent. Still, the life and work of the church is valorized in a new way as the connection with election is made explicit. Then in the theological scheme the *Christian Ethics* as the locus of critical reflection on the church's life and work, as a description of ecclesial actions, has a heightened importance. Ethics is charged with the task of helping the individual Christian, and particularly the church as a living community of piety, get clear about how it can best fulfill its role in the divine economy. In a very real way the *Christian Ethics* is the culmination of Schleiermacher's theology, giving direction as to how the church might envision and fulfill its inner mission to cultivate piety and its outer mission to transform the world. It helps the church become self-conscious about its vocation, that to which it has been elected—to be the agent of salvation for the race and thereby to manifest the glory of God. That, it would seem, qualifies the *Christian Ethics* as an exemplar of ethics in a Reformed key.

NOTES

1. Cf. Martin Redeker, who says that "Dilthey saw the determined, rigorous, manly piety as evidence that something of the spirit of his Reformed ancestors lived in him" (*Schleiermacher: Life and Thought*, trans. John Wallhausser [Philadelphia: Fortress Press, 1973], 90). And "In his ethics are found the resources for bring-

ing the aggressive spirit of Reformed religion into the right relationship with the other motifs of Christianity" (Friedrich Schleiermacher, *Aus Schleiermachers Leben: In Briefen*, 4 vols., ed. Ludwig Jonas and Wilhelm Dilthey [Berlin: G. Reimer, 1860–63] 1: 830).

2. Particularly important in this regard is the critique of Emil Brunner that Schleiermacher sells out a Reformation theology of the word for a sub-Christian mysticism. Karl Barth makes similar but more nuanced criticisms.

3. B. A. Gerrish, *Tradition and the Modern World: Reformed Theology in the Nineteenth Century* (Chicago: University of Chicago Press, 1978), 121.

4. Ibid., 15.

5. *Sämmtliche Werke*, ed. Ludwig Jonas (Berlin: G. Reimer, 1834–64) div. 1, vol. 12, 383–484.

6. Gerrish, 119.

7. For a fuller discussion of this issue, see my unpublished essay, "Ethics in a Reformed Key." This characterization of Reformed ethics is developed on the basis of a study of representative scholars in and of the Reformed tradition, including Abraham Kuyper, the Dutch statesman of a century ago and a leading light in the Neo-Calvinist movement; John Leith, Professor Emeritus at Union Theological Seminary in Virginia; Nicholas Wolterstorff, Professor at Yale University; John de Gruchy, South African theologian; and Allan Boesak, also of South Africa, a Reformed pastor and leader in the eventual overthrow of Apartheid.

8. H. Richard Niebuhr, *The Responsible Self* (New York: Harper & Row, 1963). Niebuhr formulates his ethics of response this way: "Responsibility affirms: God is acting in all actions upon you. So respond to all actions upon you as to respond to [God's] action" (126). For a helpful perspective on Niebuhr's ethics of response in relation to persons on the margin of society, see Darryl M. Trimiew, *Voices of the Silenced: The Responsible Self in a Marginalized Community* (Cleveland: Pilgrim Press, 1933).

9. For a theocentric ethics with a "Preference for the Reformed Tradition," Chapter 4 of Vol. 1, see James M. Gustafson, *Ethics from a Theocentric Perspective*, 2 vols. (Chicago: University of Chicago Press, 1981 and 1984).

10. Friedrich Schleiermacher, *Grundlinien einer Kritik der bisherigan Sittenlehre*, in *Sämmliche Werke* (Berlin: G. Reimer, 1846) div. 1, vol. 3: 261.

11. For example, in the *Christian Ethics* under representational action in the outer sphere, Schleiermacher analyzes artistic expression—both plastic arts and performing arts broadly considered (*Kunst und Spiel*)—and social relations ("free sociality.") The configuration of the *Philosophical Ethics* has been rearranged. There art was considered together with religion under individual-symbolizing rubric, whereas free sociality occupied its own, individual-organizing sphere. In all this we see that the distinctions that provide the philosophical work with its structure are not left intact in the move to Christian ethics. The *Christian Ethics* sets forth its own structure, and one must examine it in some detail to see how the different elements of its outer sphere correspond with the different kinds of moral action identified in the *Philosophical Ethics*.

12. Hans-Joachim Birkner, *Schleiermachers Christliche Sittenlehre im Zusammenhang seines Philosophisch-Theologischen Systems*. Theologische Bibliothek Töpelmann. Edited by Kurt Aland et al. (Berlin: Alfred Töpelmann, 1964), 113.

13. Friedrich Schleiermacher, *Die christliche Sitte nach den Grundsätzen der evangelischen Kirche im Zusammenhange dargestellt*, ed. Ludwig Jonas in *Sämmtliche*

Werke, div. 1, vol. 12 (Berlin: G. Reimer, 1843), 631. Hereafter referred to as the *Christian Ethics.*
 14. Gerrish, 6 and 48.
 15. Ibid., 15.
 16. *Christian Ethics,* 8–9.
 17. Ibid., 10.
 18. Ibid., 9.
 19. Ibid., 95.

BIBLIOGRAPHY

Works by Friedrich Schleiermacher

Aus Schleiermacher's Leben: In Briefen. Edited by Ludwig Jonas and Wilhelm Dilthey. 4 vols. Berlin: G. Reimer, 1860–63. Reprint edition, Berlin: G. Reimer 1974.
Briefwechsel 1775–96. Edited by Andreas Arndt and Wolfgang Virmond. 2 vols. Berlin and New York: Walter de Gruyter, 1985 and 1988.
Christliche Sittenlehre: Einleitung. Edited by Hermann Peiter. Stuttgart: Verlag W. Kohlhammer, 1983.
Das christliche Leben nach den Grundsätzen der evangelischen Kirche Im Zusammenhänge dargestellt. Edited by Herman Peiter. Berlin: Humboldt-Universität, 1969.
Der christliche Glaube nach den Grundsätzen der evangelischen Kirche im Zusammenhänge dargestellt. 7th ed., based on the 2d ed. of 1830–31. Edited by Martin Redeker. 2 vols. Berlin: Walter de Gruyter, 1960.
Dialektik. Edited by Isidor Halpern. Berlin: Mayer and Mueller, 1903.
Dialektik. Sämmtliche Werke 3:4. Edited by Ludwig Jonas. Berlin: G. Reimer, 1839.
Die christliche Sitte nach den Grundsätzen der evangelischen Kirche im Zusammenhänge dargestellt. Sämmtliche Werke 1:12. Edited by Ludwig Jonas. Berlin: G. Reimer, 1843. Reprint edition, Waltrop: Verlag Hartmut Spenner, 1999.
Die Praktische Theologie nach den Grundsätzen der evangelischen Kirche im Zusammenhänge dargestellt. Sämmtliche Werke 1:13. Edited by Jacob Frerichs. Berlin: G. Reimer, 1850. Reprint edition, Berlin: Walter de Gruyter, 1983.
Entwürfe zu einem System der Sittenlehre. 2d ed. Vol. 2. *Friedrich Ernst Daniel Schleiermacher Werke: Auswahl in vier Bänden.* Edited by Otto Braun and Johannes Bauer. Leipzig: Feliz Miner, 1927–28.
Friedrich Schleiermachers Dialektik. Edited by Rudolf Odebrecht. Leipzig: J. C. Hinrichs Verlag, 1942.
F. Schleiermachers philosophische Sittenlehre. Edited and introduced by J. H. v. Kirchmann. Philosophische Bibliothek 85. Berlin: Heimann, 1870.
Friedrich Schleiermachers Reden über die Religion. Critical edition by G. Ch. Bernhard Pünjer. Kritische Ausgabe Brunswick: C. A. Schwetschke and Son (M. Bruhn), 1879.
Grundlinien einer Kritik der bisherigen Sittenlehre. Sämmtliche Werke 3:1. Berlin: G. Reimer, 1846.
Kurze Darstellung des theologischen Studiums zum Behuf einleitender Vorlesungen. Third critical edition by Heinrich Scholz. 1910. Reprint edition, Darmstadt: Wissenschaftliche Buchgesellschaft, 1961.

Schleiermachers Sendschreiben über seine Glaubenslehre an Lücke. Edited by Hermann Mulert. Studien zur Geschichte des neueren Protestantismus, Quellenheft 2. Giessen: Alfred Töpelmann (J. Ricker), 1908.
"Über die Lehre von der Erwählung, besonders in Beziehung auf Herrn Dr. Bretschneiders Aphorismen." *Sämmtliche Werke* 1:2. Berlin: G. Reimer, 1843, 393–484.
"Vorschlag zu einer neuen Verfassung der protestantischen Kirche in preussischen Staate." In *Kleine Schriften und Predigten.* Edited by H. Gerdes and E. Hirsch. Berlin: Walter de Gruyter, 1969–70, 113ff.

Works by Friedrich Schleiermacher: English Translation

Brief Outline on the Study of Theology. Translated by Terrence N. Tice. Richmond: John Knox Press, 1966.
The Christian Faith. Edited by H. R. Mackintosh and J. S. Stewart. Edinburgh: T. & T. Clark, 1928.
Christmas Eve: Dialogue on the Incarnation. Translated by Terrence N. Tice. Richmond: John Knox Press, 1967.
Dialectic, or The Art of Doing Philosophy. Translated by Terrence N. Tice. Atlanta: Scholars Press, 1996.
Friedrich Schleiermacher: Introduction to Christian Ethics. Translated by John Shelley. Nashville: Abingdon Press, 1989.
Hermeneutics: The Handwritten Manuscripts. Edited by Heinz Kimmerle. Translated by James Duke and Jack Forstman. Atlanta: Scholars Press, 1977.
The Life of Schleiermacher, as Unfolded in His Autobiography and Letters. Translated by Frederica Rowan. 2 vols. London: Smith, Elder and Co., 1859–1860.
On the Glaubenslehre. Translated by James Duke and Francis Fiorenza. Chico, Calif.: Scholars Press, 1981.
On Religion: Addresses in Response to Its Cultured Critics. Translated by Terrence N. Tice. Richmond: John Knox Press, 1969.
On Religion: Speeches to Its Cultured Despisers. Translated by John Oman. 1894. Reprint edition, New York: Harper & Row, 1958.
On Religion: Speeches to Its Cultured Despisers. Translated by Richard Crouter. Cambridge: Cambridge University Press, 1988.

Schleiermacher: Secondary Sources

Barth, Karl. *The Theology of Schleiermacher.* Edited by Dietrich Ritschl. Translated by Geoffrey W. Bromiley. Grand Rapids: Eerdmans, 1982.
Birkner, Hans-Joachim. *Schleiermachers Christliche Sittenlehre im Zusammenhang seines Philosophisch-Theologischen Systems.* Theologische Bibliothek Töpelmann. Edited by Kurt Aland et al., 8. Berlin: Alfred Töpelmann, 1964.
Blackwell, Albert L. *Schleiermacher's Early Philosophy of Life: Determinism, Freedom, and Phantasy.* Chico, Calif.: Scholars Press, 1982.
Brandt, James M. "Ritschl's Critique of Schleiermacher's Theological Ethics." *Journal of Religious Ethics* 17, no. 2 (Fall 1989): 51–72.
Brunner, Emil. *Die Mystik und das Wort: Der Gegensatz Zwischen moderner Religion-*

auffassung und christlichem Glauben dargestellt an der Theologie Schleiermachers. Tübingen: J. C. B. Mohr (Paul Siebeck), 1924.
Clements, Keith W. "Schleiermacher: A Life in Outline." In *Friedrich Schleiermacher: Pioneer of Modern Theology.* London and San Francisco: Collins, 1987.
Crossley, John P., Jr. "Calvin's Idea of Freedom in the Ethics of Schleiermacher and Barth." In *Anxiety, Guilt, and Freedom.* Edited by B. Hubbard and B. Starr. Lanham, Md.: University Press of America, 1990.
———. "Schleiermacher's Christian Ethics in Relation to His Philosophical Ethics." *The Annual of the Society of Christian Ethics* (Fall 1998).
———. "Schleiermacher's Critique of Ethical Reason: Toward a Systematic Ethic." *The Journal of Religious Ethics* 12, no. 7 (Fall 1989): 5–24.
———. "Religion, Science, and Ethics: Schleiermacher's Study of the Structure of Mind." *The Annual of the Society of Christian Ethics* (1991).
Crouter, Richard. "Hegel and Schleiermacher at Berlin: A Many-Sided Debate." *Journal of the American Academy of Religion* 48, no. 1 (March 1980): 29–30.
———. "Schleiermacher and the Theology of Bourgeois Society: A Critique of the Critics." *Journal of Religion* 66, no. 2 (July 1986): 302–23.
Dawson, Jerry F. *Friedrich Schleiermacher: The Evolution of a Nationalist.* Austin and London: University of Texas Press, 1966.
Duke, James. "The Christian and the Ethical in Schleiermacher's Christian Ethics." *Encounter* 46, no. 1 (Winter 1985): 51–69.
Gerrish, B. A. *Continuing the Reformation: Essays on Modern Religious Thought.* Chicago: University of Chicago Press, 1993.
———. *The Old Protestantism and the New: Essays on the Reformation Heritage.* Chicago: University of Chicago Press, 1982.
———. *A Prince of the Church: Schleiermacher and the Beginnings of Modern Theology.* Philadelphia: Fortress Press, 1984.
———. *Tradition and the Modern World: Reformed Theology in the Nineteenth Century.* Chicago: University of Chicago Press, 1978.
Graby, James K. "The Problem of Ritschl's Relationship to Schleiermacher." *Scottish Journal of Theology* 19, no. 3 (September 1966): 257–68.
Herms, Eilert. "Reich Gottes und menschliches Handeln." In *Friedrich Schleiermacher 1768–1834.* Göttingen: Vandenhoeck & Ruprecht, 1985.
Internationaler Schleiermacher Kongress: Berlin 1984. Edited by Kurt-Victor Selge. Berlin and New York: Walter de Gruyter, 1985.
Jorgenson, Poul. *Die Ethik Schleiermachers: Forschungen zur Geschichte und Lehre des Protestantismus.* Edited by Ernst Wolf. Munich: Kaiser Verlag, 1959.
Kantzenbach, F. W. *Friedrich Daniel Ernst Schleiermacher.* Reinbek bei Hamburg: Rowolt Taschenbuch Verlag GmbH, 1967.
Lamm, Julia A. *The Living God: Schleiermacher's Theological Appropriation of Spinoza.* University Park: Pennsylvania State University Press, 1996.
Malfèr, Benno. *Das Handeln des Christen: Theologische Ethik am Beispiel von Schleiermachers Christlicher Sitte.* Münsterschwarzach: Vier-Türme-Verlag, 1979.
Niebuhr, Richard R. *Schleiermacher on Christ and Religion.* New York: Charles Scribner's Sons, 1964.
Park, Sung M. *Christ and Christian Conduct: A Study of Friedrich Schleiermacher's Christology and Theological Ethics.* Ann Arbor: U.M.I., 1995.
Redeker, Martin. *Friedrich Schleiermacher: Leben und Werk.* Berlin: Walter de Gruyter, 1968.

———. *Schleiermacher: Life and Thought*. Translated by John Wallhausser. Philadelphia: Fortress Press, 1973.
Reich, Andreas. *Friedrich Schleiermacher als Pfarrer an der Berliner Dreifaltigkeitskirche 1809–1834*. Berlin and New York: Walter de Gruyter, 1992.
Samson, Holger. *Die Kirche als Grundbegriff der theologischen Ethik Schleiermachers*. Zollikon-Zürich: Evangelische Verlag, 1958.
Spiegel, Yorick. *Theologie der bürgerlichen Gesellschaft: Sozialphilosophie und Glaubenslehre bei Friedrich Schleiermacher*. Munich: Kaiser Verlag, 1968.
Spiegler, Gerhard. *The Eternal Covenant: Schleiermacher's Experiment in Cultural Theology*. New York, Evanston, and London: Harper & Row, 1967.
Thandeka. *The Embodied Self: Friedrich Schleiermacher's Solution to Kant's Problem of the Empirical Self*. Albany: State University of New York Press, 1995.
Thiel, John E. *God and World in Schleiermacher's Dialektik and Glaubenslehre: Criticism and the Methodology of Dogmatics*. Basler und Berner Studien zur historischen und systematischen Theologie. Bern: Peter Lang, 1981.
Tice, Terrence N. *Schleiermacher Bibliography*. Princeton: Princeton Theological Seminary, 1966.
Von Willich, Ehrenfried. *Aus Schleiermachers Hause: Jugenderinnerungen seines Stiefsohnes*. Berlin: G. Reimer, 1909.
Williams, Robert R. *Schleiermacher the Theologian: The Construction of the Doctrine of God*. Philadelphia: Fortress Press, 1978.
Wyman, Walter E., Jr. *The Concept of Glaubenslehre: Ernst Troeltsch and the Theological Heritage of Schleiermacher*. Chico, Calif.: Scholars Press, 1983.

Other Works

Barth, Karl. *Church Dogmatics*. Vol. 2. *The Doctrine of God*, pt. 2. Translated by G. W. Bromiley and T. F. Torrance. Edinburgh: T. & T. Clark, 1957.
———. *Protestant Theology: From Rousseau to Ritschl*. Translated by Brian Cozens. New York: Clarion Books, 1969.
Bigler, Robert M. *The Politics of German Protestantism: The Rise of the Protestant Church Elite in Prussia, 1815–1848*. Berkeley: University of California Press, 1972.
Browning, Don S. *A Fundamental Practical Theology*. Minneapolis: Augsburg Fortress Press, 1991.
Brunner, Emil. *Das Gebot und die Ordnungen*. Tübingen: Verlag von J. C. B. Mohr (Paul Siebeck), 1933.
———. *The Divine Imperative*. Translated by Olive Wyon. Philadelphia: The Westminster Press, 1947.
Calvin, John. *Institutes of the Christian Religion*. Edited by John T. McNeill and translated by Ford Lewis Battles. 2 vols. Library of Christian Classics, Vols. 20–21. Philadelphia: The Westminster Press, 1960.
Campbell, Ted. *The Religion of the Heart*. Columbia: University of South Carolina Press, 1991.
Ellison, Julie. *Delicate Subjects: Romanticism, Gender and the Ethics of Understanding*. Ithaca: Cornell University Press, 1990.
Farley, Edward. *Theologia: The Fragmentation and Unity of Theological Education*. Philadelphia: Fortress Press, 1983.

BIBLIOGRAPHY 153

Gerrish, Brian A. *Grace and Reason: A Study in the Theology of Luther.* Oxford: Oxford University Press, 1962. Midway reprint, Chicago: University of Chicago Press, 1979.
Godsey, John. *The Promise of H. Richard Niebuhr.* Philadelphia and New York: J. B. Lippincott, 1970.
Goeters, Johann F. G. "Der reformierte Pietismus in Bremen und am Niederrhein im 18. Jahrhundert." In *Der Pietismus im achtzehnten Jahrhundert.* Edited by Martin Brecht and Klaus Deppermann. Göttingen: Vandenhoeck & Ruprecht, 1995.
Goethe, Johann Wolfgang von. *The Sorrows of Young Werther and Selected Writings.* Translated by Catherine Hutter. New York: New American Library, 1962.
Gustafson, James M. *Ethics from a Theocentric Perspective.* 2 vols. Chicago: University of Chicago Press, 1981 and 1984.
Handy, Jim. *Gift of the Devil: A History of Guatemala.* N.p. South End Press, 1984.
Hertz, Deborah. *Jewish High Society in Old Regime Berlin.* New Haven: Yale University Press, 1988.
Herzog, Frederick. *Justice Church: The New Function of the Church in North American Christianity.* Maryknoll, N. Y.: Orbis Books, 1980.
Holborn, Hajo. *A History of Modern Germany.* 3 vols. New York: Alfred Knopf, 1959–69.
Hodgson, Peter C. *G. W. F. Hegel: Theologian of the Spirit.* Minneapolis: Augsburg Fortress Press, 1997.
Jodock, Darrell. "Metaphysics and Theology in Albrecht Ritschl." Berkeley: AAR Nineteenth Century Theology Working Group Papers, 1983.
Kant, Immanuel. *Critique of Practical Reason.* Translated by Lewis White Beck. Indianapolis: Bobbs-Merrill Educational Publishing, 1956.
———. *Critique of Pure Reason.* Translated by Lewis White Beck. Indianapolis: Bobbs-Merrill Educational Publishing, 1956.
———. *Prolegomena to Any Future Metaphysics that Will Be Able to Present Itself as a Science.* Translated by Peter G. Lucas. Manchester: Manchester University, 1953.
Kelsey, David H. *Between Athens and Berlin: The Theological Education Debate.* Grand Rapids: Eerdmans, 1993.
Lehmann, Paul. *Ethics in a Christian Context.* New York: Harper & Row, 1963.
McClelland, Charles E., *State, Society, and University in Germany 1700–1914.* Cambridge: Cambridge University Press, 1980.
Meyer, Dietrich. "Zinzendorf und Herrnhut." In *Der Pietismus im achtzehnten Jahrhundert.* Edited by Martin Brecht and Klaus Deppermann. Göttingen: Vandenhoeck & Ruprecht, 1995.
Niebuhr, H. Richard. *Christ and Culture.* New York: Harper & Row, 1951.
———. *The Responsible Self.* New York: Harper & Row, 1963.
———. "Theology and Psychology: A Sterile Union" *The Christian Century*, 1927.
Reiss, H. S. *The Political Thought of the German Romantics, 1793–1815.* New York: The Macmillan Company, 1955.
Ritschl, Albrecht. *The Christian Doctrine of Justification and Reconciliation: The Positive Development of the Doctrine.* Translated by H. R. Mackintosh and A. B. Macaulay. Clifton, N.J.: Reference Book Publishers, 1966.
———. *A Critical History of the Christian Doctrine of Justification and Reconciliation.* Translated by John S. Black. Edinburgh: Edmonston and Douglas, 1872.

———. *Three Essays*. Translated by Philip Hefner. Philadelphia: Fortress Press, 1972.
Rogerson, John W. *W. M. L. de Wette, Founder of Modern Biblical Criticism: An Intellectual Biography*. Sheffield: JSOT Press, an imprint of Sheffield Academic Press, 1992.
Schellong, Dieter. *Bürgertum und christliche Religion: Anpassungsprobleme der Theologie seit Schleiermacher*. Munich: Kaiser Verlag, 1975.
Spener, Philip Jacob. *Pia Desideria*. Translated by Theodore G. Tappert. Philadelphia: Fortress Press, 1964.
Stoeffler, F. Ernest. *The Rise of Evangelical Pietism and the German Pietism of the Eighteenth Century*. Leiden: Brill, 1973.
Thiemann, Ronald F. "Piety, Narrative, and Christian Identity." *Word and World* 3, no. 2 (Spring 1983): 148–59.
Trimiew, Darryl M. *Voices of the Silenced: The Responsible Self in a Marginalized Community*. Cleveland: Pilgrim Press, 1993.
von der Luft, Eric. *Hegel, Hinrichs, and Schleiermacher on Feeling and Reason in Religion: The Texts of Their 1821–22 Debate*. Lewiston and Queenstown: Edwin Mellen Press, 1987.
Wallmann, Johannes. *Der Pietismus*. Vol. 4, *Die Kirche in Ihrer Geschichte*. Göttingen: Vandenhoeck & Ruprecht, 1990.
———."Was ist Pietismus?" *Pietismus und Neuzeit* 20 (1994): 11–27.
Welch, Claude. *Protestant Thought in the Nineteenth Century*. Vol. 1, 1799–1870. New Haven and London: Yale University Press, 1972. Vol. 2, 1870–1914. Ibid., 1985.

INDEX OF SUBJECTS

absolute dependence, feeling of, xiii, 48, 87, 138
aesthetic religion, 49–50
agrarian crises, 111
art, xv, 53, 76–77, 123–124, 147 n.11
atheism controversy, 25

blessedness, 100
broadening action, xv, 52–53, 90, 91, 96–100, 117, 122–23, 124–27
Christian experience, 26–27, 36, 37, 45
Christian permeation of culture, 127–30, 143
Christian principle, the, 22, 55, 104, 117, 128–29, 141
Christianity, 21, 26, 35, 49, 64
christology, 27, 37, 61–62, 87–88
church (inner sphere), xv, 34, 36, 37, 52–54, 73–74, 139, 146
church, doctrine of, 86–105
church discipline, xv, 53, 93–94
church polity, 95, 104
church reform, xv, 53, 93, 94–95
coercion, 121, 122
colonization, xv, 119, 121–22
community, 37, 73–75, 84–85, 87, 88, 92, 96, 111
competition, 124
consciousness of sin and grace, 50, 76, 87–88, 92, 142
criminal justice, 53, 76

death penalty, xv, 119–20
dehumanization of workers, 123
Deism, 21–22
Demagogenverfolgung (period of persecution), 114

dueling, 124, 134 n.62
Dialectical Theology, 3
disposition, Christian, 98, 104–5
divorce, 122–23
doctrinal theology (dogmatics), xiii, 6, 8, 12 n.26, 34, 45–47, 90, 139

economics (commerce), 53, 124, 125–27
education, 112, 124, 125–27
education, Christian, xv, 53, 98–99
effectual action, 52–53, 74
election, doctrine of, xvi, 89, 136–37, 146
empirical knowledge, 68–69
Enlightenment, 14, 17–18, 20, 32, 37, 59, 110, 145
ethical activity, 28, 46–47
ethics, Christian, xiii, 6–8, 12 n.26, 45–47, 51–55, 62–78, 109, 144–46
ethics of duty, 71
ethics of the highest good, 71–73
ethics of virtue, 71
ethics, philosophical, xiv, 62–78
ethics, Reformed, 138–46
equality (egalitarian impulse), 129, 130, 142
Evangelical Revival, 42

family, xv, 53, 122–23
force, use of, 120

gambling, 124
gender equality, 122
God, 5, 18, 30, 36, 37–39, 44, 45, 47, 51, 62, 89, 98, 101, 139, 124, 127, 138–41, 146
grace, 51, 138–39, 142
"gymnastic," spiritual, 93–94

INDEX OF SUBJECTS

Hasidism, 42
hermeneutics, 32
historical consciousness, 144–46
historical theology, 34
Holy Spirit, 37, 75, 89, 92, 98, 102, 146

incarnation, doctrine of, 61–62
individuality, 29, 86
international relations, 53

Jansenism, 42
John, Gospel of, 92, 130
Junkers, 14, 111

kingdom of God, 7, 49, 74, 89, 96, 98, 100, 118, 124, 126–27

liturgy controversy, 29, 31, 116
Landsturm, 113
Landswehr (national guard), 113
Lutheran church, xv-xvi, 13, 26, 103, 136

marriage, 24–25, 29, 122–23, 134 n.56
Matthew, Gospel of, 94
missions, xv, 53, 98, 99–100
Moravian pietism, 14, 41–45, 56 n.8, 84, 135
mutuality, 120, 124, 129, 130
mysticism, 43

nationalism, 125–26, 133 n.54
nature formation, 124, 126
natural religion, 21
natural/supernatural, 96–98
Neo-Pietist awakening, 114
New Protestantism, 4, 18, 36

Orthodoxy, Protestant, 17, 18, 21, 32, 36–37, 59, 145

pantheism, 24
peasants, 110–11
Pelagianism, 38
Pietism, 18, 22, 36, 41–45, 145
piety, xvi, 5–7, 11 n.21, 21, 36, 41–55, 56 n.12, 56 n.14, 56 n.16, 67, 84, 99, 101–2, 138
philosophical theology, 35
philosophy of culture, 70–74
pneuma, 97–98, 117
positive religion, 21–22

practical theology, 34
priesthood of all believers, 85
prophetic critique, 118–24, 143
Protestant church, xv-xvi, 85, 93, 95, 98, 99–100, 102, 103
protestant principle, 22
Prussia, history of, 13–15, 27–28, 109–16
Prussian Reform Movement, 2, 10 n.4, 28, 109–14
Prussian Union Church, xv-3, 13, 30–31, 83, 115–16, 136
public communication, freedom of, 120
punishment, corporeal, 118–19

Quakers, 102

Rationalism, 4, 17, 32, 145
redemption (salvation), xiv, 8, 37–38, 51, 62, 92, 96, 104, 137, 138, 139–40, 146
representational action, xv, 52–53, 74–75, 90, 91, 100–105, 123–24, 127–30
reprobation, 38, 44
Reformation, Protestant, 37, 94–95
Reformed church, xv-xvi, 13, 26, 38–39, 42, 136
restoring action, xv, 52–53, 76, 90, 91, 92–95, 118–22
revisionism, 37–39, 137, 143–46
revolution, xv, 119–20
Roman Catholic Church, xv-xvi, 85, 93, 94–95, 99–100, 102, 103
Romanticism, 1–2, 18–20, 23 n.9, 31, 59

salon society, 19
Scripture, 145
sectarianism, 127
Seven Years' War, 14
slavery, 123, 145
social change, 76, 120
social relations, 53, 76, 127–30, 133 n.45, 147 n.11
society (the outer sphere), xv, 53, 76, 116–30, 140, 142–43
Speculative Idealism, 31, 59
speculative knowledge, 68–69
spirit and flesh, 52
state, the, xv, 76, 125–27, 133 n.50

talent formation, 124, 126
teleological religion, xiv, 49–50
tradition, 143–46

transformation, 9, 39, 55, 74, 99, 109, 116–30, 135, 138, 142–43
transvaluation of cultural goods, 124–27, 143
Trinity, doctrine of, 38, 61–62, 88

virtue, Christian, 103, 128–29, 134 n.61, 141

violence, 119, 122
vocation, 139–40
volksschule, 112

war, xv, 53, 76, 118, 119–21, 132 n.31, 132 n.33
worship, Christian (see also representational action), 53, 75, 94, 100–105

INDEX OF NAMES

Arndt, Ernst Moritz, 115
Aristotle, 123
Aquinas, St. Thomas, 36
  Summa Theologiae, 36
Augustine, Saint, 98, 130

Barby, 14, 44–45
Barth, Karl, 4, 37, 133 n.40, 133 n.44, 147 n.2
Beethoven, Ludwig van, 59
Berlin, 13, 17–19, 22, 24, 28, 60, 111
Berlin Academy of Sciences, 33, 60
Berlin, University of, (Humboldt University), 1, 2, 28–29, 31–32, 55, 58, 109, 112, 135
Biglar, Robert, 110
Birkner, Hans-Joachim, 56 n.14, 63, 67, 75, 80 n.28, 120, 140
Blackwell, Albert, 3, 20, 107 n.42
Boesak, Allan, 147 n.7
Brunner, Emil, 4, 86, 147 n.2
Burschenschaften (student unions), 60, 113–14, 130

Calvin, John, xv, 36, 130, 136–137, 141, 143
  Institutes of the Christian Religion, 36
Campbell, Ted, 55–56 n.5
collegia pietatis, 43
Crouter, Richard, 10 n.3, 10 nn.10, 59–60, 131 n.2, 132 n.25

Dawson, Jerry F., 133 n.54
Dilthey, Wilhelm, xvi, 135, 146–47 n.1
de Gruchy, John, 147 n.7
de Wette, W. M. Leberecht, 58, 115
Dohna, Count Friedrich, 16, 24
Dohna, Frederika, 16

Duke, James, 80 n.50

Elberfeld sect (Children of Zion), 42
Eller, Elias, 42
Eller, Anna, 42

Feuerbach, Ludwig, 79 n.11
Fichte, Johann Gottlieb, 3, 25, 31, 32, 59, 71, 112
Follen, Karl, 114
Friedrich II (the "Great"), 13, 17, 19, 28, 112
Friedrich Wilhelm I, 13–14, 83
Friedrich Wilhelm II, 17
Friedrich William III, xv, 1, 13–14, 17, 28, 30–31, 33, 83, 109, 110–11, 112, 113, 115, 136
Friedrich William IV, 1
Fries, J. F., 58, 59

Gerrish, B. A., 27, 36, 40 n.22, 56 n.12, 80 n.35, 136, 143, 144
Goethe, Johann Wolfgang von, 1, 3, 14, 19, 44, 58
  The Sufferings of the Young Werther, 44
Grimm, Jakob and Wilhelm, 23 n.11
Grunow, Eleonore, 2, 10 n.5, 24–26, 58

Halle, 15, 26–28
Halle, University of, 15, 26–28
Handy, Jim, 10 n.4
Hardenburg, Prince Karl August von, 112, 115
Hegel, Georg Wilhelm Friedrich, 9, 31, 48, 55, 58–62, 67–68, 71, 77–78, 78 nn.7, 11, 135
  Encyclopedia of the Philosophical Sciences, 58

158

INDEX OF NAMES 159

Science of Logic, 58
The Phenomenology of Spirit, 58
Hegel, Ludwig, 58
Hegel, Marie von Tucher, 58
Herder, Johann Gottfried, 59
Herz, Henriette, 19–20
Herz, Markus, 19
Hinrichs, H. F. W., 60
Hodgson, Peter, 78 n.7
Hölderlin, Friedrich, 19, 58, 59
Humboldt, Wilhelm von, 32, 112

Jacobi, Friedrich Heinrich, 16
Jahn, Ludwig, 107 n.47
Jean Paul, 19, 59
Jesus Christ, 22, 27, 37–38, 44, 50, 54, 62, 73–74, 87–89, 91, 96–98, 100–101, 139, 141
  God-consciousness, 27, 38, 54, 62, 73, 88, 96–97, 100–101
Jonas, Ludwig, xiii, 6, 11 n.22, 80 n.29, 117
Jorgensen, Poul, 63

Kant, Immanuel, 5, 14, 16, 18, 21, 31, 33, 43, 44, 59, 66
  Critique of Practical Reason, 5
  Prolegomena to Any Future Metaphysics, 44
Karlsbad Decrees, 109, 114
Kleist, Heinrich von, 59
Kotzebue, August von, 114
Kuyper, Abraham, 147 n.7

Laurer, Quentin, S. J., 79 n.11
Leibniz, Gottfried Wilhelm, 17–18, 66
Leith, John, 147 n.7
Lessing, Gotthold Ephraim, 59
Louise, Queen of Prussia and wife of Friedrich Wilhelm III, 17, 31
Louis XVI, 132 n.25
Luther, Martin, xv, 116, 143

Maurice, F. D., 130
Mozart, Wolfgang Amadeus, 17

Napoleon, 2, 14, 17, 27–29, 33, 58, 110, 112, 115, 130
Nicolovius, Ludwig, 114–15
Niebuhr, H. Richard, 4, 10 n.10, 109, 117, 130, 138, 143, 147 n.8

The Responsible Self, 138
Niesky, 14, 43, 44–45
Novalis, 19, 59

Oman, John, 10 n.3

Paul, the Apostle, xiv, 97, 108 n.70
Plato, 3, 33
Pischon, August, 85

Reardon, Bernard, 79 n.11
Reich, Andreas, 82, 83, 84, 105 n.5, 106 n.6, 112, 131 n.10
Reimer, Georg, 83
Redeker, Martin, 26, 29, 33, 84
Ritschl, Albrecht, 4
Romantic circle, 19–20, 24
Rousseau, Jean-Jacque, 14

Sack, Friedrich Samuel Gottfried, 24–25
Sand, Karl Ludwig, 114, 115
Samson, Holger, 88, 106 n.19
Schelling, Friedrich Wilhelm, 31, 59
Schiller, Friedrich, 59
Schlegel, A. W., 19, 59
Schlegel, Dorothea Veit, 20, 24–25, 33
Schlegel, Friedrich, 3, 19, 20, 24, 59
  Lucinde, 24–25
Schleiermacher, Charlotte, 42, 43
Schleiermacher, Daniel, 15, 41–42
Schleiermacher, Friedrich,
  and the poor, 111
  as Reformed, xvi-xvii, 9, 13, 83, 95, 102, 109–30, 135–46
  as pastor, 29–31, 78, 82–86, 135
  lecture style, 63,
  Plato Translation, 33
  political activity, xv, 29–30, 109–16, 135
  political consciousness, 28
  work in the academy, 29, 31–34
  Brief Outline on the Study of Theology, 4, 7, 11 n.21, 18, 34–36, 46, 69, 80 n.34, 141, 144
  Christian Ethics, xiii, 4–9, 11 n.22, 28, 33, 41, 46, 48, 51–55, 60–61, 67–78, 86, 90–105, 109, 116–30, 135–46, 147 n.11
  Christian Faith, xiii, 4–8, 11 n.23, 21, 34, 36–39, 45, 46, 48–51, 60, 83, 86–90, 91

Schleiermacher, Friedrich (continued)
  Christmas Eve: Dialogue on the Incarnation, 26–27, 36, 37
  Confidential Letters on Schlegel's Lucinde, 25
  Dialektik, 33, 67–68
  Grundlinien einer Kritik der bisherigen Sittenlehre, 71
  Hermeneutics, 33
  On Religion: Speeches to the Cultured Among its Despisers, 2, 4–5, 18–22, 24–25, 26, 28, 34, 36, 46, 83
  On the Doctrine of Election, with Special Reference to the Aphorisms of Dr. Bretschneider, 136
  Philosophical Ethics, 28, 33, 67–74, 140, 142, 147 n.11
Schleiermacher, Gottlieb, 13, 15, 41–42, 45
Schleiermacher, Henriette von Willich, 3, 28–29, 58
Schleiermacher, Karl, 42
Schleiermacher, Katherine-Maria, 13
Schleiermacher, Nathaniel, 29
Shelley, John C., xiv
Sigismund, Elector John, 13
Spiegler, Gerhard, 79 n.22
Spener, Philip Jacob, 42
  Pia Desideria, 42
Spinoza, Baruch, 16, 25,

Stein, Baron Karl Freiherr vom, 109–12, 130
Stoeffler, F. Ernest, 55 n.1
Stolp, 25
Stubenrauch, Samuel, 15–16, 24

Thiele, Karl Friedrich, 82
Tice, Terrence, 10 n.3
Tieck, Ludwig, 19
Tillich, Paul, 22
Trimiew, Darryl M., 147 n.8
Trinity Church, 2, 9, 28, 31, 32, 82–86, 109, 111
Troeltsch, Ernst, 36, 86

Voltaire, 14
von Arnim, Bettina Brentano, 3, 10 n.7
von der Luft, Eric, 78 n.11
von Willich, Ehrenfried, 10 n.7
von Willich, Ernst, 29

Wallman, Johannes, 55 n.1, 56 n.7
Wesley, John, 42
Wolff, Christian, 14, 66
Wolterstorff, Nicholas, 147 n.7
Würzburg, University of, 26

Zinzendorf, Count Ludwig von, 43
Zwingli, Ulrich, 137, 141, 143

www.ingramcontent.com/pod-product-compliance
Lightning Source LLC
Chambersburg PA
CBHW071924290426
44110CB00013B/1463